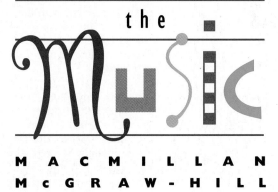

SHARE the Music

MACMILLAN McGRAW-HILL

AUTHORS

Judy Bond,
Coordinating Author

René Boyer-White

Margaret Campbelle-duGard

Marilyn Copeland Davidson,
Coordinating Author

Robert de Frece

Mary Goetze,
Coordinating Author

Doug Goodkin

Betsy M. Henderson

Michael Jothen

Carol King

Vincent P. Lawrence,
Coordinating Author

Nancy L. T. Miller

Ivy Rawlins

Susan Snyder,
Coordinating Author

Macmillan/McGraw-Hill School Publishing Company
New York • Columbus

ACKNOWLEDGMENTS

Grateful acknowledgment is given to the following authors, composers, and publishers. Every effort has been made to trace the ownership of all copyrighted material and to secure the necessary permissions to reprint these selections. In the case of some selections for which acknowledgment is not given, extensive research has failed to locate the copyright holders.

Hooshang Bagheri for *Haji Firuz.* Copyright © Hooshang Bagheri.

Elizabeth Barnett for *Travel* by Edna St. Vincent Millay. From COLLECTED POEMS, HarperCollins. Copyright 1921, 1948 by Edna St. Vincent Millay. Reprinted by permission of Elizabeth Barnett, literary executor.

Irving Berlin Music Company for *Alexander's Ragtime Band* by Irving Berlin, page 239. Copyright © 1911 by Irving Berlin. Copyright Renewed. International Copyright Secured. Used by Permission. All Rights Reserved. For *There's No Business Like Show Business* by Irving Berlin, page 188. Copyright © 1946 by Irving Berlin. Copyright renewed. International Copyright Secured. Used by Permission. All Rights Reserved.

Boosey & Hawkes, Inc. for *Autumn Canon* by L. Bardos. © Copyright 1933 by Magyar Korus, Budapest; Copyright Renewed. Copyright & Renewal assigned 1950 to Editio Musica Budapest. Reprinted by permission of Boosey & Hawkes, Inc. English translation © Sean Deibler. For *Concerto for Orchestra* by Béla Bartók. Copyright © 1946 by Hawkes & Son (London) Ltd. Copyright Renewed. Reprinted by permission of Boosey & Hawkes, Inc. For *The Lobster Quadrille* by Carolyn Jenkins. © 1990 by Boosey & Hawkes, Inc. Reprinted by permission. For *Old Abram Brown.* Text by Walter de la Mare from TOM TIDDLER'S GROUND. Music by Benjamin Britten. © Copyright 1936 by Boosey & Co., Ltd.; Copyright Renewed. Reprinted by permission of Boosey & Hawkes, Inc. For *Old Joe Clark,* arr. by Mary Goetze. © 1984 by Boosey & Hawkes, Inc. Reprinted by permission. For *Seventeen Come Sunday* from ENGLISH FOLK SONG SUITE by Ralph Vaughan Williams. Copyright © 1924 by Boosey & Co. Ltd. Copyright renewed. Reprinted by permission of Boosey & Hawkes, Inc.

Cherio Corp. for *Bandstand Boogie,* Words by Barry Manilow and Bruce Sussman, Music by Charles Albertine. © 1954 (Renewed), 1975 CHERIO CORP. All Rights Reserved. Used by Permission.

Cherry Lane Music Publishing Company, Inc. for *Day-O* by Irving Burgie and William Attaway. ©1955, Renewed 1983 Cherry Lane Music Publishing Company, Inc./Lord Burgess Music Publishing Co. This Arrangement © 1994 Cherry Lane Music Publishing Company, Inc./Lord Burgess Music Publishing Co. For *Earth Day Every Day (Celebrate)* by John Denver. Copyright © 1990 Cherry Mountain Music (ASCAP). International Copyright Secured. All Rights Reserved.

CPP/Belwin, Inc. for *Carol from an Irish Cabin* by Dale Wood. Copyright © 1970 by BELWIN-MILLS PUB. CORP., c/o CPP/BELWIN, INC., Miami, FL 33014. International Copyright Secured. Made in U.S.A. All Rights Reserved. For *Every Morning When I Wake Up* by Avon Gillespie. Copyright © 1976 BELWIN MILLS PUBLISHING CORPORATION. All Rights Assigned to and Controlled by BEAM ME UP MUSIC. International Copyright Secured. Made in USA. All Rights Reserved. Used by Permission of CPP/BELWIN, INC., P.O. Box 4340, Miami, FL 33014. For *From a Distance* by J. Gold. © 1987 WING AND WHEEL MUSIC & JULIE GOLD MUSIC (BMI). All Rights Administered by IRVING MUSIC, INC. (BMI). International Copyright Secured. Made in USA. All Rights Reserved. For *The Greatest Love of All* by Michael Masser and Linda Creed. Copyright © 1977 by GOLD HORIZON MUSIC CORP., A Division of Filmtrax Copyright Holdings Inc. and GOLDEN TORCH MUSIC CORP., A Division of Filmtrax Copyright Holdings Inc. International Copyright Secured. Made in USA. All Rights Reserved. For *It Don't Mean a Thing (If It Ain't Got That Swing),* D. Ellington & I. Mills. © 1932 (Renewed 1960) Mills Music, Inc., c/o EMI MUSIC PUBLISHING, worldwide print rights controlled by CPP/BELWIN, INC., Miami, FL 33014. Used by Permission. All Rights Reserved. For *Trav'ler* by Mark Foster and Jane Foster Knox. Copyright © 1988 Studio 224, Inc., c/o CPP/BELWIN, INC., Miami, FL 33014. International Copyright Secured. Made in USA. All Rights Reserved. For *A Voice from a Dream* by Joyce Elaine Eilers. Copyright © 1976 Schmitt Music Center, Inc., c/o CPP/BELWIN, INC., Miami, FL 33014. International Copyright Secured. Made in USA. All Rights Reserved.

Sean Deibler for *Autumn Canon* by L. Bardos. © Copyright 1933 by Magyar Korus, Budapest; Copyright Renewed. Copyright & Renewal assigned 1950 to Editio Musica Budapest. Reprinted by permission of Boosey & Hawkes, Inc. English translation © Sean Deibler.

continued on page 436

Macmillan/McGraw-Hill School Division
10 Union Square East
New York, New York 10003

Printed in the United States of America
ISBN 0-02-295055-9 / 6
3 4 5 6 7 8 9 VHJ 99 98 97 96 95

SPECIAL CONTRIBUTORS

Contributing Writer
Janet McMillion

Consultant Writers
Teri Burdette, Signing
Brian Burnett, Movement
Robert Duke, Assessment
Joan Gregoryk, Vocal Development/
  Choral
Judith Jellison, Special Learners/
  Assessment
Jacque Schrader, Movement
Kathy B. Sorensen, International Phonetic
  Alphabet
Mollie Tower, Listening

Consultants
Lisa DeLorenzo, Critical Thinking
Nancy Ferguson, Jazz/Improvisation
Judith Nayer, Poetry
Marta Sanchez, Dalcroze
Mollie Tower, Reviewer
Robyn Turner, Fine Arts

Multicultural Consultants
Judith Cook Tucker
JaFran Jones
Oscar Muñoz
Marta Sanchez
Edwin J. Schupman, Jr., of ORBIS
  Associates
Mary Shamrock
Kathy B. Sorensen

Multicultural Advisors
Shailaja Akkapeddi (Hindi), Edna Alba
(Ladino), Gregory Amobi (Ibu), Thomas
Appiah (Ga, Twi, Fanti), Deven Asay
(Russian), Vera Auman (Russian, Ukrainian),
David Azman (Hebrew), Lissa Bangeter
(Portuguese), Britt Marie Barnes (Swedish),
Dr. Mark Bell (French), Brad Ahawanrathe
Bonaparte (Mohawk), Chhanda Chakroborti
(Hindi), Ninthalangsonk Chanthasen
(Laotian), Julius Chavez (Navajo), Lin-Rong
Chen (Mandarin), Anna Cheng (Mandarin),
Rushen Chi (Mandarin), T. L. Chi (Mandarin),
Michelle Chingwa (Ottowa), Hoon Choi
(Korean), James Comarell (Greek), Lynn
DePaula (Portuguese), Ketan Dholakia
(Gujarati), Richard O. Effiong (Nigerian),
Nayereh Fallahi (Persian), Angela Fields
(Hopi, Chemehuevi), Gary Fields (Lakota,

Cree), Siri Veslemoy Fluge (Norwegian),
Katalin Forrai (Hungarian), Renee Galagos
(Swedish), Linda Goodman, Judith A. Gray,
Savyasachi Gupta (Marati), Elizabeth Haile
(Shinnecock), Mary Harouny (Persian),
Charlotte Heth (Cherokee), Tim Hunt
(Vietnamese), Marcela Janko (Czech), Raili
Jeffrey (Finnish), Rita Jensen (Danish), Teddy
Kaiahura (Swahili), Gueen Kalaw (Tagalog),
Merehau Kamai (Tahitian), Richard Keeling,
Masanori Kimura (Japanese), Chikahide
Komura (Japanese), Saul Korewa (Hebrew),
Jagadishwar Kota (Tamil), Sokun Koy
(Cambodian), Craig Kurumada (Balkan),
Cindy Trong Le (Vietnamese), Dongchoon Lee
(Korean), Young-Jing Lee (Korean), Nomi Lob
(Hebrew), Sam Loeng (Mandarin, Malay),
Georgia Magpie (Comanche), Mladen Marič
(Croatian), Kuinise Matagi (Samoan), Hiromi
Matsushita (Japanese), Jackie Maynard
(Hawaiian), David McAllester, Mike
Kanathohare McDonald (Mohawk),
Khumbulani Mdlefshe (Zulu), Martin Mkize
(Xhosa), David Montgomery (Turkish), Kazadi
Big Musungayi (Swahili), Professor Akiya
Nakamara (Japanese), Edwin Napia (Maori),
Hang Nguyen (Vietnamese), Richard Nielsen
(Danish), Wil Numkena (Hopi), Eva Ochoa
(Spanish), Drora Oren (Hebrew), Jackie
Osherow (Yiddish), Mavis Oswald (Russian),
Dr. Dil Parkinson (Arabic), Kenny Tahawisoren
Perkins (Mohawk), Alvin Petersen (Sotho),
Phay Phan (Cambodian), Charlie Phim
(Cambodian), Aroha Price (Maori), Marg Puiri
(Samoan), John Rainer (Taos Pueblo, Creek),
Lillian Rainer (Taos Pueblo, Creek, Apache),
Winton Ria (Maori), Arnold Richardson
(Haliwa-Saponi), Thea Roscher (German),
Dr. Wayne Sabey (Japanese), Regine Saintil
(Bamboula Creole), Luci Scherzer (German),
Ken Sekaquaptewa (Hopi), Samouen Seng
(Cambodian), Pei Shin (Mandarin), Dr. Larry
Shumway (Japanese), Gwen Shunatona
(Pawnee, Otoe, Potawatomi), Ernest Siva
(Cahuilla, Serrano [Maringa']), Ben Snowball
(Inuit), Dr. Michelle Stott (German), Keiko
Tanefuji (Japanese), James Taylor
(Portuguese), Shiu-wai Tong (Mandarin),
Tom Toronto (Lao, Thai), Lynn Tran
(Vietnamese), Gulavadee Vaz (Thai), Chen
Ying Wang (Taiwanese), Masakazu Watabe
(Japanese), Freddy Wheeler (Navajo), Keith
Yackeyonny (Comanche), Liming Yang
(Mandarin), Edgar Zurita (Andean)

CONTENTS

v

MUSIC

MAKERS

FROM

WE ARE THE MUSIC MAKERS

We are the music makers
We are the dreamers of dreams
We are the movers and shakers
of the world, forever, it seems.

—*Arthur O'Shaughnessy*

Music MOVES

Let's get together, movers and shakers!

MOVE along with the sections of this song. Show the contrast and repetition in the form of the song with contrasting and repeated movements.

Dancin' on the Rooftop

Words and Music by
Teresa Jennings

I'm danc-in' on the roof-top, roof-top, roof-top.

Danc-in' in my sneak-ers, heel and toe.— I'm swing-in' on a tree-top,

tree-top, tree-top. Hang-in' by my shoe-strings. Watch me go!— The

weath-er's fine on ol' Cloud Nine. All the birds are danc-in',

too. But I won't come down to the ground_ till I find my par-a-

heel and toe.— I'm swing-in' on a tree-top, tree-top, tree-top.

Hang-in' by my shoe-strings. Watch me go!— Hang-in' by my shoe-strings.

Watch me go!— Hang-in' by my shoe-strings. Watch me go!—

Hang-in' by my shoe-strings.———— Watch

me go! Watch me go! Yeah!

The famous big band,
The Sweethearts of Rhythm

4

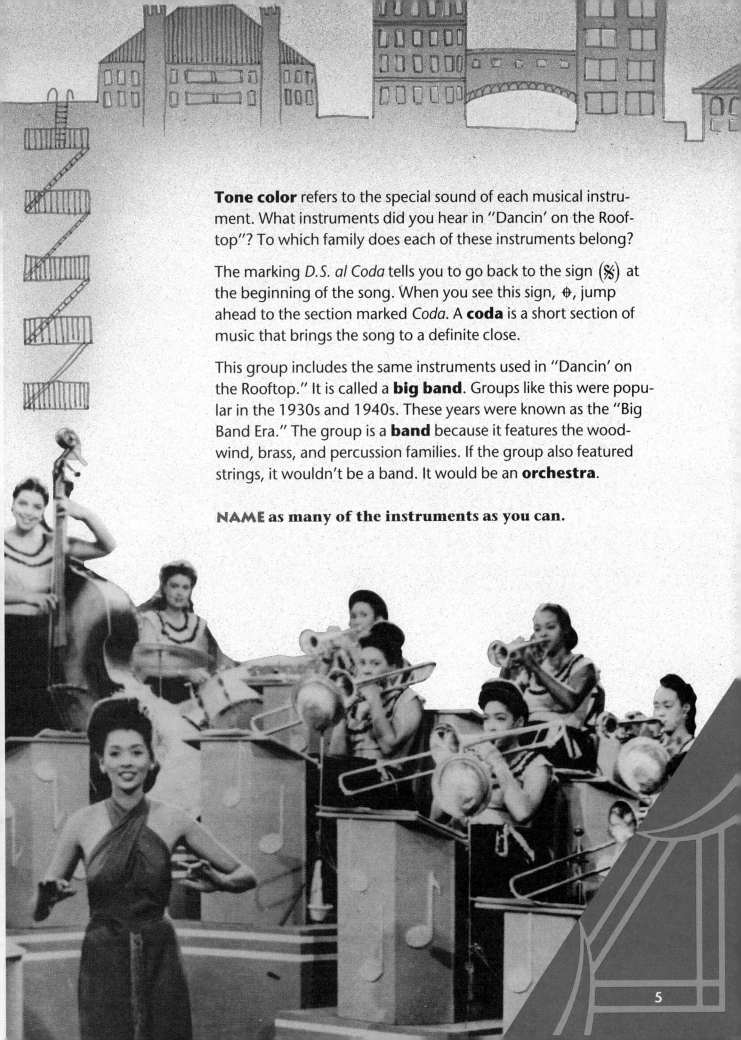

Tone color refers to the special sound of each musical instrument. What instruments did you hear in "Dancin' on the Rooftop"? To which family does each of these instruments belong?

The marking *D.S. al Coda* tells you to go back to the sign (𝄋) at the beginning of the song. When you see this sign, ⊕, jump ahead to the section marked *Coda*. A **coda** is a short section of music that brings the song to a definite close.

This group includes the same instruments used in "Dancin' on the Rooftop." It is called a **big band**. Groups like this were popular in the 1930s and 1940s. These years were known as the "Big Band Era." The group is a **band** because it features the woodwind, brass, and percussion families. If the group also featured strings, it wouldn't be a band. It would be an **orchestra**.

NAME as many of the instruments as you can.

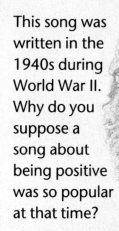

This song was written in the 1940s during World War II. Why do you suppose a song about being positive was so popular at that time?

LISTEN for the instruments that accompany the singer.

ACCENTUATE THE POSITIVE

Music by Harold Arlen
Words by Johnny Mercer

With a Swing

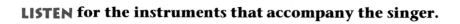

You've got to ac - cen - tu - ate the pos - i - tive,

E - lim - i - nate the neg - a - tive,

Latch on to the af - firm - a - tive,

Don't mess with Mis - ter In - be - tween.___ You've got to spread joy

Step to the Music

Here's a marching band. This group is from Bavaria, in southern Germany. What families of instruments are shown below?

Most music in **march form** goes something like this:

Introduction   AA   BB   Trio Trio

An **introduction** lets us hear the style, key, and tempo before the main part of the piece starts. The **trio** of a march contrasts with the sections that come before it. Trios were once played by only three instruments.

LISTENING

Muss i denn   German March

The melody of a popular German folk song is heard in the trio of this march.

Introduction

‖: A :‖

‖: B :‖

Trio 1

Trio 2

LISTENING MAP   *Listen for the form and follow the map as you hear this Bavarian band.*

These performers belong to a group called a **samba bateria.** The music they are performing is samba. Samba was invented in Brazil and was influenced by African music. It is especially popular at carnival time, in February or March. Which family of instruments is pictured here?

Describe the form of this song using letters of the alphabet. How many sets of words are there in the section marked verse? In the refrain? A song that has more than one set of words for one section and only one set of words for another section is in **verse-refrain form.**

You've seen marching bands in parades and during halftime at football games. Drum majors, baton twirlers, and elaborate movements add to the excitement of marching band performances. Which family of instruments is missing in this band?

LISTENING

National Emblem

by E. E. Bagley

How is the form of this march the same as or different from the form of "Muss i denn?"

GOTTA GET Rhythm

Think about the kinds of musical groups you've seen so far and take a look at the lyrics of "Rock Around the Clock." What kind of group might play and sing this song? Which instruments do you think they would play?

PLAY percussion instruments along with this song as you sing.

14

Rock Around the Clock

Words and Music by Max Freedman
and Jimmy De Knight

One, two, three o'clock, four o'clock, rock.
Five, six, seven o'clock, eight o'clock, rock.
Nine, ten, eleven o'clock, twelve o'clock, rock.
We're gonna rock around the clock tonight.

1. Well, get your glad rags on, join me hon,' we're gonna
   have some fun when the clock strikes one,
   We're gonna rock around the clock tonight, we're gonna
   rock, rock, rock 'til the broad daylight,
   We're gonna rock, gonna rock around the clock tonight.

2. When the clock strikes two, three and four, and the band
   slows down we'll yell for more,
   We're gonna rock around the clock tonight, we're gonna
   rock, rock, rock 'til the broad daylight,
   We're gonna rock, gonna rock around the clock tonight.

3. When the chimes ring five, six, and seven, we'll be rockin'
   up' in seventh heaven
   We're gonna rock around the clock tonight, we're gonna
   rock, rock, rock 'til the broad daylight,
   We're gonna rock, gonna rock around the clock tonight.

4. When it's eight, nine, ten, eleven too, I'll be going strong
   and so will you,
   We're gonna rock around the clock tonight, we're gonna
   rock, rock, rock 'til the broad daylight,
   We're gonna rock, gonna rock around the clock tonight.

5. When the clock strikes twelve we'll cool off, then, start
   a-rockin' 'round the clock again,
   We're gonna rock around the clock tonight, we're gonna
   rock, rock, rock 'til the broad daylight,
   We're gonna rock, gonna rock around the clock tonight.

All music has one thing in common—that all-important element, **rhythm**. Rhythm is created by organizing sounds and silences of different lengths. Composers write rhythm using notes and rests. People who can read and write rhythm know how much time one note or rest takes in relation to other notes or rests. Look at the chart below and see if you can figure out why there is only one whole note but 16 sixteenth notes.

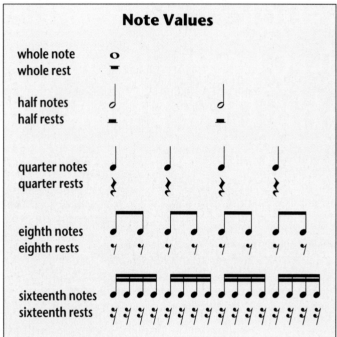

Note Values

whole note	
whole rest	
half notes	
half rests	
quarter notes	
quarter rests	
eighth notes	
eighth rests	
sixteenth notes	
sixteenth rests	

THINK IT THROUGH

Imagine that you are in a band. How would you use an understanding of note values?

READ and clap these rhythms.

Bill Haley (right) and the Comets recorded "Rock Around the Clock" in 1954.

MAKING A PITCH FOR PITCH

If music were just rhythm, there would be drumming, hand clapping, and rap. But could we sing? Could trumpets play melodies? For these we need **pitch.**

Pitch is the highness or lowness of a tone in relation to other tones. When you string pitches together, you can make a melody.

In melodies, pitches can:

- move by step, up or down.

- skip pitches going up or down.

- take long leaps up or down.

- stay the same as the previous pitch.

When you talk about pitches moving, you are talking about the shape of melody— its direction, or **melodic contour**.

PLAY the music below with the first three sections (ABA) of "Dancin' on the Rooftop." The example below can remind you of the pitch name of each line and each space of the staff.

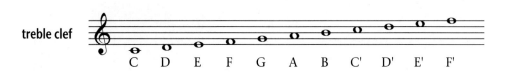

treble clef

C D E F G A B C' D' E' F'

playalong

The marking *D.C. al Fine* tells you to go back to the beginning of the song and then stop when you see the word *Fine*. *Fine* means "end" in Italian.

Here is a new
song to read and
sing. It is part of a very
old tradition of street performances
in China. The music is called "Fung Yang
Song" because it comes from Fung Yang, a
district in northern China. Since about 1700,
songs like this have been popular all over China.

LISTEN for the rhythm and melodic contour
of this song.

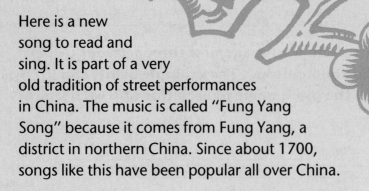

Chinese Folk Song
Arranged by
Marilyn Davidson

BREAK THE CODES

Now that you've learned something about rhythm and pitch, it's time to do a bit of song sleuthing. The mystery is . . . What song does the measure below come from?

Here are some clues that could help you break both the rhythm and pitch codes.

- The measure is from a song you know.
- The rhythm and the melody of the measure appear more than once in the song.

How did you arrive at your answer?

Here's an even more challenging mystery. On the next page are four song fragments. Your assignment is to identify one of the songs.

FOLLOW the steps below as you work with others to break the codes. Use a pitched instrument to help you.

- Describe the melodic contour.
- Name the pitches.
- Play the fragment on an instrument.
- Sing it with pitch letter names.
- Identify the song (but don't tell the other groups).

PLAY and sing your fragment for the other groups. See if they can identify it.

Mystery Melody 1

Mystery Melody 2

Mystery Melody 3

Mystery Melody 4

23

Here's a brand-new song to read. It has a **countermelody**, marked "Part 2." The countermelody is a second melody designed to be sung with Part 1. Find the parts of the melody that repeat. Are any rhythms repeated? Are the rhythms and pitches the same in the countermelody as they are in the melody? Break the rhythm and pitch codes and sing this song.

I Shall Sing

Words and Music
by Van Morrison
Arranged by
Nancy Ferguson

The notation of the countermelody of this song uses **ledger lines**. Ledger lines are short pieces of staff lines that help you read the notes that are too high or low to fit on the regular staff. In this countermelody, a ledger line is needed for the note C.

What is the form of this song?

**CREATE your own countermelody for "Fung Yang Song."
Use one of these rhythm patterns with the pitches D, E,
F♯, and A:**

MUSIC ON A

String

Listen for the instruments in this country string group. They are: fiddle, string bass, dulcimer, guitar, and banjo. How many voice parts are in this song?

YOU SING FOR ME

Words and Music
by Raymond K. McLain

1. I've come through storm-y weath-er, I'm sure you've seen it too.
2. I'll nev - er be more read - y to sing a - long with you.

But now we're here to - geth - er and it's good to be with you.
To keep each oth - er stead - y,— well, this is what to do.

Well, here I am and there you are with noth - ing much to say.
You lis - ten to the rhy - thm, then start mov - in' to the beat.

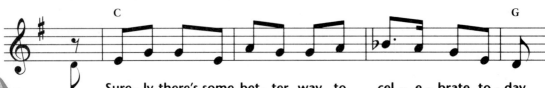

Sure - ly there's some bet - ter way to cel - e - brate to - day.
Come on, sweet mu - sic mak - er,— let's give our - selves a treat.

When you described the number of voice parts in "You Sing for Me," you were talking about **texture.** Musicians use the term *texture* to describe the number of sounds going on at one time and how these sounds relate to each other.

At the beginning of the refrain, each group sings a phrase while the other holds a pitch. In the notation of the refrain melody, curved lines called **ties** tell the singers to hold the note.

STRINGS AND MORE STRINGS

In a symphony orchestra, the string section is the heart of the sound. An orchestra might have 65 string players, 16 woodwind players, 15 brass players, and two percussionists. With a full symphony orchestra, you can hear the contrast between many instruments playing at once and only one or two instruments at a time.

Capriccio espagnol (excerpt)

by Nicolai Rimsky-Korsakov

Listen for the thick and thin textures in this 1887 orchestral piece. Sometimes only one instrument is played. At other times, you will hear the entire orchestra. Notice when instruments are played by themselves or with just one or two others. Which families of instruments (brass, woodwinds, percussion, strings) are featured most prominently?

strings

MAKING HARMONY

Harmony is often provided by **chords**, groups of three or more pitches that sound at the same time. Listen for the organ accompaniment in order to hear the chords in this recording of "Walk Together Children."

WALK TOGETHER CHILDREN

African American Spiritual
Arranged by René Boyer-White

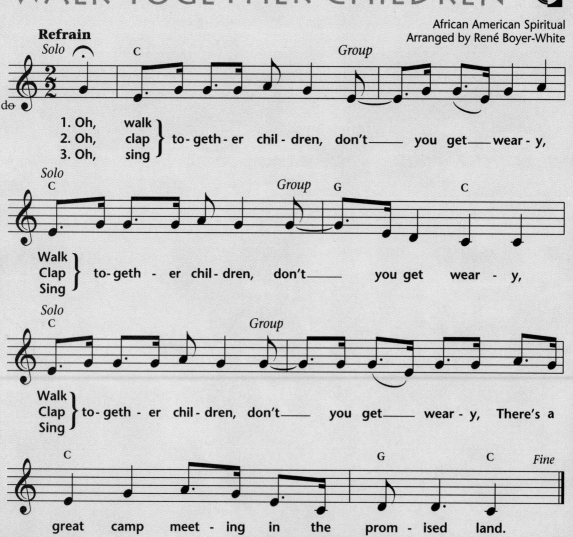

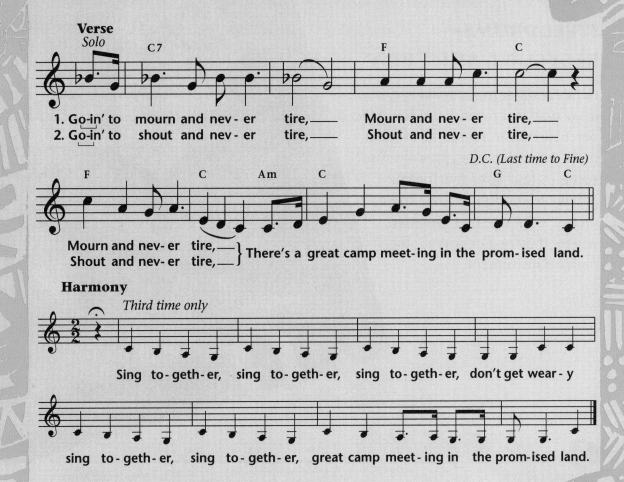

Verse
Solo

C7

1. Go-in' to mourn and nev-er tire,___ Mourn and nev-er tire,___
2. Go-in' to shout and nev-er tire,___ Shout and nev-er tire,___

F   C   Am   C   G   C

D.C. (Last time to Fine)

Mourn and nev-er tire,___ } There's a great camp meet-ing in the prom-ised land.
Shout and nev-er tire,___

Harmony

Third time only

Sing to-geth-er, sing to-geth-er, sing to-geth-er, don't get wear-y

sing to-geth-er, sing to-geth-er, great camp meet-ing in the prom-ised land.

Did you hear the two different chords in the refrain? They are named with Roman numerals: I and V. Since this song is in the key of C, the **root**, or starting tone, of the I chord is C, the first pitch of that scale. The fifth pitch of the C scale is G, and G is the root of the V chord. The basic chord, the **triad**, is built with three pitches. The I chord in the key of C is made up of the pitches C, E, and G. The V chord is G, B, and D.

C major scale

1 2 3 4 5 6 7 8
C D E F G A B C'

The I and V triads in C major

I   V
C   G

31

STEEL DRUMS—
RECYCLING AT ITS BEST

Here's another music-making group. It's a steel drum band and has only percussion instruments, all of them made from oil barrels. Steel drums come in four sizes that produce pitches from high to low. These drums originated in Trinidad, where they're considered the national instrument.

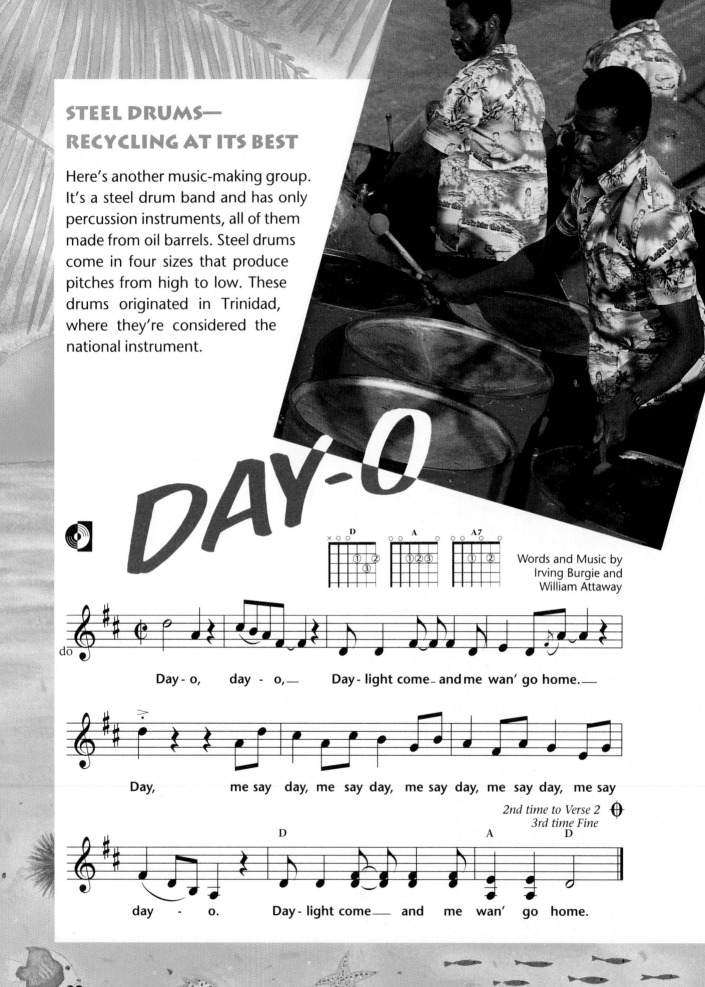

DAY-O

Words and Music by
Irving Burgie and
William Attaway

do

Day - o,   day - o,—   Day - light come— and me wan' go home.—

Day,   me say   day, me say day,   me say day,   me say day,   me say

2nd time to Verse 2
3rd time Fine

day - o.   Day - light come—— and   me   wan'   go   home.

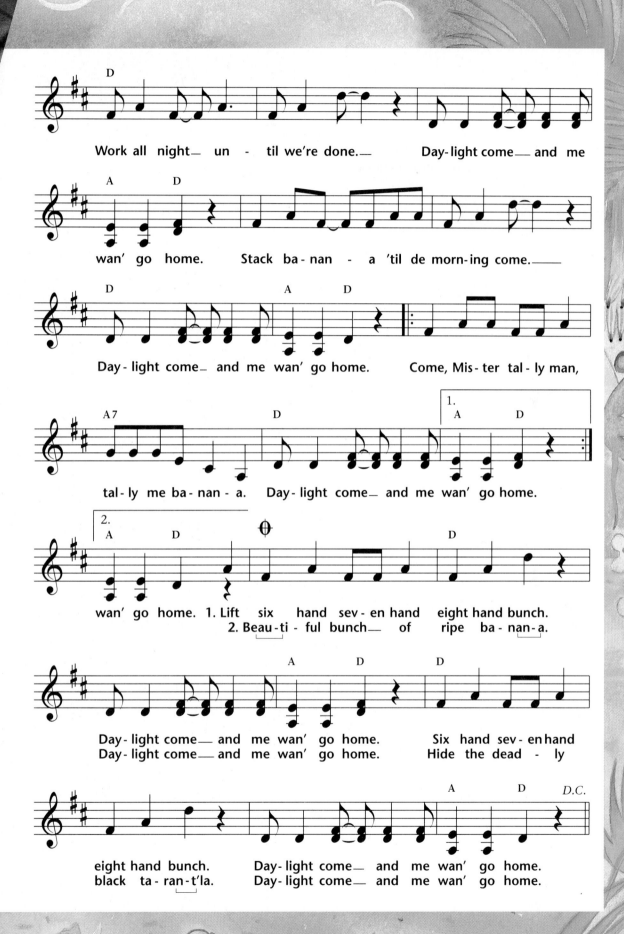

ARRANGE IT!

Here's one more musical group to hear.
What performers do you hear in this recording?

Music for the World

Words and Music by
Gene Grier and Richard Derwingson

Bright Rock

1. Mel - o - dy mak - ers   all join in___ and sing out with a smile!___
2. Strike up the band__ and start to play__ a   song for all to share.___

Har - mo - ny shap - ers, let's be - gin___ to sing it with some style!___
Or - ches - tra lead - ers, show the way.__ Let mu - sic fill   the   air!___

Rhy - thm and tem - po set the pace.__ So ev' - ry - one can fly.___
Play   it with feel - ing, show our class,__ no mat - ter what the style.___

So - pra - no and al - to, ten - or, bass,__ let's give it our best try.___
      Wood - winds, per - cus - sion, strings and brass,__ to - geth - er with a smile!___

Refrain

We're sing - ing } mu - sic for the world,___   so ev' - ry - one can hear.___
(2.) We're play - ing }

34

Many people behind the scenes help to create the sound of your favorite recordings. For example, Quincy Jones worked on some of Michael Jackson's greatest hits. Jones arranged the music to get that Jackson sound. Many popular music stars, past and present, from big bands to the Beatles, have used arrangers to get the sound they want from their instrumentalists and singers.

SPOTLIGHT ON
QUINCY JONES

Quincy Jones is an American who is active in many areas of music. He is a pianist, trumpeter, bandleader, composer, arranger, and producer. As a jazz musician, he played with Lionel Hampton and Dizzy Gillespie. He has worked with musicians in many styles, including jazz, pop, and rap.

What does an **arranger** do? An arranger makes choices that determine how a musical performance will sound. These choices might include the style of the accompaniment, the rhythms and pitches in the accompaniment parts, the number of singers and players, the instruments and the parts they play, and the texture.

"MUSIC FOR THE WORLD" (AS YOU LIKE IT)

This is your chance to be an arranger. The song is "Music for the World." The choices are:

What style of accompaniment do I want? Big band, orchestra, country string band, samba bateria, pop-style band?

What instruments should I use? Woodwinds, brass, percussion, strings? Clarinets? Violins? You are choosing the **instrumentation** of the song.

Should part of the arrangement feature an instrument or section of instruments? Drum solo, electronic keyboard interlude, rhythm pattern for tambourine? When in the music should it happen?

The texture—thick, thin, or both? Soloist with back-up singers, two-part chorus, melody with countermelody? The texture could change partway into the song. What change would sound best?

THINK IT THROUGH
How can these choices help express the meaning of the words?

MAKING YOUR OWN MUSIC

Music-making groups come in many shapes and sizes. Listen to and sing "Dancin' on the Rooftop" and discuss the instruments that you hear. Now do the same for "Accentuate the Positive." How are the instrumental groups accompanying these two songs similar?

Both "Dancin' on the Rooftop" and "Accentuate the Positive" come from the United States. But music-makers come from all over the world. "A Zing-a Za" is accompanied by the sound of a Brazilian band. Listen for the Chinese music-makers in "Fung Yang Song." Which instrument families are heard in both recordings?

Music-makers create harmony by adding a countermelody to a song. Sing "I Shall Sing," with its countermelody. What other songs in this unit had countermelodies?

CHECK IT OUT

1. Which instruments do you hear?

   a. brass and percussion **c.** strings

   b. woodwinds and brass **d.** percussion

2. Which type of musical group do you hear?

   a. band **b.** orchestra **c.** something else

3. Which rhythm pattern do you hear?

4. Which example shows the pitches you hear?

CREATE

Play Your Own Accompaniment

Work in groups. First choose a song in Unit 1 to accompany.

• Develop a rhythm for your accompaniment patterns using half, quarter, and eighth notes. The patterns should be either four or eight beats long. Write your rhythm patterns down using music notation.
• Choose instruments for each pattern. If you choose pitched instruments, select any pitches on the treble staff.
• Organize your patterns to fit the form of the song. For each section of the song, change the rhythm pattern or the instrumentation.

PRACTICE your accompaniment with the song. Make any changes or improvements you see fit.

PERFORM your arrangement for the class.

CREATE movement to the song if you wish. If the song is in more than one section, there should be a change of movement or number of people in each section.

Write

Write a paragraph about a music-making group you have heard. Where does this group perform? Who might be listening to their music? Discuss what instruments were in the group and to what families they belong.

Carmina

THE BREVIARY OF QUEEN ISABELLA OF CASTILE
This miniature painting from about 1495 comes from an illustrated prayer book once owned by Queen Isabella of Castile (employer of Christopher Columbus). Illustrated books such as this were prepared with special colors and decorations that made the paintings glow.

# Burana

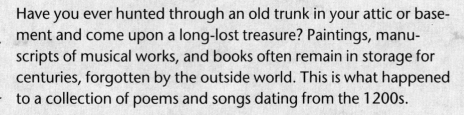

Have you ever hunted through an old trunk in your attic or basement and come upon a long-lost treasure? Paintings, manuscripts of musical works, and books often remain in storage for centuries, forgotten by the outside world. This is what happened to a collection of poems and songs dating from the 1200s.

During that time, groups of students and young monks wandered about the countryside, entertaining themselves, and anyone who cared to listen, with amusing songs. The songs were sung in Latin, French, and German.

Many of these songs were not written down but were passed from one group of singers to another through the oral tradition. About 700 years ago, someone assembled manuscripts for a number of these works and placed the collection in the Library of the Benedictine Monastery at Beuren, in Germany, for safekeeping. The manuscript contained words to the songs, with some medieval musical notation.

In the mid-1800s, a scholar discovered the manuscript and published it under the title "Carmina Burana," which means "Songs of Beuren." In 1936, the German composer Carl Orff took the texts for some of these songs and composed a new musical version of "Carmina Burana" for chorus and orchestra. Through the popularity of Orff's work, these ancient Latin poems have become familiar to people all over the world.

Carl Orff

LISTENING

Ecce gratum

(excerpt) from *Carmina Burana*
by Carl Orff

READ the translation as you listen to a song from Orff's "Carmina Burana."

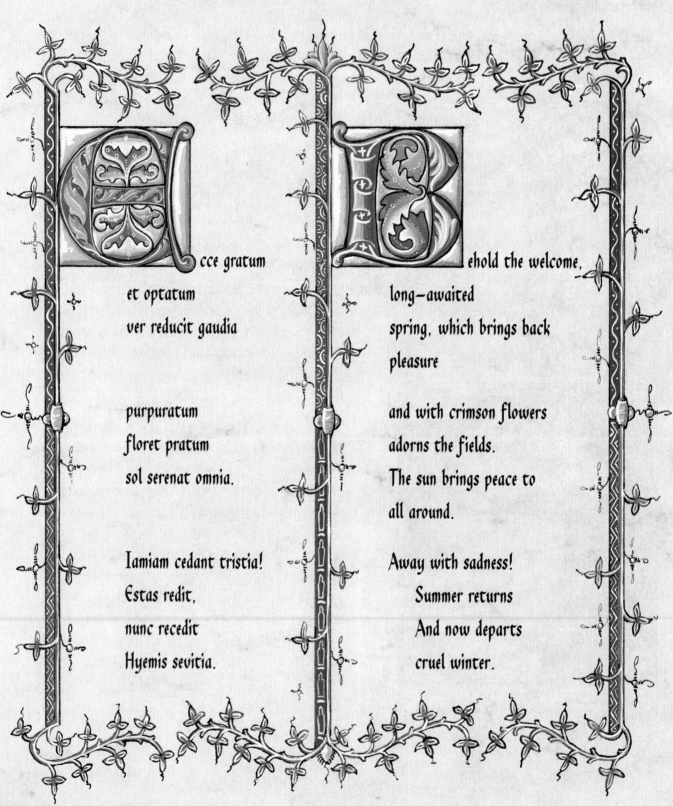

Ecce gratum
et optatum
ver reducit gaudia

purpuratum
floret pratum
sol serenat omnia.

Iamiam cedant tristia!
Estas redit,
nunc recedit
Hyemis sevitia.

Behold the welcome,
long–awaited
spring, which brings back
pleasure

and with crimson flowers
adorns the fields.
The sun brings peace to
all around.

Away with sadness!
Summer returns
And now departs
cruel winter.

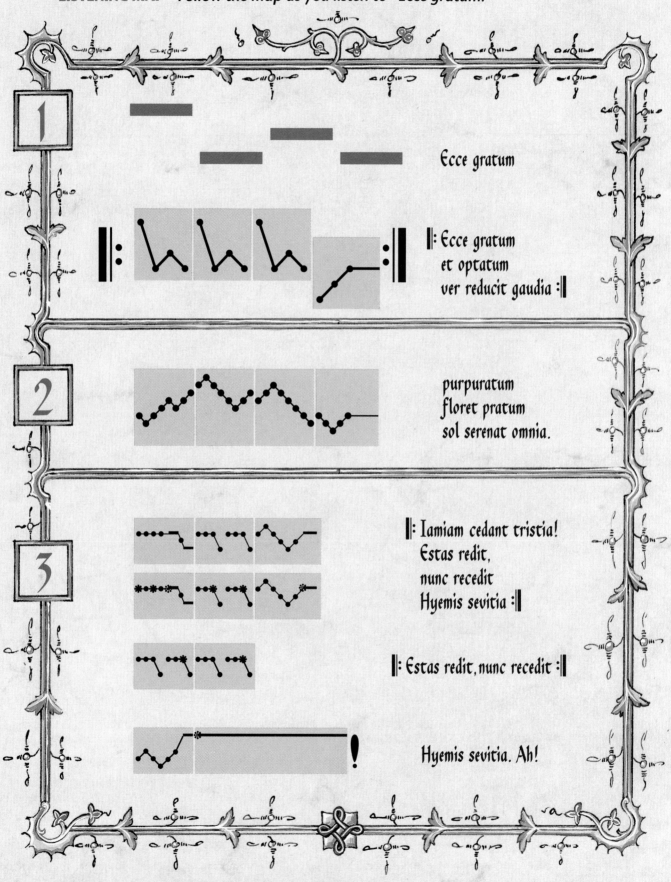

1

Ecce gratum

‖: Ecce gratum
et optatum
ver reducit gaudia :‖

2

purpuratum
floret pratum
sol serenat omnia.

3

‖: Iamiam cedant tristia!
Estas redit,
nunc recedit
Hyemis sevitia :‖

‖: Estas redit, nunc recedit :‖

Hyemis sevitia. Ah!

DESCRIBE each of the sections in "Ecce gratum."

MUSICAL ADVEN

TURES

YOUR WORLD

Your world is as big as you make it.
I know, for I used to abide
In the narrowest nest in a corner,
My wings pressing close to my side.

But I sighted the distant horizon
Where the skyline encircled the sea.
And I throbbed with a burning desire
To travel this immensity.

I battered the cordons around me
And cradled my wings on the breeze
Then soared to the uttermost reaches
With rapture, with power, with ease!

—Georgia Douglas Johnson

MOMENTS IN TIME

Do you ever feel as though your world is just too small, too limiting, and you want to be off to other places or other times? Music is a way you can travel with your ears. It can take you to far-away places, introduce you to other ways of life, and teach you different languages. Music can show you what people have in common, no matter where they are.

Just as planes and spaceships have changed how we travel and the kinds of adventures that are possible, the invention of CDs, tapes, and videos allows us to travel through music more often, more easily, and to more distant places.

ONE MOMENT IN TIME

Words and Music by Albert Hammond and John Bettis

Each day I live I want to be a day to give the best of me.
I'm only one, but not alone. My finest day is yet unknown.
I broke my heart for ev'ry gain. To taste the sweet, I faced
    the pain.
I rise and fall, yet through it all this much remains:

I want one moment in time when I'm more than I thought
    I could be,
when all of my dreams are a heartbeat away
and the answers are all up to me.
Give me one moment in time when I'm racing with destiny.
Then, in that one moment in time, I will feel, I will feel eternity.

I've lived to be the very best. I want it all, no time for less.
I've laid the plans, now lay the chance here in my hands.

I want one moment in time when I'm more than I thought
    I could be,
when all of my dreams are a heartbeat away
and the answers are all up to me.
Give me one moment in time when I'm racing with destiny.
Then, in that one moment in time, I will feel, I will feel eternity.

You're a winner for a lifetime if you seize that one moment in time,
    make it shine.

Give me one moment in time when I'm more than I thought
    I could be,
when all of my dreams are a heartbeat away
and the answers are all up to me.
Give me one moment in time when I'm racing with destiny.
Then, in that one moment in time,
I will be, I will be, I will be free. I will be free.

"One Moment in Time" became famous when it was recorded by Whitney Houston.

Spotlight on *Whitney Houston*

Whitney Houston was born in 1963. Her mother, Cissy Houston, was in a singing group that appeared with Elvis Presley and sang often with Aretha Franklin. As a child, Whitney would accompany her mother to the recording studio to hear her sing.

Whitney Houston made her solo singing debut at age 11 in church. By her late teens, she was singing with her mother at clubs in New York City. In 1985, Whitney Houston made her first album. It was a hit, selling 14 million copies. The album also won a Grammy award. Between 1985 and 1988, Whitney Houston had seven consecutive number-one hits on the music charts, breaking a record set by the Beatles.

A **scale** is a series of pitches in order. Look at the white keys on the keyboard. Those are the notes of the C **major scale.** Notice that between E and F, and between B and C, there is no black key. The distance between these pitches is called a **half step**.

A **whole step** equals two half steps added together. It's the distance between the other pitches in the C major scale. You can see that the distance, or **interval,** between whole steps is greater, because there is a black key in between the two pitches.

Whitney Houston has received many recording industry awards for her musical achievements.

THE C SCALE IN HISTORY

LISTENING

Canon *by Henry Purcell*

A **canon** *is a melody that is imitated exactly in one or more parts. The English composer Henry Purcell wrote this canon in the late 1600s.*

PLAY this with the Purcell Canon, first alone and then with the recording. It uses every pitch in the C major scale.

PLAY a C major scale on bells, keyboard, piano, or on another pitched instrument.

The **tonal center**, or starting and ending point, of the C major scale is C. But what if you wanted to play a major scale starting on another pitch, such as D? Could you just start on D and play only white keys?

A **sharp** (♯) before a note raises it a half step. A **flat** (♭) lowers it a half step. You can see on the keyboard that each black key has both a sharp name and a flat name.

By using sharps and flats, you can make the half and whole steps fall in the right places, no matter what major scale you are playing.

LISTENING

Tune in a CAGe *by Norm Sands*

Practice reading these notes by playing "Tune in a CAGe" on the recorder. You've seen them before. What notes are they?

RHYTHM OF TIME

This song was written in the 1970s. It expresses the appeal of music as a universal language. Music can be a bridge, spanning distances between people and ideas.

SNAP this rhythm with "I Believe in Music":

I Believe in Music

For guitar, transpose to key of D.

Words and Music by Mac Davis
Words adapted by Marilyn Davidson

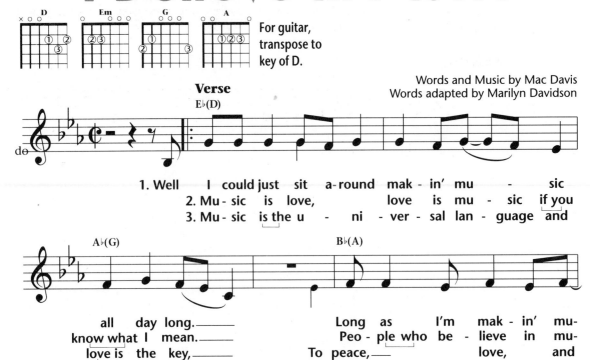

Verse

1. Well I could just sit a-round mak-in' mu - sic
2. Mu - sic is love, love is mu - sic if you
3. Mu - sic is the u - ni - ver - sal lan - guage and

all day long._____ Long as I'm mak-in' mu-
know what I mean._____ Peo - ple who be - lieve in mu-
love is the key,_____ To peace,_____ love, and

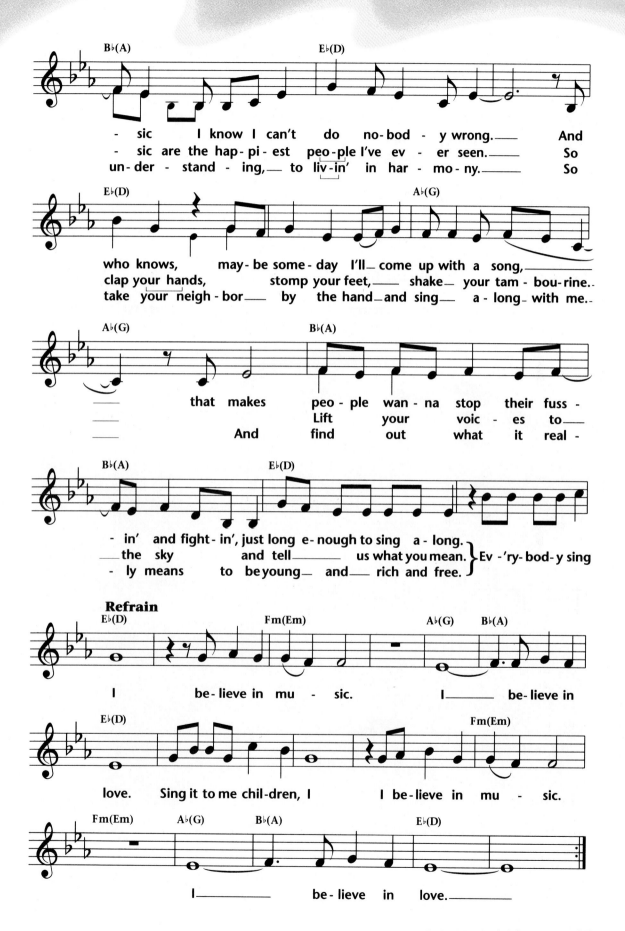

Music can let us travel back in time.

Cancan
from *Gaité parisienne* (excerpt)
by Jacques Offenbach

The dance pictured below is the cancan, which has a lot of high kicks. Offenbach composed his "Cancan" in 1866. Listen for a major scale at the end of the dance theme.

LISTEN to "Cancan."

READ the rhythm of the theme, saying:

■ *I'm* for ♩   ■ *dancing* for ♫   ■ *here in Paris* for ♬

AT THE MOULIN ROUGE: THE DANCE

Henri de Toulouse-Lautrec painted scenes of life in Paris in the late 1800s. He is famous for his paintings of cafés and theaters. Toulouse-Lautrec made this theater scene in 1890.

Philadelphia Museum of Art; The Henry P. McIlhenny Collection in memory of Frances P. McIlhenny.

"Kokoleoko" is a folk song from Liberia, in western Africa. Though "Kokoleoko" and "Cancan" originated miles away from each other, the two pieces are alike in some ways, too. Look for groups of four sixteenth notes in "Kokoleoko." They were in "Cancan," too.

KOKOLEOKO

Liberian Folk Song

Verse

1. Ko - ko - le - o - ko, ma - ma, ko - ko - le - o - ko.
2. Let me sleep some more, ma - ma, let me sleep some more.

Ko - ko - le - o - ko, chick - en crow - ing for day.
Let me sleep some more, chick - en crow - ing for day.

Refrain

A - by,— ma - ma, a - by,— a - by,— chick - en crow - ing for day.

PLAY this rhythm on a drum.

Into the Past

Through musical adventures we can revisit great events in history. The Battle of Jericho was fought in southwestern Asia between 1400 and 1200 B.C. Today the city of Jericho is in Jordan. In this song, how many times is the refrain section sung? The verse section?

Joshua Fit the Battle of Jericho

African American Spiritual
Additional Words by MMH

Refrain

Dm *Swing it*   A7   Dm

Josh-ua fit the bat-tle of— Jer-i-cho,— Jer-i-cho,— Jer-i-cho.—

Last time to Coda ⊕

Dm   A7   Dm

Josh-ua fit the bat-tle of— Jer-i-cho— and the walls came tum-blin' down.

Verse

Dm

1. You may talk a-bout your king of Gid-e-on,—— You may
2. Up to the walls of Jer-i-cho—— He—
3. Then the ram horns— they be-gan to blow,—— And the

Dm

talk a-bout your man of Saul. There's none like good ol'
marched with a spear in hand, "Go blow those ram horns,"
trum-pets— be-gan to sound, Then Josh-ua com-mand-ed the

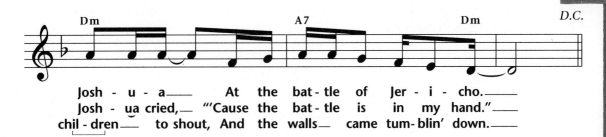

Josh - u - a—— At the bat - tle of Jer - i - cho.——
Josh - ua cried,— "'Cause the bat - tle is in my hand."——
chil - dren—— to shout, And the walls— came tum - blin' down.——

And the walls came a - tum - bl - in', a - tum - bl - in' down, And the walls came a - tum - bl -

in' down.   And the walls came a - tum - bl - in', a - tum - bl - in' down. And the

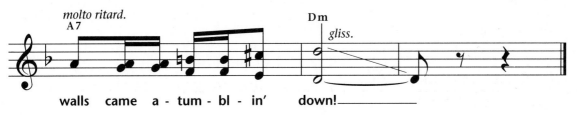

walls came a - tum - bl - in'   down!————

PERFORM an introduction to "Joshua Fit the Battle of Jericho." Speak this pattern four times.

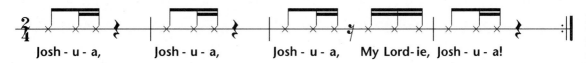

Josh - u - a,   Josh - u - a,   Josh - u - a,   My Lord - ie, Josh - u - a!

The second time through add this pattern.

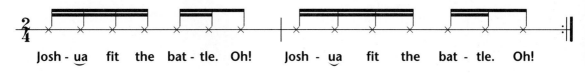

Josh - ua   fit the bat - tle. Oh!   Josh - ua   fit   the   bat - tle.   Oh!

The third time through add this sung part.

Josh   -   u - a! ————

The celebrated composer Wolfgang Amadeus Mozart was a child prodigy who started playing keyboard instruments at age three and wrote large pieces for orchestra by age nine. Here Mozart, aged thirteen, is seated at the keyboard, perhaps working on a new composition. The year is about 1770. Later he composed the rondo "Alla turca" ("in Turkish style") that you're about to hear. Mozart wanted to give his European audiences a sense of the fascinating sounds of Turkey.

LISTENING

Alla turca from Piano Sonata in A Major, K. 331
by Wolfgang Amadeus Mozart

READ this rhythm from the rondo and play it. Use drumsticks or another sound source.

Say: ■ *March* for ♩   ■ *Everybody* for ♫♫

Rondo form is usually ABACA or a simple variation of that idea. But Mozart really varied the form for the rondo "Alla turca." One way to describe it is:
ABA C DED C ABA C Coda.

LISTENING MAP *Listen for the repetitions of the A, or rondo, theme as you follow the map of the rondo "Alla turca."*

‖: A :‖   ‖: B   A' :‖   ‖: C :‖

‖: D :‖   ‖: E   D' :‖   ‖: C :‖

‖: A :‖   ‖: B   A' :‖   ‖: C' :‖

Coda

Listening Map Concept by Barb Stevanson

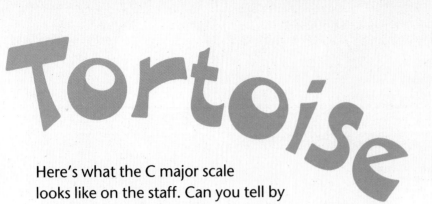

Tortoise Tales

Here's what the C major scale
looks like on the staff. Can you tell by
looking at the pitches where the half steps are?

PLAY and sing the C major scale.

Each note in the major scale also
has a pitch syllable name.

Which pitch syllables are a half
step apart?

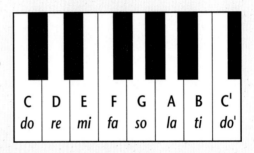

C	D	E	F	G	A	B	C'
do	re	mi	fa	so	la	ti	do'

PLAY and sing these pitches. Perform the bell part
below with the refrain of "One Moment in Time."

LISTENING

🎵 **Tortoises** from *The Carnival of the Animals* by *Camille Saint-Saëns*

How would you describe the tempo, or speed of the beat, of "Cancan"?

Let's visit Paris, France, in the late 1800s to hear "Cancan" performed again. Listen especially for the tempo this time.

The "Cancan" melody was there, but how was it changed?

Saint-Saëns borrowed the "Cancan" melody for a new piece, which he called "Tortoises."

SING the beginning of "Tortoises" with pitch syllables.

THINK IT THROUGH

Why do you think this piece is considered a musical joke?

Would someone who had not heard "Cancan" get the joke?

Music can take you to wherever
you want to be, even . . .

Flying Free

Words and Music by Don Besig

C   G   Am   C

1. There is a place I call my own _____ where I can
2. But life is not a dis-tant sky _____ with-out a
3. So life's a song that I must sing, _____ a gift of

Descant on 3rd verse only

So life's a song, a gift of

F   B♭   G7

stand _____ by the sea, _____
cloud, _____ with - out rain, _____
love _____ I must share. _____

love _____ I must share. _____

C   G   Am   C

And look be-yond the things I've known, _____ and dream that
And I can nev-er hope that I _____ can trav-el
And when I see the joy it brings, _____ my spir-its

And when I see, my spir-its

LOOK for similar and different parts of the song.
Describe the form with letters.

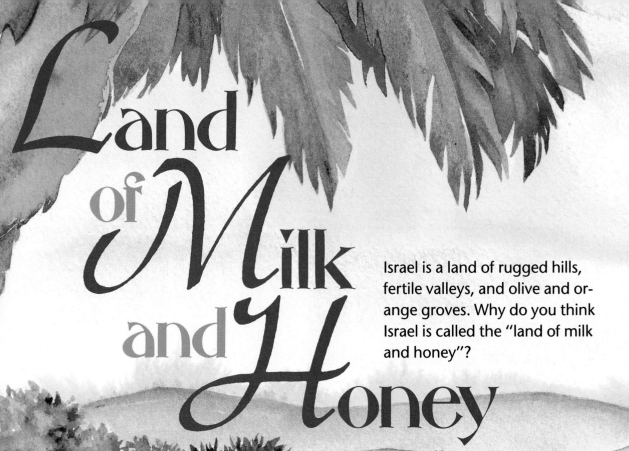

Land of Milk and Honey

Israel is a land of rugged hills, fertile valleys, and olive and orange groves. Why do you think Israel is called the "land of milk and honey"?

SING the melody of this folk song all together, in unison.

Tumbai

Israeli Folk Song

Hebrew: טום - בַּי, טום - בַּי, טום - בַּי, טום - בַּי, טום - בַּי, טום - בַּי, טום - בַּי,
Pronunciation: tum baı tum baı tum baı tum baı tum baı tum baı tum baı

Tra la la la la la la la la la la la la la.

Tra la la la la la la la la la la la la la la la.

READ and clap these note values. Some of them can be found in the rhythms of "Tumbai."

READ the same rhythms from the notation of "Tumbai." Work in groups to practice these rhythms.

THINK IT THROUGH

How are the rhythms in the chart like the rhythms in the song? Could rhythms from the chart be played at the same time as those from the song? Why or why not?

LET'S MOVE!

LEARN this dance step.

1
step right

2
cross back

3
step right

4
hop right

MOVE to show each phrase of "Tumbai."

- Phrase 1: walk right 4 counts, walk left 4 counts.
- Phrase 2: right, back, right, hop; left, back, left, hop as shown above.
- Phrase 3: move forward 3 steps and clap, back 3 steps and clap.

Now try this movement as a circle dance.

8
hop left

7
step left

6
cross back

5
step left

The recording of "Tumbai" is in ABA form. The song is the A section and an instrumental melody is the B section.

CREATE sixteen beats of movement to do with a partner during the B section.

Now dance the big ABA form.
- Do the circle dance with the A section.
- Do your own partner movement with the B section.

Major Talk About Minor

There is a **key signature** at the beginning of every staff. It shows which notes must be sharped or flatted in a particular key. In the key of C major, there are no sharps or flats.

Check the key signature in "Tumbai." The sharp on the F line tells you that every F must be played as an F♯.

E is the tonal center, and you might guess that the key is E major. But "Tumbai" doesn't sound like a major song. Look at all the pitches from E to E' written with the F♯ in the key signature.

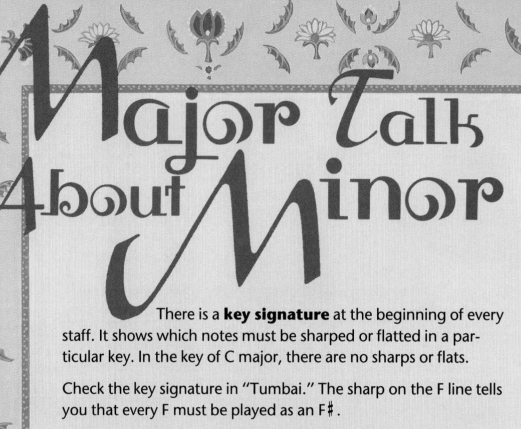

Notice that the half steps fall between pitches 2 and 3, and 5 and 6. This is a **minor scale**. (Remember that in the major scale the half steps fall between pitches 3 and 4, and 7 and 8.) "Tumbai" is written in E minor. We know it is minor because:

- the half steps fall between pitches 2 and 3, and 5 and 6
- *la* is the tonal center

1 2 3 4 5 6 7 8

la, ti, do re mi fa so la
       ∨   ∨
half step   half step

In minor, the half steps still fall between *mi* and *fa,* and *ti* and *do,* just as they do in major. When you are trying to tell if music is in major or in minor, listen for a half step between pitches two and three of the scale.

TALK ABOUT TEXTURE

Sing "Tumbai" as a canon in three groups. All the groups sing lines 1, 2, and 3, but start at different times. All three groups stop singing at the same time when a signal is given. Each group will be at a different place when the music stops.

Think about the difference between the sound of everyone singing "Tumbai" as a three-part canon and the sound of everyone singing the melody in unison. The difference that you observe is a difference in texture.

Unaccompanied unison singing has a very thin texture. Adding accompaniment makes a somewhat thicker texture. Singing in canon is even thicker. So, texture is changed by changing the number of things that are going on at once.

MOVE in canon as you sing. Each group moves in its own circle.

This song mentions Üsküdar, the city in Turkey pictured at left.

SING this song.

Üsküdar

Popular Turkish Song
English Version by MMH

Turkish:	Üs - kü - dar' a gi - der i ken	al - di - da bir yağ mur,
Pronunciation:	üs kü dɑɾ ɑ gi dɛɾ i kɛn	al di dɑ biɾ ya muɾ
English:	Üs - kü - dar, a dis - tant cit - y.	I walk a - long the road.

Ka - ti - bi - min se - tre - si u - zun e - te - gi - ça -
ka ti bi min sɛ tɾɛ si u zun ɛ tɛ gi jɑ
On a rain - y morn - ing there I met my

mur. e - te - gi - ça - mur.
muɾ ɛ tɛ gi jɑ muɾ
friend. there I met my friend.

Do you hear something familiar about this song? In what way does it sound like "Tumbai"?

Many of the rhythm patterns in "Üsküdar" and "Tumbai" are the same.

- Identify the rhythms in "Üsküdar" that you recognize from "Tumbai."
- What is the rhythm pattern that is not found in "Tumbai"?
- Another way to write ♩♫ is ♬♬ How many beats does it take to play this rhythm? This rhythm occurs in the song on the word *Üsküdar*.

TAP this rhythm while listening to the song.

Through THICK & THIN

Anything you study—math, meteorology, medicine—has its own vocabulary. Music is no exception. You already know and understand many of these specialized terms.

DESCRIBE what you know about the term *texture* as it's used in music, using the pictures below.

Here are the three words describing texture: *monophony, homophony, polyphony. Mono-* means alone or single in Greek. *Homo-* means the same. *Poly-* means many.

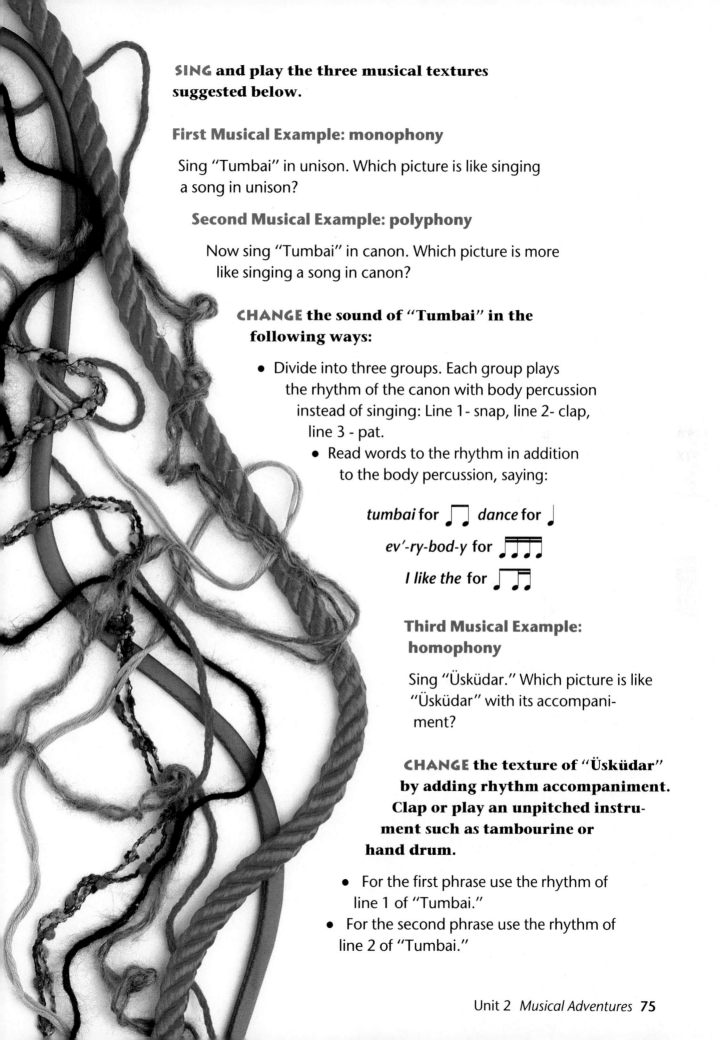

SING and play the three musical textures suggested below.

First Musical Example: monophony

Sing "Tumbai" in unison. Which picture is like singing a song in unison?

Second Musical Example: polyphony

Now sing "Tumbai" in canon. Which picture is more like singing a song in canon?

CHANGE the sound of "Tumbai" in the following ways:

- Divide into three groups. Each group plays the rhythm of the canon with body percussion instead of singing: Line 1- snap, line 2- clap, line 3 - pat.
  - Read words to the rhythm in addition to the body percussion, saying:

tumbai for ♫ *dance* for ♩

ev'-ry-bod-y for ♫♫

I like the for ♩♫

Third Musical Example: homophony

Sing "Üsküdar." Which picture is like "Üsküdar" with its accompaniment?

CHANGE the texture of "Üsküdar" by adding rhythm accompaniment. Clap or play an unpitched instrument such as tambourine or hand drum.

- For the first phrase use the rhythm of line 1 of "Tumbai."
- For the second phrase use the rhythm of line 2 of "Tumbai."

Joshua Fit the Battle of Jericho

Two Versions
African American Spiritual

"Joshua Fit the Battle of Jericho" is a well-known spiritual. It was created in the early days of the United States, and is still being performed today. Spirituals, also called "sorrow songs," were written by enslaved African Americans to express their suffering and their wish for a better life. These songs were also used to send secret messages. The spiritual "Deep River" was sung to announce a meeting near a river. The song "Wade in the Water" told people trying to escape to walk in the river, so that the search dogs could not locate them.

LISTEN to two different versions of "Joshua" and think about the texture of each.

- Which version had the thinner texture?
- Which version had the thicker texture?
- Which version was not homophonic?

Opera singer Florence Quivar
and pianist Armen Guzelimian

Vonetta Green, vocalist

One Last Adventure

Almost all of the music you've encountered on your musical adventures so far used only two different meter signatures: $\frac{2}{4}$ and $\frac{4}{4}$. This music moved in groups of twos rather than threes.

In the meter signature $\frac{3}{4}$, the 3 means that there are three beats to a measure, and the 4 means that each beat has a quarter-note value.

How would you like to meet a troll king in a mountain cave, a chieftain in a desert tent, become fabulously wealthy, and then lose it all? This is what happens to Peer Gynt, the main character in an 1867 play by the Norwegian playwright Henrik Ibsen. The background music for the play was written in 1874 by Ibsen's fellow countryman, Edvard Grieg.

Peer Gynt's adventures take him to northern Africa. It is the late 1800s. A chieftain's tent is spread with a lavish feast. Musicians are entertaining assembled guests. The music is in a minor key, but there is something different about the meter.

IDENTIFY the meter of this music. How can you tell?

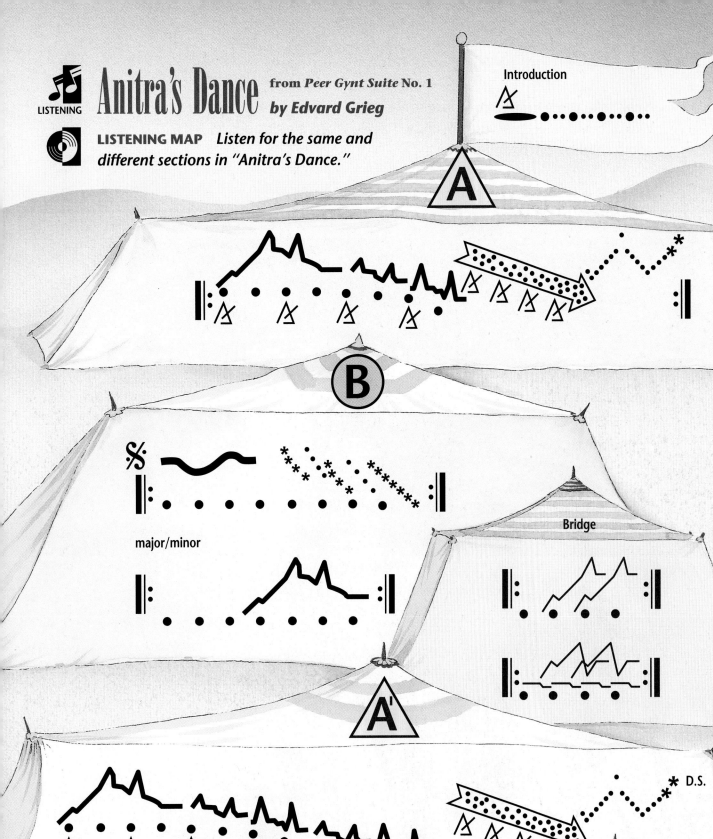

LISTENING

Anitra's Dance
from *Peer Gynt Suite* No. 1
by Edvard Grieg

LISTENING MAP *Listen for the same and different sections in "Anitra's Dance."*

Introduction

A

B

major/minor

Bridge

A'

D.S.

last time

Listening Map concept by Kay Greenhaw

Now, take some time to compose some music of your own. Working with a partner, use what you have learned in this unit about rhythm, pitch, and form.

CREATE a B section for an ABA form with "Kokoleoko" as the A section.

- Make up an eight-beat rhythm pattern.
- Use sixteenth notes in at least one of those beats.

PLAY YOUR RHYTHM PATTERN

- Choose instruments or other sound sources that make short sounds.
- Combine your pattern with the pattern of another pair of students who have an instrument that is different from yours. Play the patterns one after the other, or both at the same time. The choice is yours.
- Practice until the combined patterns are easy to play.

PLAY your pattern on a pitched instrument such as bells, xylophone, or keyboard.

- Choose three to five pitches from the C major scale.
- Transfer the rhythm pattern you created to the pitched instrument, using the pitches you have chosen. Hint: make your phrase sound like C major by ending it on C, E, or G.
- Play your pattern with another pair of students who have instruments with contrasting tone colors.
- Make any changes you and your partners think would make your patterns sound better.

Here it is! The final production!

A Sing "Kokoleoko" twice.

B Play your pitched pattern twice.

A Sing "Kokoleoko" twice more.

This art is based on a batik cloth design from the Ivory Coast.

REVIEW

MUSIC IS ADVENTURE

Music can take you on a journey through time and space—and you don't even have to leave your room. Today's journey revisits some of the places you discovered on your travels in this unit.

Begin with "One Moment in Time."

Liberia, on the west coast of Africa, was founded in the early 1800s to be a home for formerly enslaved African Americans. "Kokoleoko" is very popular in Liberia. What note values do you hear in its melody?

Musical journeys take you as far as your imagination can go. The words of "Flying Free" describe soaring like a bird in the sky. What is the form of "Flying Free"?

"Tumbai" comes to us from Israel. Perform "Tumbai," creating an ABA form with song and dance.

The words of "I Believe in Music" express the belief that music has the power to bring people together. People all over the world speak the language of music.

CHECK IT OUT

1. Which rhythm do you hear?

   a.

   b.

   c.

   d.

2. Which rhythm do you hear?

   a.

   b.

   c.

   d.

3. Do you hear a major scale?

   a. Yes   **b.** No

4. Do you hear a major scale?

   a. Yes   **b.** No

5. Do you hear ABA form?

   a. Yes   **b.** No

6. Do you hear ABA form?

   a. Yes   **b.** No

CREATE

Mood Music

When you're watching a movie or television mystery story, the music is often the first thing that tells you, "Watch out! Something is about to happen." Look at the picture below. If this were a scene in a movie, what might the next scene be?

CREATE some music in ABA form to go with this picture. Use tones from the major scale for the melodies and rapidly moving patterns, using sixteenth notes, for the rhythms.

- The A section should be music to set the mood.
- The B section should be background music for a story inspired by this picture.
- Return to the mood music of the A section to end your piece.

Write

Using the picture below as a starting point, write down some ideas for a mystery movie. Then write a brief dialogue for the part of the story that would go with the music you developed above.

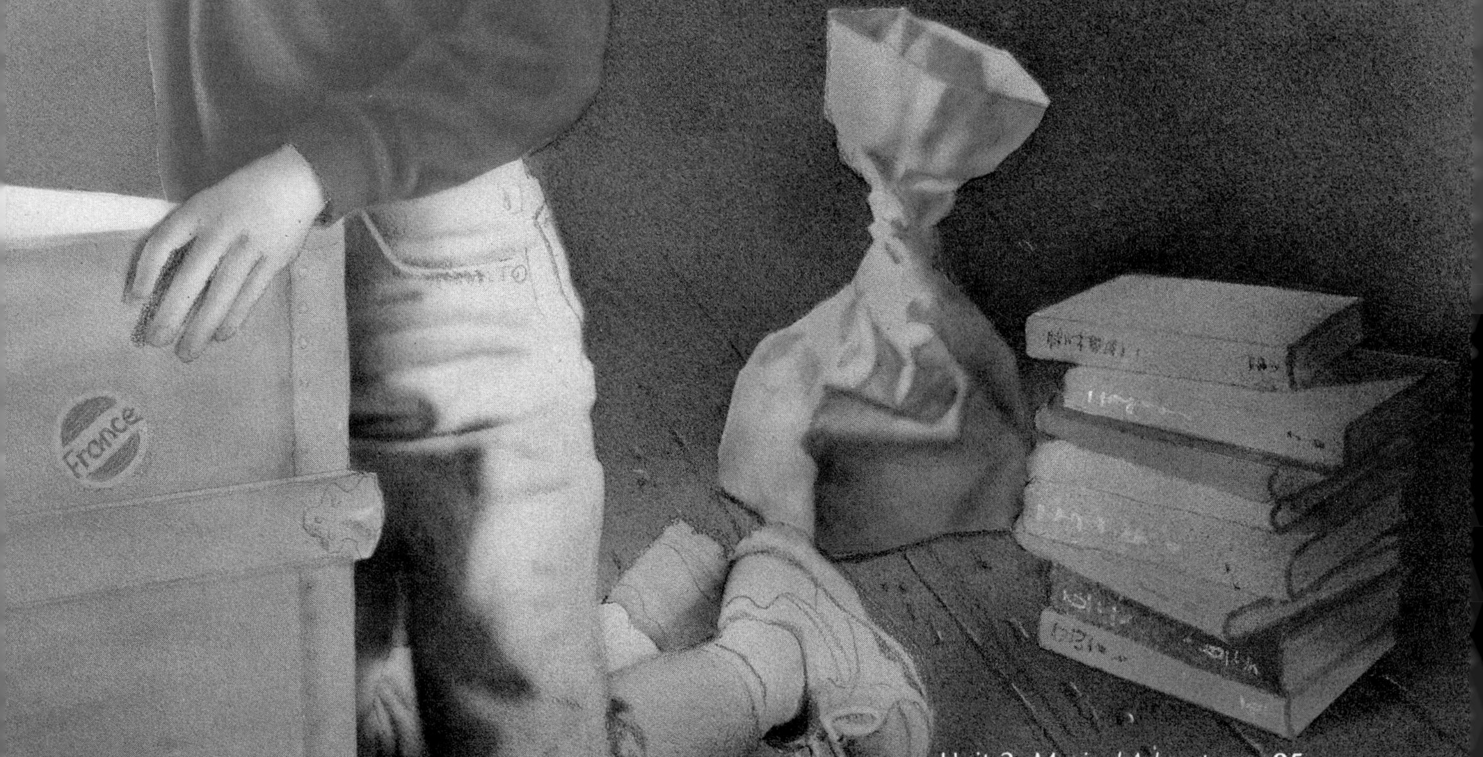

ENCORE DRUMMIN'

Have you ever started your own jam session? Perhaps you and several friends began by rapping on a table. Some of you may have slapped your hands on your thighs and perhaps others stomped their feet in a rhythmic pattern against the floor. You created an instant percussion band. Percussion instruments are those that produce sound when they are struck or shaken.

The drum is, perhaps, the most popular percussion instrument. All cultures have some form of drum. Drums vary greatly in shape, size, and method of playing. Some drums are struck with the fingers, others are shaken, and still others are rattled. The sound of the drum is affected by the material of the drumhead and the kind of wood used for the frame. In some cultures, the drum solo is the most important part of a performance.

G ALONG

Indian tablas

African talking drum

Korean changko

Middle-Eastern dumbek

Frame drums are portable instruments with circular frames. They are small enough to be held in one hand and struck with the other.

The tambourine, which originated in Southwest Asia, is a very simple and versatile instrument. It is one of the more popular frame drums. In addition to a drum head, the tambourine has jingles on it that ring when the instrument is struck.

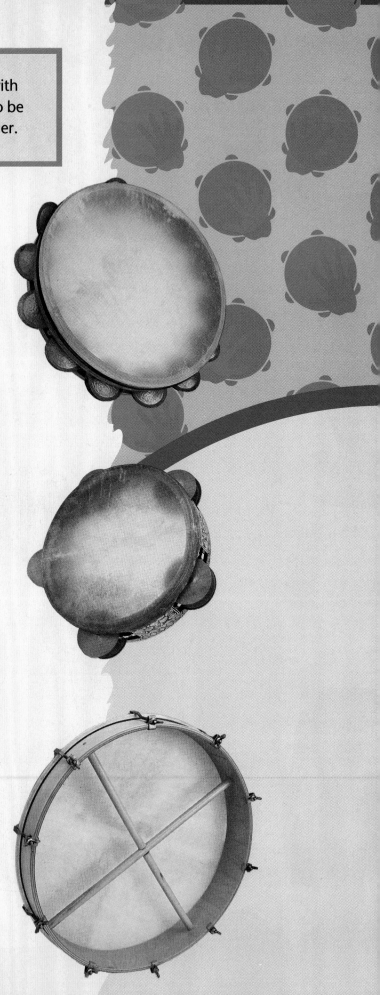

The riq, a drum from Egypt, resembles the tambourine. It is used in dance music, concert music, and religious music. The pitch of this drum can be raised or lowered.

Popular for more than a hundred years, the bodhran is a frame drum from Ireland. It has a low, deep sound, but brighter, ringing sounds can be drawn from it as well. Traditionally, this drum is played with a double-headed stick and is used in Irish folk music.

Meet GLEN VELEZ

Glen Velez, who first started studying the drums with his uncle at the age of eight, is an internationally known drummer, composer, scholar, and teacher. He has combined his background in Western percussion with the study of tambourine performance styles from around the world. For 15 years, Velez performed with the Steve Reich ensemble. He has been the percussionist with the Paul Winter Consort since 1983.

LISTEN to Glen Velez talk about his career and demonstrate some of the drums he has collected from around the world.

The Keyboard Connection

TO CATALINA

Love thy piano, Oh girl,
It will give you back
Note for note
The harmonies of your soul.
It will sing back to you
The high songs of your heart.
It will give
As well as take . . .

—Frank Horne

Jeunes filles au piano (detail),
by Pierre Auguste Renoir

91

THE KEY TO KEY

What do the piano, organ, and harpsichord have in common? They all have keyboards. Keyboard instruments are popular because you can play harmony on them, accompanying yourself. What keyboard instrument is used in "Harmony"?

Harmony

Words and Music by
Artie Kaplan and
Norman J. Simon

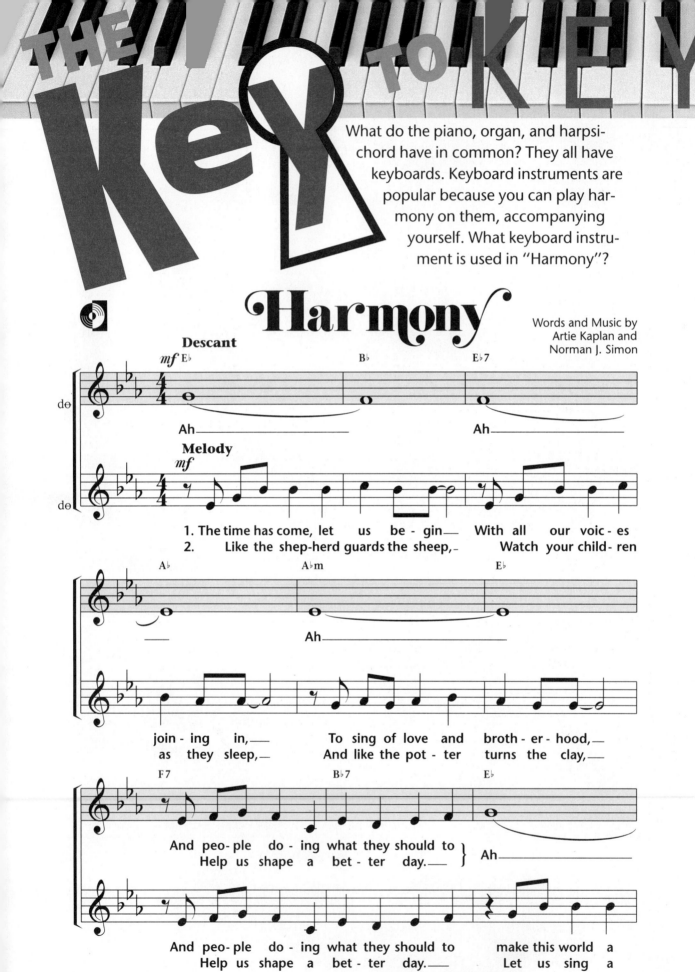

Descant

Ah_____ Ah_____

Melody

1. The time has come, let us be-gin___ With all our voic-es
2. Like the shep-herd guards the sheep,___ Watch your child-ren

Ah_____

join-ing in,___ To sing of love and broth-er-hood,___
as they sleep,___ And like the pot-ter turns the clay,___

And peo-ple do-ing what they should to
Help us shape a bet-ter day.___ } Ah_____

And peo-ple do-ing what they should to make this world a
Help us shape a bet-ter day.___ Let us sing a

har - mo - ny,___ And sing a - way___ the hurt and fear,___ A

har - mo - ny,___ And sing a - way___ the hurt and fear,___ A

great new day will soon be here._____

great new day will soon___ be___ here._____

LISTENING

Heart and Soul *by Hoagy Carmichael*

This song was written in 1938. Many beginning pianists learn to play it and its accompaniment as a duet.

FOLLOW this keyboard to play the bass line for "Heart and Soul." Touch one key on each beat. Play these notes in sequence: C E A₁ C D F G₁ B₁

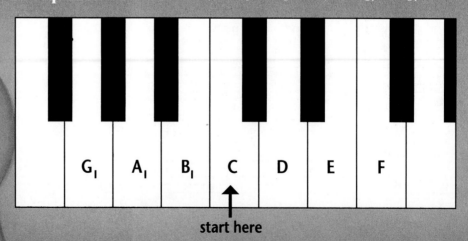

G₁ A₁ B₁ C D E F

start here

THE GIANT OF KEYBOARDS: THE PIPE ORGAN

Keyboard instruments have developed over hundreds of years. One of the oldest is the organ.

Pipe **organs** are the largest of all musical instruments. When organ keys are pressed, air is forced through pipes shaped like long tubes. The air vibrates in the tubes, creating sound. Organists play two or more keyboards, called *manuals,* as well as large, wooden foot pedals. Different tone qualities are produced by devices called *stops.* Stops control which pipes are used. Imagine playing an organ in a cathedral. By controlling hundreds of different-sized organ pipes, you can produce a great number of sounds.

AN ANCESTOR OF THE PIANO: THE HARPSICHORD

If you had attended a party at George Washington's home, you might have danced to the sounds of the **harpsichord.** The harpsichord is similar to the piano in shape, but it is smaller and much lighter. When the keys are pressed, metal strings inside the instrument are plucked, much like the strings of a harp.

LISTENING

Rondeau

by Elizabeth-Claude Jacquet de la Guerre

This composition is from a 1707 collection of harpsichord pieces dedicated to King Louis XIV of France. De la Guerre (1664–1729) was a child prodigy who often performed for the king.

THE AMAZING PIANO

The **piano** was invented in the 1700s, and within a hundred years or so it had replaced the harpsichord as the most popular keyboard instrument. *Piano* is short for *pianoforte,* which means "soft-loud" in Italian. The piano was the first keyboard instrument to be able to play a range of volume from soft to loud. When one of its eighty-eight keys is struck, small padded hammers hit strings inside the instrument. The strings vibrate and produce sound. The harder the key is struck, the louder the sound. As soon as the key is released, a felt pad, called a *damper,* touches the strings and stops the sound.

Genius at the Keyboard

The canon "Alleluia" is adapted from a soprano solo written by Wolfgang Amadeus Mozart.

Alleluia

Words and Music by
Wolfgang Amadeus Mozart

Spotlight on

Wolfgang Amadeus

Mozart

This portrait of Wolfgang, his sister Maria Anna, and their father, Leopold, was painted when Wolfgang was 7 or 8 years old.

When Wolfgang Amadeus Mozart (1756–1791) was only three years old, he was writing music for the harpsichord and violin. His father recognized his son's great talent and started giving him lessons on the harpsichord. Soon afterwards, his father began taking Mozart and his older sister to play concerts throughout Europe.

There are many stories about Mozart's musical genius. One is about an extraordinary feat he accomplished when he was fourteen. Mozart visited the Sistine Chapel in Rome. He heard a long composition for solo voices. The Pope had ruled that this piece could only be performed in the Sistine Chapel. He carefully guarded the music. After the performance, Mozart returned to his hotel room and wrote out the entire piece from memory. When the Pope learned of this accomplishment, he was not angry. Instead, he awarded Mozart a medal.

When Mozart was grown, he worked as an organist, pianist, music director, and composer. Although Mozart died at the early age of 35, he wrote a large number of compositions during his life, including several operas and many symphonies.

THE BLACK KEYS

To play the C major scale on the piano, only the white keys are used. However, to play a major scale from any other pitch, you need to use black keys. Play an F major scale. First, listen as someone plays a scale from F to F' without using any black keys. Does it sound correct?

Figure out which pitch is wrong in this F to F' scale by remembering where half steps should occur in a major scale.

Decide where you need to substitute a black key for a white key.

PLAY the F major scale.

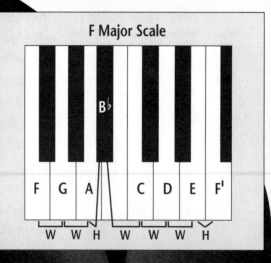

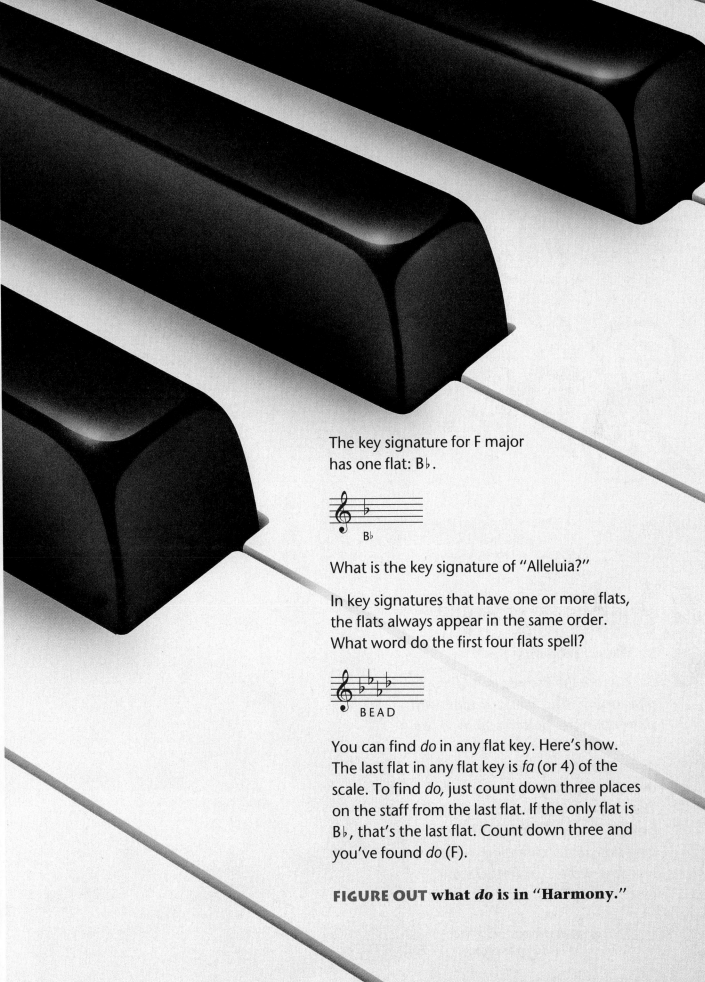

The key signature for F major has one flat: B♭.

B♭

What is the key signature of "Alleluia?"

In key signatures that have one or more flats, the flats always appear in the same order. What word do the first four flats spell?

BEAD

You can find *do* in any flat key. Here's how. The last flat in any flat key is *fa* (or 4) of the scale. To find *do,* just count down three places on the staff from the last flat. If the only flat is B♭, that's the last flat. Count down three and you've found *do* (F).

FIGURE OUT what *do* is in "Harmony."

The Pipes Speak

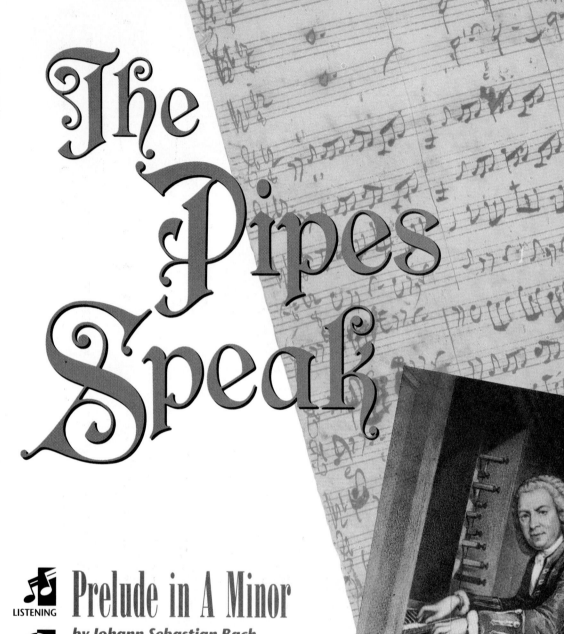

Prelude in A Minor

by Johann Sebastian Bach

Bach wrote the Prelude in A Minor for pipe organ. The music begins with sixteenth-note patterns played on the manuals. Soon you will hear six or eight notes to a beat, tumbling over one another like a waterfall. Then the low pedals play a **pedal point**—*a single pitch held for a long time under changing chords and fast scales. Later there are more pedal points.*

Bach was famous throughout Germany for his skill as an organist.

Remember the pitches in the C major scale and where the half steps occur.

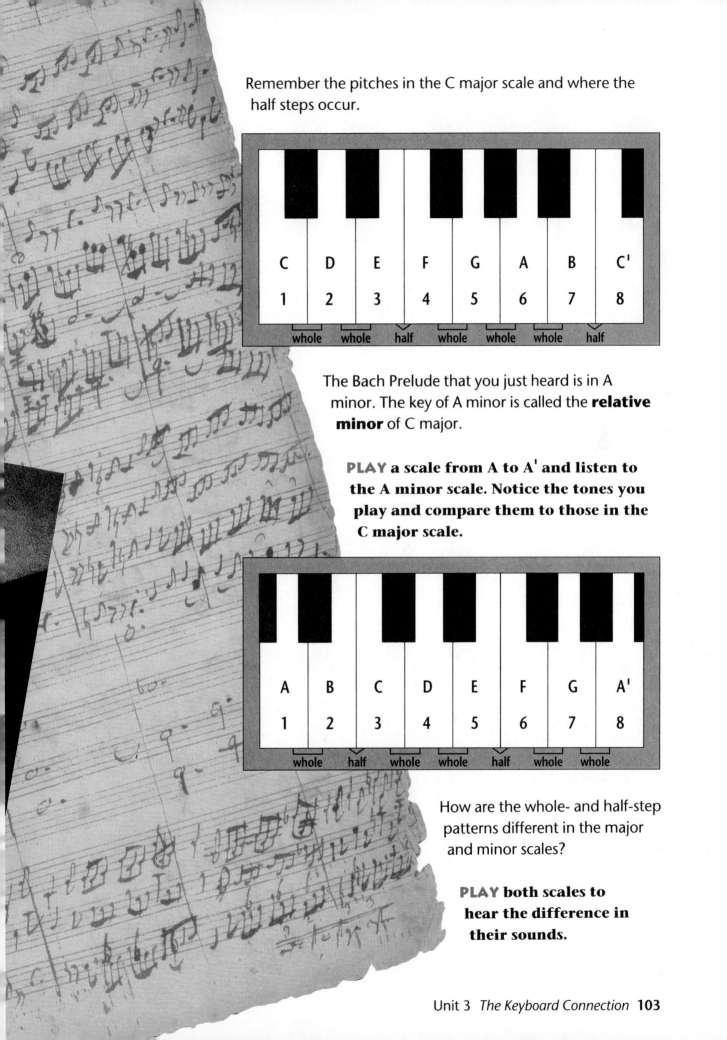

The Bach Prelude that you just heard is in A minor. The key of A minor is called the **relative minor** of C major.

PLAY a scale from A to A' and listen to the A minor scale. Notice the tones you play and compare them to those in the C major scale.

How are the whole- and half-step patterns different in the major and minor scales?

PLAY both scales to hear the difference in their sounds.

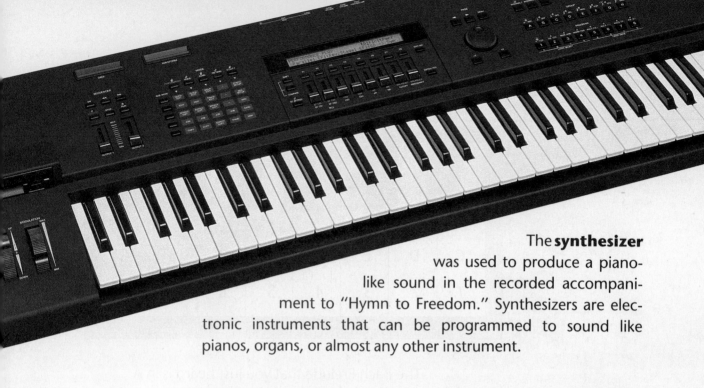

The synthesizer was used to produce a piano-like sound in the recorded accompaniment to "Hymn to Freedom." Synthesizers are electronic instruments that can be programmed to sound like pianos, organs, or almost any other instrument.

HYMN TO FREEDOM

Music by
Oscar Peterson
Words by
Harriette Hamilton

When ev'-ry heart joins ev'-ry heart and to-geth-er yearns for lib-er-ty,— that's when we'll be free.

When ev'-ry hand joins ev'-ry hand and to-geth-er moulds our des-ti-ny,— that's when we'll be free.

An-y hour, an-y day the time soon will come when we will live in

dig - ni - ty, — that's when we'll be free. When ev' - ry one

joins in our song, and to - geth - er sing - ing

har - mo - ny, — that's when we'll be free.

that's when we'll be free. — We'll be free.

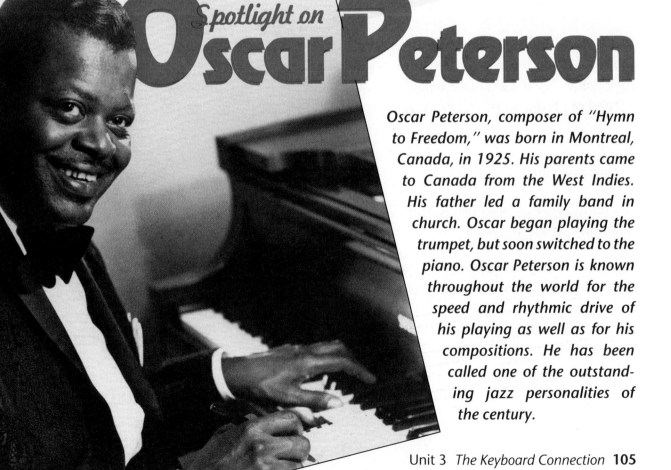

Spotlight on Oscar Peterson

Oscar Peterson, composer of "Hymn to Freedom," was born in Montreal, Canada, in 1925. His parents came to Canada from the West Indies. His father led a family band in church. Oscar began playing the trumpet, but soon switched to the piano. Oscar Peterson is known throughout the world for the speed and rhythmic drive of his playing as well as for his compositions. He has been called one of the outstanding jazz personalities of the century.

A DOT MAKES A Difference

SAY the following rhythm patterns, and you'll see what a difference a dot makes.

First try this pattern, made up of equal sounds.

Sing   my   song

Now try the same pattern, with the second beat divided equally into two parts.

Sing   me a song

Sometimes, rhythm patterns with unequal sounds are needed. Dots after notes lengthen their value. Try the example below. This time, instead of saying "me" out loud, just think it.

Sing——— (me) a song

Try clapping or playing this pattern with the recording of "Harmony."

A **dotted** note is lengthened by half its value. Here's some musical math for you:

♩ = ♪ ♪   (A quarter note is as long as two eighth notes.)

♩. = ♪ ♪ ♪   (A dotted quarter note is as long as three eighth notes.)

A KEYBOARD INSTRUMENT IN FOLK MUSIC—THE ACCORDION

Cajuns are French-speaking residents of Louisiana. This Cajun song describes going by horse and buggy to get supplies from Mamou, a small town that specialized in rice and crawfish.

Tee galop pour Mamou

Gallop On to Mamou

Cajun Folk Dance
English Version by MMH

French:	Tee ga - lop, tee ga -	lop pour Ma - mou!___	J'ai ven - du mon tee mu -
Pronunciation:	ti ga lo ti ga	lo puɾ ma mu	ʒe vã dü mɔ̃ ti mü
English:	Gal - lop on, gal - lop	on to Ma - mou!___	Sold my mule for on - ly

let pour quinze sous.___	J'ai ache - té du can - di rouge pour les tee,___
le puɾ kãz su	ʒe ash te dü kã di ɾuʒ puɾ le ti
fif - teen pen - nies.___	Bought red can - dy for the lit - tle chil - dren,

___	du su - cre et du ca - fé	pour les vieux.
	dü sü kɾə e dü ka fe	puɾ le vyö
___	sug - ar and some cof - fee for	the old folks.

You know that: ♩. = ♪ ♪ ♪
So, it stands to reason that: ♪. = ♪ ♪ ♪

Look for dotted notes in this song.
Is the pattern ♩. ♪ or ♫ . ?

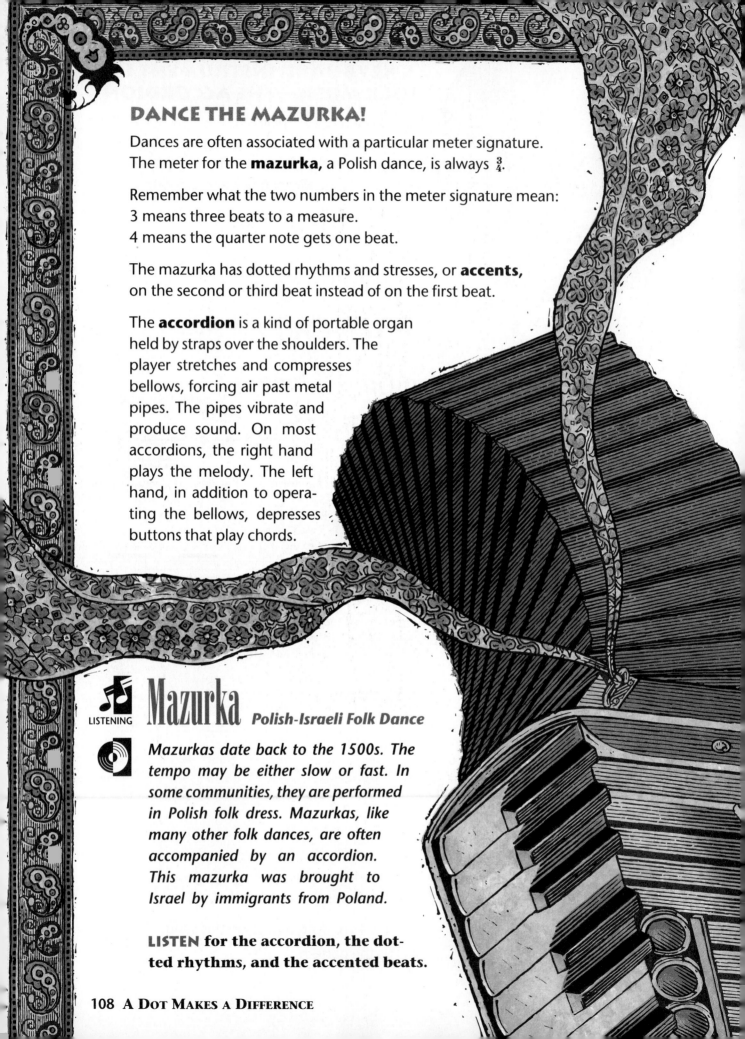

DANCE THE MAZURKA!

Dances are often associated with a particular meter signature. The meter for the **mazurka,** a Polish dance, is always $\frac{3}{4}$.

Remember what the two numbers in the meter signature mean:
3 means three beats to a measure.
4 means the quarter note gets one beat.

The mazurka has dotted rhythms and stresses, or **accents,** on the second or third beat instead of on the first beat.

The **accordion** is a kind of portable organ held by straps over the shoulders. The player stretches and compresses bellows, forcing air past metal pipes. The pipes vibrate and produce sound. On most accordions, the right hand plays the melody. The left hand, in addition to operating the bellows, depresses buttons that play chords.

LISTENING

Mazurka _Polish-Israeli Folk Dance_

Mazurkas date back to the 1500s. The tempo may be either slow or fast. In some communities, they are performed in Polish folk dress. Mazurkas, like many other folk dances, are often accompanied by an accordion. This mazurka was brought to Israel by immigrants from Poland.

LISTEN for the accordion, the dotted rhythms, and the accented beats.

SPOTLIGHT ON Frédéric Chopin

Frédéric Chopin (1810–1849) was born in Warsaw, Poland. Like Mozart, he showed great musical talent at an early age. When he was eight, he gave his first public performance on the piano. Chopin left Warsaw and settled in Paris, France.

Almost all of Chopin's compositions are for solo piano. They explore a wide expressive range—from the quiet and dreamlike to the very bold and dramatic. For this reason, Chopin is called the "Poet of the Piano."

FRÉDÉRIC CHOPIN
This portrait by Eugène Delacroix (1798–1863) contrasts light and shadow to focus attention on the composer's face.

LISTENING

Mazurka, Op. 68, No. 3

by Frédéric Chopin

During the 1800s the mazurka became so popular that it was danced throughout Europe. Chopin's mazurkas were intended for listening.

IDENTIFY the beat with the dotted rhythm. What is the form of this mazurka?

A Piano that Plays Itself

Player pianos were very fashionable during the late 1800s and early 1900s. A player piano uses a roll of paper with patterns of holes that correspond to the different pitches in a piece of music. The roll moves over a cylinder, which also has small holes. Air is sucked through the matching holes in the moving roll and the cylinder. The air causes the piano's hammers to move and strike the strings, producing musical sounds.

With a player piano, listeners could be entertained by their favorite piano music without having to play the instrument themselves.

PLAYER PIANO

My stick fingers click with a snicker
As, chuckling, they knuckle the keys,
Light-footed, my steel feelers flicker
And pluck from the keys melodies.

My paper can caper, abandon
Is broadcast by dint of my din,
And no man or band has a hand in
The tones I turn on from within.

At times I'm a jumble of rumbles,
At others I'm light like the moon,
But never my numb plunker fumbles,
Misstrums me, or tries a new tune.

—*John Updike*

Player pianos in the old days often played popular songs in a style called "ragtime." This style often used the dotted-rhythm pattern ♪.♪

LISTEN for this dotted rhythm in "The Old Piano Roll Blues." Then sing the song.

The Old Piano Roll Blues

Words and Music by Cy Coben

I wanna hear it again, I wanna hear it again,
The Old Piano Roll Blues.
We're sittin' at an upright, my buddy and me,
Pushin' on the pedals, makin' sweet harmony,
When we hear rinkity tink, and we hear plinkity plink,
The music's better it seems.
And while we sing, sing, sing away all our cares,
The player piano's playin' razzamatazz,
I wanna hear it again, I wanna hear it again,
The Old Piano Roll Blues.

Franz Joseph Haydn

Franz Joseph Haydn (1732–1809) showed musical talent on the violin and harpsichord as a child. At the age of eight, Haydn went to Vienna, Austria, to study music. As an adult Haydn conducted an orchestra, composed music, and ran musical activities for a Hungarian noble family for over thirty years.

Haydn composed works for orchestra, chorus, keyboard instruments, and singers. He also wrote **chamber music.** This is music performed by smaller groups in homes or other small spaces. A piano trio is one kind of chamber music group. It is made up of a violin, a cello, and a piano.

LISTENING

Trio No. 39
Finale (Gypsy Rondo)
by Franz Joseph Haydn

*Listen to a piano trio by Franz Joseph Haydn. The piano you hear was made in 1797 and is called a **fortepiano.** It is smaller and quieter than modern pianos. This movement is called the "Gypsy Rondo." Perform the rhythm below whenever you hear the A section of the rondo. Where have you played the rhythm of the first two measures before?*

A fortepiano built in
Vienna, Austria, around 1790

113

The Envelope, Please

meet  Ellis Marsalis

Ellis Marsalis, born in 1934, is a pianist, composer, and music teacher from New Orleans, Louisiana. While he was studying to be a music teacher, Marsalis played jazz in clubs around New Orleans. Later, he played with jazz greats Ornette Coleman, Don Cherry, and others. Since the 1970s, Ellis Marsalis has been very successful as a teacher, helping many young jazz musicians to develop their talents. Among Ellis's students are his sons Wynton and Branford, and the singer-pianist Harry Connick, Jr. All have become famous jazz musicians.

LISTENING

This Can't Be Love

by Lorenz Hart and Richard Rodgers

Listen to Ellis Marsalis and his band perform this song from the 1938 musical The Boys from Syracuse. *Jason Marsalis, the youngest son of Ellis Marsalis, is playing drums in this recording.*

THE SHAPE OF SOUND

Every sound we hear has the same parts. It has a beginning, a middle, and an end. These parts are called *attack, decay, sustain,* and *release.*

DEMONSTRATE these stages by playing tones on a resonator bell. The picture below represents four stages of any sound.

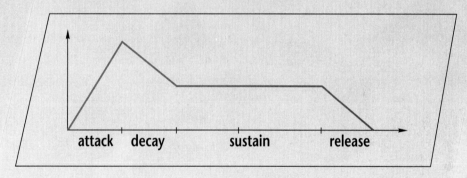

attack decay sustain release

Attack: The pitch begins with the sharp sound of the mallet hitting the bell.

Decay: The sound fades a bit.

Sustain: As the pitch sounds, it rings and sustains.

Release: The sound gradually fades away.

Attack, decay, sustain, and release help give all instruments and voices their own unique character. The combination of these four stages is called an **envelope**. The same pitch played on a piano, an organ, and a harpsichord will have a completely different envelope.

This song brings a message of good news. It is in a style known as *gospel.* Gospel music is often accompanied by both piano and electric organ. Gospel may be sung in a call-and-response style. In this vocal style, each phrase is sung by a soloist, then answered by a chorus. "Said I Wasn't Gonn' Tell Nobody" is in call-and-response style.

Said I Wasn't Gonn' Tell Nobody

African American Gospel Song
Arranged by René Boyer-White

FLIGHTS OF FANCY

The **fugue** is a musical form used by Bach and other composers. The word *fugue* means "flight." In a fugue, the parts seem to be trying to get away from each other. Parts of a fugue sound like a canon, because the different voices enter one at a time and imitate one another. To create a fugue, a composer must follow a set of rules of musical form.

PERFORM this four-part spoken fugue from the chart below.

1. At a signal, each person reads parts **A**, **B**, and **C** all the way through. Reader 1 begins alone. When each reader reaches **B**, the next reader begins. When the readers finish **C**, they repeat it until everyone is reading **C** together.

2. At a signal, the readers perform step 1 again.

3. At a signal, the readers perform a **stretto**. To do this, Reader 1 begins **A** alone. Every few seconds another reader begins **A**. The readers repeat **A** until a signal is given to say, all together, "the end." The stretto makes the end of a fugue exciting.

A The main theme of a fugue is called the **subject**. This tune is usually easy to recognize and remember.

B The subject is followed by a **countersubject**. This tune is also easy to recognize and remember. It usually accompanies the subject.

C Sometimes, no one is performing the subject or the countersubject. This part is called an **episode**.

Sonata in G Minor (The Cat's Fugue)
by Domenico Scarlatti

Domenico Scarlatti was born in 1685, the same year as J. S. Bach. Scarlatti was Italian, but lived and worked much of his life at the Spanish royal court in Madrid. He wrote over 500 short pieces for the harpsichord. This is his only fugue. It is called "The Cat's Fugue" because the subject sounds like a cat walking across the keyboard.

LISTENING MAP *Point to either "subject-countersubject" or to "episode" in the map when you hear those parts of "The Cat's Fugue." Which keyboard instrument do you hear?*

subject-countersubject

episode

All Thumbs!

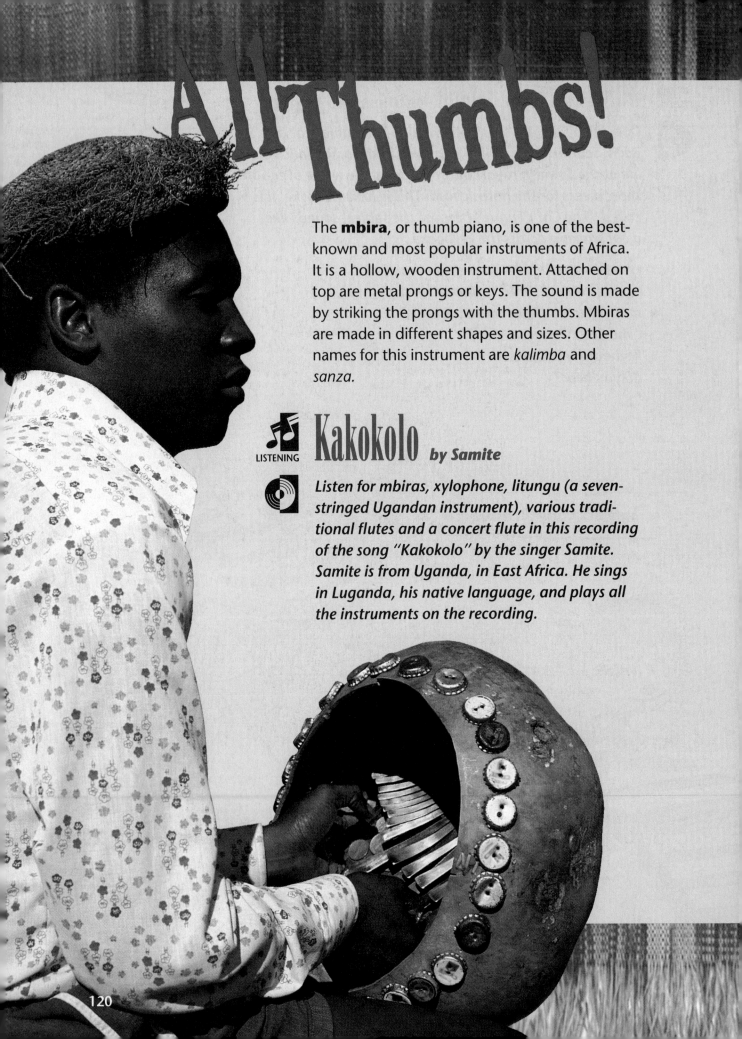

The **mbira**, or thumb piano, is one of the best-known and most popular instruments of Africa. It is a hollow, wooden instrument. Attached on top are metal prongs or keys. The sound is made by striking the prongs with the thumbs. Mbiras are made in different shapes and sizes. Other names for this instrument are *kalimba* and *sanza*.

LISTENING

Kakokolo *by Samite*

Listen for mbiras, xylophone, litungu (a seven-stringed Ugandan instrument), various traditional flutes and a concert flute in this recording of the song "Kakokolo" by the singer Samite. Samite is from Uganda, in East Africa. He sings in Luganda, his native language, and plays all the instruments on the recording.

Kakokolo

Words and Music by Samite

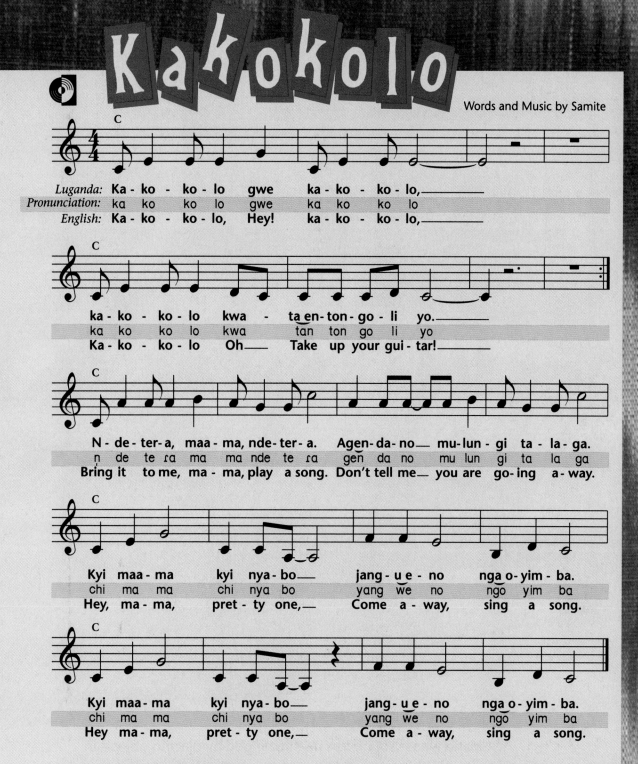

Luganda: **Ka - ko - ko - lo gwe ka - ko - ko - lo,**_____
Pronunciation: ka ko ko lo gwe ka ko ko lo
English: **Ka - ko - ko - lo, Hey! ka - ko - ko - lo,**_____

ka - ko - ko - lo kwa - ta en - ton - go - li yo._____
ka ko ko lo kwa tan ton go li yo
Ka - ko - ko - lo Oh___ Take up your gui - tar!

N - de - ter - a, maa - ma, nde - ter - a. Agen - da - no___ mu - lun - gi ta - la - ga.
n de te ɾa ma ma nde te ɾa gen da no mu lun gi ta la ga
Bring it to me, ma - ma, play a song. Don't tell me___ you are go - ing a - way.

Kyi maa - ma kyi nya - bo___ jang - u e - no nga o - yim - ba.
chi ma ma chi nya bo yang we no ngo yim ba
Hey, ma - ma, pret - ty one,___ Come a - way, sing a song.

Kyi maa - ma kyi nya - bo___ jang - u e - no nga o - yim - ba.
chi ma ma chi nya bo yang we no ngo yim ba
Hey ma - ma, pret - ty one,___ Come a - way, sing a song.

CREATE and perform a dance for "Kakokolo."
**Step to the rhythm pattern you used for
"Harmony" and the "Gypsy Rondo."**

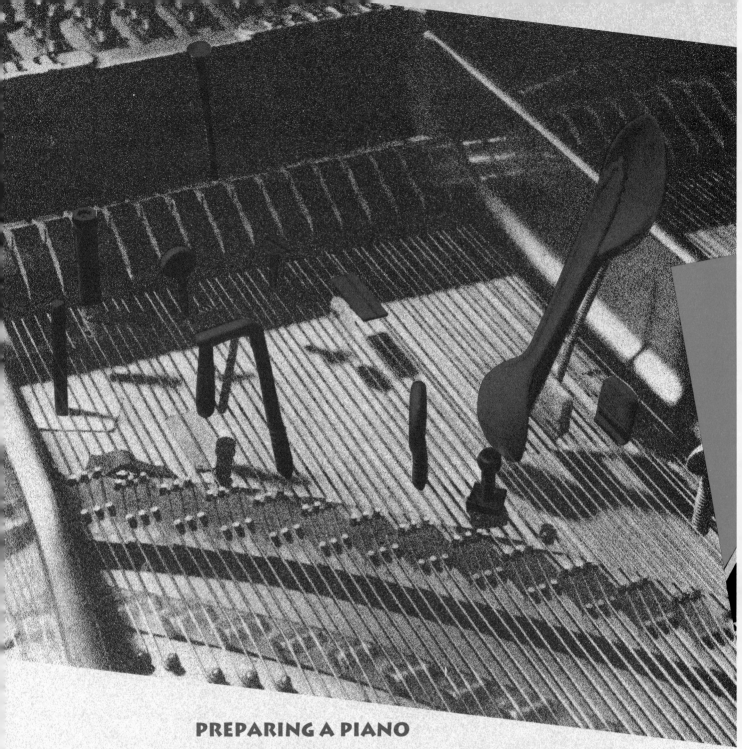

PREPARING A PIANO

A piano whose sound has been changed by placing objects in contact with the strings is called a **prepared piano.** Items such as pieces of paper, coins, spoons, or erasers are placed on or between the piano's strings. This causes the instrument to produce sounds that are completely different from those a piano usually makes. In addition to striking the keys, the performers hit wooden parts of the piano and reach inside the instrument to pluck, strum, or tap the strings.

The idea of the prepared piano was introduced by American composer John Cage in the early 1940s.

Spotlight on

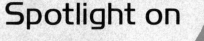
John Cage

John Cage (1912–1992) was the son of an inventor. As a young man he studied composition. Like his father, he saw new ways to use old materials. In addition to the prepared piano, he developed what is called chance music. The performer is given the task of making major decisions about the music. A player might choose some of the pitches, or decide the order in which to perform the parts of a composition.

John Cage had many other innovative ideas. Sometimes he invited the audience to join in on the performance. Once, he asked them to go out and get garbage cans because they were needed for percussion sounds.

LISTENING

Three Dances for Two Amplified Prepared Pianos (excerpt)
by John Cage

Cage used the sounds of Asian music in this piece, which he wrote in the mid-1940s.

THINK IT THROUGH

What musical instruments or other sounds do you think the prepared pianos sound like?

KEYS FOR TWO

Music for keyboards generally covers a wide range of notes, from very low to very high. Because of this, keyboard players must read music in both the **treble clef** and **bass clef**. Notes on the top staff (with the treble clef) are higher, and are usually played by the right hand. The bottom staff (with the bass clef) is for the lower notes. Lower pitches are usually played by the left hand. Middle C is usually considered to be the dividing line between treble and bass clefs.

These notes can be found on what is called the **grand staff,** a staff that combines both clefs.

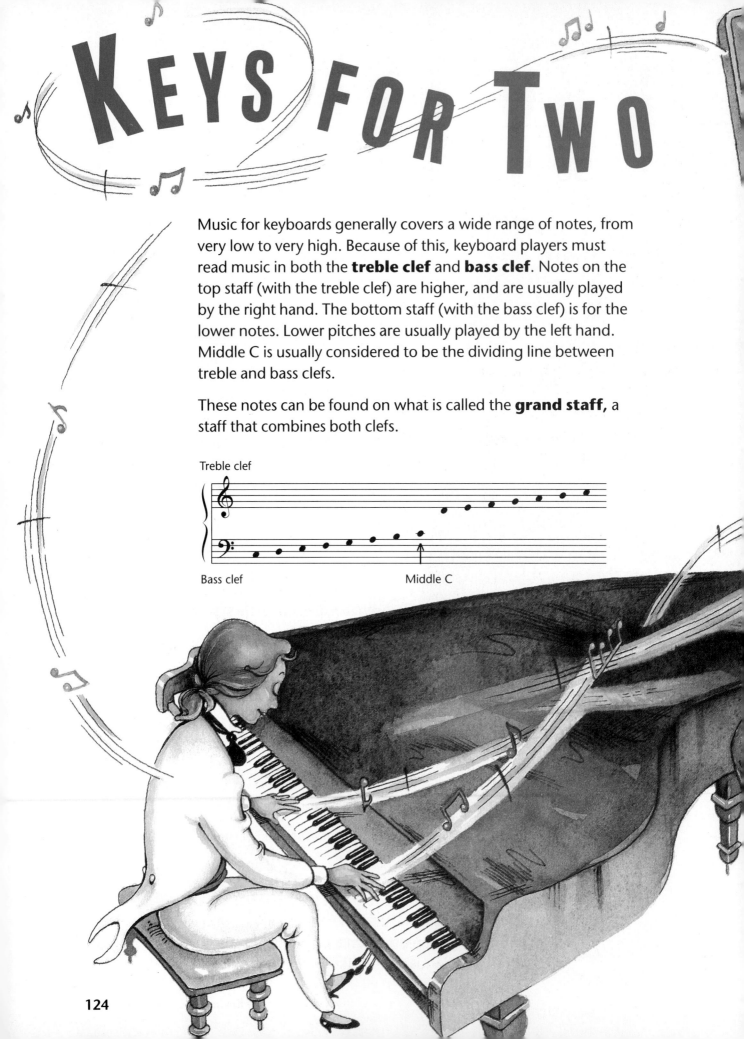

Treble clef

Bass clef

Middle C

SPOTLIGHT ON

Katia & Marielle Labèque

Katia and Marielle Labèque are French sisters who play together as **duo-pianists.** *Using two pianos, they get a thick, full sound. One pianist plays melody parts with both hands. The other plays accompaniment parts with both hands. Sometimes, the pianos exchange melody and accompaniment roles.*

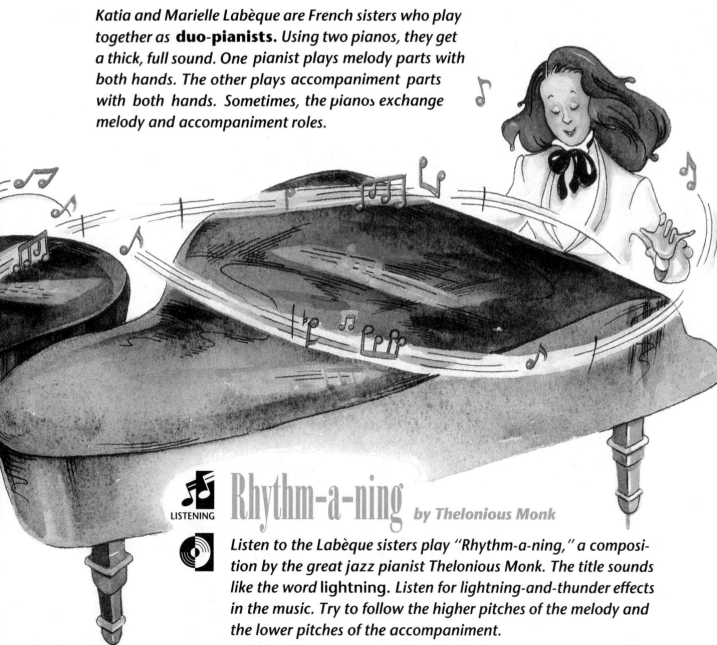

LISTENING

Rhythm-a-ning *by Thelonious Monk*

*Listen to the Labèque sisters play "Rhythm-a-ning," a composition by the great jazz pianist Thelonious Monk. The title sounds like the word **lightning.** Listen for lightning-and-thunder effects in the music. Try to follow the higher pitches of the melody and the lower pitches of the accompaniment.*

PLAY the melody of this song on a keyboard with a chordal accompaniment underneath it.

Lean on Me

Words and Music
by Bill Withers

Some-times in our lives ___ we all have pain ___ we all have sor-

row. ___ But if we are wise ___ we know that there's ___

___ al-ways to-mor - row. ___ Lean on me when you're not strong ___

and I'll be your friend ___ I'll help you car - ry ___ on

for it won't be long ___ 'til I'm gon-na need ___ some-bod-y to lean ___

___ on. Please ___ swal-low your pride ___ if I have things ___

you need to bor - row ___ for no one can fill ___

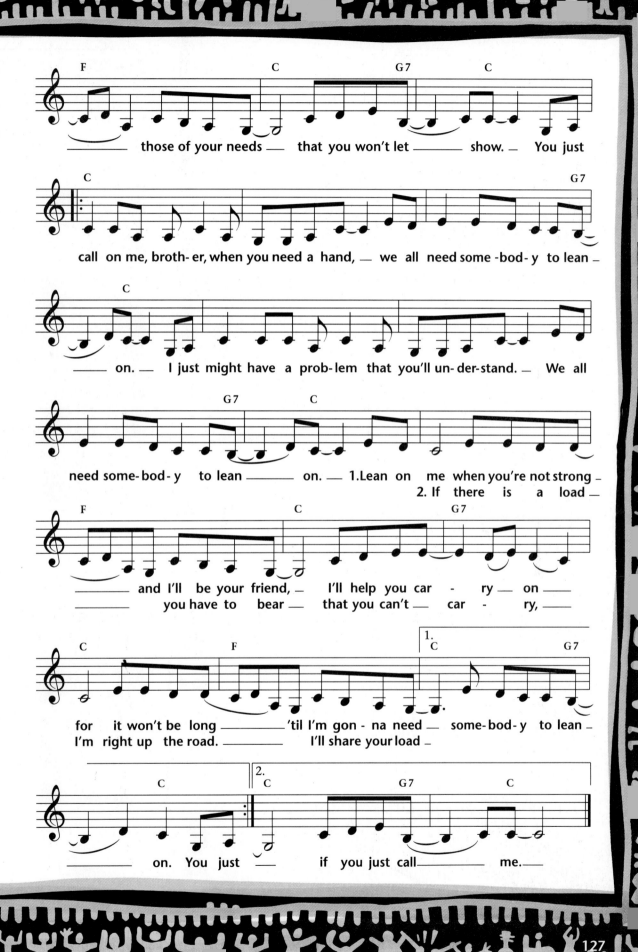

those of your needs — that you won't let — show. — You just

call on me, broth-er, when you need a hand, — we all need some-bod-y to lean —

— on. — I just might have a prob-lem that you'll un-der-stand. — We all

need some-bod-y to lean ——— on. — 1. Lean on me when you're not strong —
2. If there is a load —

——— and I'll be your friend, — I'll help you car - ry — on —
you have to bear — that you can't — car - ry, —

1.
for it won't be long ——— 'til I'm gon - na need — some-bod-y to lean —
I'm right up the road. ——— I'll share your load —

2.
——— on. You just — if you just call——— me.—

KEYBOARD COLLECTION

Press a key and what sound comes out? Depending on whether it's a piano, organ, harpsichord, accordion, or synthesizer, the sound might be very different indeed.

The heart and soul of the organ, harpsichord, and piano are their keyboards. Listen to "Heart and Soul" and perform the bass line with it.

With keyboard instruments you can play several pitches at the same time, creating harmony. Make some harmony by singing "Harmony" in two parts.

Some keyboard instruments, such as the organ, have been around for several centuries. "Alleluia," a song more than two centuries old, was written by Mozart. Listen for the organ accompanying the song on the recording.

The accordion is also a keyboard instrument, but it is much more portable than the piano or organ! "Tee galop pour Mamou" comes from the southern part of Louisiana, where French is spoken. In this area the accordion is a favorite instrument.

For the player piano, you don't need to press down a key at all. Player pianos became popular at the beginning of the twentieth century because they played all by themselves. Sing "The Old Piano Roll Blues" and imagine that a player piano is playing it.

CHECK IT OUT

1. Which rhythm do you hear?

    a. (rhythm notation)   c. (rhythm notation)

    b. (rhythm notation)   d. (rhythm notation)

2. Which rhythm do you hear?

    a. (rhythm notation)   c. (rhythm notation)

    b. (rhythm notation)   d. (rhythm notation)

3. Which keyboard instrument do you hear?

    a. piano   **b.** pipe organ   **c.** harpsichord

4. How is this keyboard sound produced?

    a. A hammer hits a string.

    b. Air vibrates in a tube.

    c. A string is plucked.

CREATE

Write a Tune in ¾ Time

CREATE your own melody in ¾ meter.
Follow these suggestions.

- The melody must be eight measures long.
- Use only the pitches C, D, E, F, and G.
- The last note of the fourth measure must be G.
- The last note of the piece must be C.
- Write your melody in notation.

How to do it? Read the rhyme below to find out.
Do you recognize this rhythm?

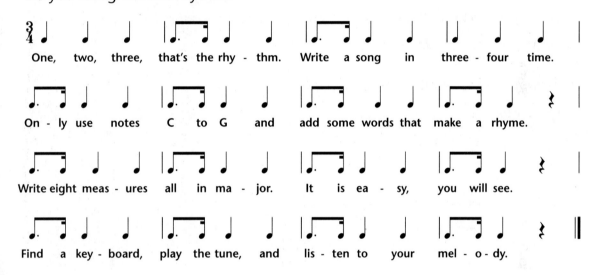

One, two, three, that's the rhy - thm. Write a song in three - four time.

On - ly use notes C to G and add some words that make a rhyme.

Write eight meas - ures all in ma - jor. It is ea - sy, you will see.

Find a key - board, play the tune, and lis - ten to your mel - o - dy.

Write

Write a paragraph comparing two different keyboard instruments that you have heard, either live or on recordings. What was the same or different about the way the two instruments sounded?

JAZZ

Jazz is a musical style that grew out of African rhythms, European harmony, and melodies from folk songs and other popular sources. Jazz focuses on individual interpretations. Within this freedom of expression, the jazz musician varies the beat, rhythm, melody, and volume as desired. This technique, known as improvisation, is a main ingredient of jazz.

As jazz became popular, it developed new forms. The variety of styles includes Dixieland, swing, big band, bebop, and jazz-rock. Meet a few of the jazz musicians who helped to develop some of these styles.

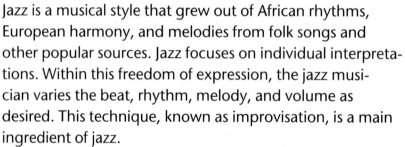

SPOTLIGHT ON *Jazz Artists*

MEMPHIS MINNIE

Memphis Minnie, a blues singer and guitarist, was born in Algiers, Louisiana. At the age of eight, she arrived in Memphis, Tennessee, where she worked as a street musician. In 1928 she moved with her husband to Chicago. Together they made many successful recordings. Memphis Minnie continued to make popular recordings with other artists for many years. She is best known for the forceful style of her guitar playing and the strong quality of her voice.

MARY LOU
WILLIAMS

The musical style of Mary Lou Williams, a jazz pianist and arranger-composer, strongly influenced modern jazz musicians. During the 1930s, she played with Andy Kirk's band, whose style was a result of Mary Lou Williams's solo performances and compositions. She also wrote arrangements for many popular swing bands of the era, including Benny Goodman's.

meet
DOROTHY
DONEGAN

Dorothy Donegan, a jazz pianist for nearly fifty years, was recently elected to the Jazz Hall of Fame. Praised for her piano technique, Donegan plays a mixture of different jazz styles.

LISTEN to Dorothy Donegan talk about her playing style.

LISTENING

A Blues Montage

Listen to examples of the twelve-bar blues. Memphis Minnie plays "When the Levee Breaks," Mary Lou Williams plays "Boogie Misterioso," and Dorothy Donegan plays "St. Louis Blues." In this style, popular in the 1930s, the bass plays a variety of patterns. The style became popular again during the early years of rock and roll. How are these selections alike? How are they different?

MAX ROACH

Max Roach, a famous jazz drummer, played an important role in the development of modern jazz. He performed in the 1940s and 1950s with world-famous musicians such as saxophonist Charlie Parker and trumpeter Dizzy Gillespie. During these years, Roach helped create a new style of drumming for bebop jazz. For nearly 40 years, he has continued to play in this tradition.

LISTENING

Brilliant Corners *by Thelonious Monk*

LISTEN to Max Roach perform in "Brilliant Corners."

The trap set, or drum set, is an important part of a jazz ensemble. The main part of the rhythmic background is carried by the cymbals. Snare drum and tom-toms fill in the background. Occasionally the bass drum plays strong accents. The solo passages usually feature the snare drums.

How many parts of the trap set can you hear the drummer play at the beginning of the piece? Notice how he waits for the saxophone player to pause, then fills in the space with drumming. Now listen to his solo.

 meet
KEITH JARRETT

Keith Jarrett is best known as a modern jazz pianist. Many of his concerts are on-the-spot improvisations at the piano. He is also skilled at many other kinds of music. In addition to performing and recording classical piano music, he plays soprano saxophone, guitar, recorders, and several different kinds of percussion instruments.

LISTEN to this famous jazz pianist talk about his career and his recording techniques.

 LISTENING
Montage of Performance Styles

LISTEN to Keith Jarrett play in four different styles.

Keith Jarrett plays the jazz standard "I Hear a Rhapsody," two pieces he composed—"Improvisation: Part 2A," and "Spirits: No. 5," and "Prelude No. 1 in C Major" by J. S. Bach. What is different about the playing styles he uses for each selection?

OUR MUSI

Love Letter to AMERICA

Dear America
    I love 10 things about you:
Your combination of cultures,
Your beautiful oceans,
Your mystical forests,
Your majestic mountains,
Your big cities,
Your small towns,
The way you open your arms
To anyone who cares to enter,
Your lovely snowflakes in the winter,
Your warm sunshine in the summer,
Your gentle breezes,
Your windy gales,
    I love you, America.
          Forever yours,

—Mattie Catherine Johnson

Coming to

"Love Letter to America" was written by Mattie Johnson, a seventh-grade student in Northfield, Minnesota. How does Mattie's letter compare with your feelings about the United States?

America

People have come to the United States from many parts of the world. With them, they have brought art, literature, and music. Imagine what music from Panama, Taiwan, England, and Tahiti might sound like. Think of the music of Native Americans, whose ancestors came to North America long before the Europeans.

LISTENING

Liberty Fanfare (excerpt) *by John Williams*

In this piece, an American composer celebrates freedom. As you listen, notice that each beat can be divided into smaller parts. The chart below shows beats divided into twos and threes.

PERFORM these beat divisions.

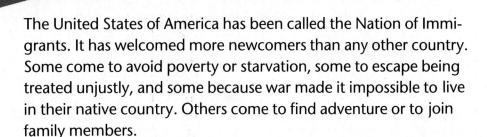

The United States of America has been called the Nation of Immigrants. It has welcomed more newcomers than any other country. Some come to avoid poverty or starvation, some to escape being treated unjustly, and some because war made it impossible to live in their native country. Others come to find adventure or to join family members.

In the late 1800s, many newcomers to our country came from the British Isles, Germany, and Scandinavia. They traveled to America by ship, and entered the country through New York Harbor.

Away to America

Words and Music by Linda Williams

1. My grand-fa-ther jour-neyed, like so man-y oth-ers, he
(2.) all he took with him was what he could car-ry, his
(3.) I've gone a-way, there was noth-ing to hold me, I

turned to the West and the sun.___ He sailed out of Bris-tol a-
books and an old vi-o-lin.___ Wait-ing to meet him: a
flew off to Lon-don and stayed.___ But still I re-mem-ber the

long with his broth-ers, a new world was there to be won.
girl he would mar-ry, a new life a-bout to be-gin.
sto-ries they told me, And think of the jour-ney he made.

(V.2 modulates.)

He'd heard of the moun-tains in far Col-o-ra-do, where
My moth-er was born there not man-y years af-ter, and
Now I miss the moun-tains when I look a-round me, And

ea-gles flew free in the air.___ He'd find a high moun-tain and
all of her sis-ters as well;___ And all of the years, all the
I real-ly can't tell you when,___ But some-how the voice of my

3rd time to Coda ⊕

live in its sha-dow, for some-thing was call-ing him there.___
tears and the laugh-ter, are there in the stor-ies they tell.___
grand-fa-ther found me And soon I'll be fly-ing a-gain.___

Refrain

"Sail a - way, a - way to A - mer - i - ca, far off o - ver the sea." There is

some - thing there in A - mer - i - ca, And it's call - ing to me. 2.&3. Now "Fly a-

way, come home to A - mer - i - ca, far off o - ver the sea."There is some - thing
a - way

there in A - mer - i - ca, And it's call - ing to me.___ "Sail a - me.___

The meter signature of "Away to America" is $\frac{6}{8}$. This means that there are two beats per measure and that each beat has been divided into three pulses. All of these rhythms equal one beat in $\frac{6}{8}$.

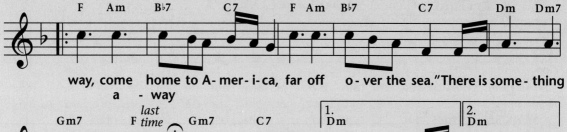

CLAP these rhythms and rearrange them to create an accompaniment for "Away to America." Save the measure that contains a rest for the end.

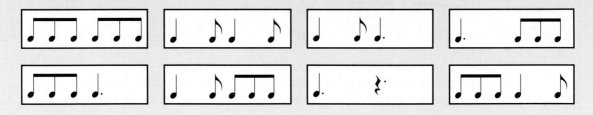

MUSIC ENRICHES US

The contributions of different cultures
have enriched life for people who live
in the United States. "El tambor"
was brought north from Panama.
Clap the strong beat and snap
the weak beat as you listen to
this song.

EL TAMBOR
THE DRUM

Panamanian Folk Song

Spanish: El tam - bor, el tam - bor, el tam - bor de a - le - grí - a. Yo
Pronunciation: el tam bor el tam bor el tam bor ðe a le gri a yo
English: El tam - bor, el tam - bor, el tam - bor the drum of glad - ness, I

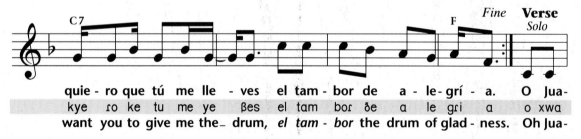

quie - ro que tú me lle - ves el tam - bor de a - le - grí - a. O Jua-
kye ɾo ke tu me ye ßes el tam bor ðe a le gri a o xwa
want you to give me the drum, el tam - bor the drum of glad - ness. Oh Jua-

ni - ta o Jua - ni - ta, Jua - ni - ta a - mi - ga mí - a
ni ta o xwa ni ta xwa ni ta a mi ga mi a
ni - ta, oh Jua - ni - ta, Jua - ni - ta my friend, a - mi - ga

Yo quie - ro que tú me lle - ves el tam - bor de a - le - grí - a.
yo kye ɾo ke tu me ye ßes el tam bor ðe a le gri a
I want you to give me the drum, el tam - bor the drum of glad - ness.

Let's review some of the rhythms you already know. Clap each of the following rhythmic building blocks.

ORGANIZE the building blocks in your own order to accompany "El tambor." Use the block that contains a quarter rest as the last measure to give the accompaniment the feeling of an ending.

This art is based on Panamanian pottery designs.

Spotlight on John Philip SOUSA

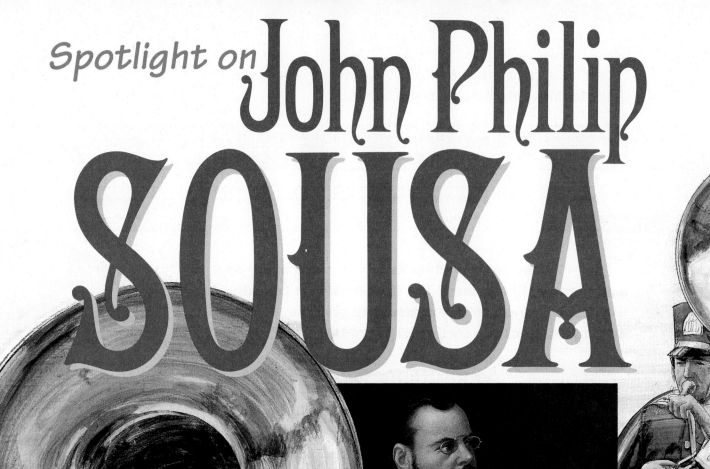

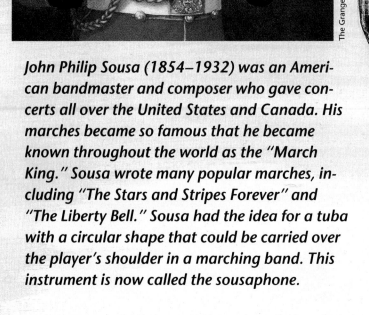

The Granger Collection

John Philip Sousa (1854–1932) was an American bandmaster and composer who gave concerts all over the United States and Canada. His marches became so famous that he became known throughout the world as the "March King." Sousa wrote many popular marches, including "The Stars and Stripes Forever" and "The Liberty Bell." Sousa had the idea for a tuba with a circular shape that could be carried over the player's shoulder in a marching band. This instrument is now called the sousaphone.

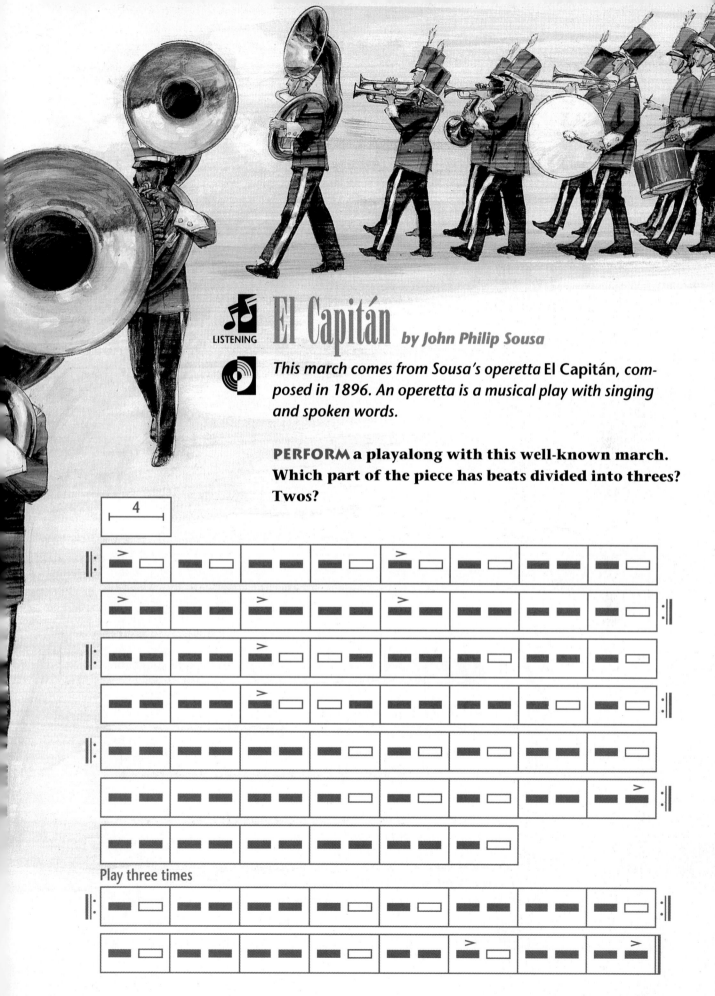

LISTENING

El Capitán *by John Philip Sousa*

This march comes from Sousa's operetta El Capitán, composed in 1896. An operetta is a musical play with singing and spoken words.

PERFORM a playalong with this well-known march. Which part of the piece has beats divided into threes? Twos?

Play three times

TRAVELING ON

Travel

The railroad track is miles away,
And the day is loud with voices speaking,
Yet there isn't a train goes by all day
But I hear its whistles shrieking.

All night there isn't a train goes by,
Though the night is still for sleep and dreaming
But I see its cinders red on the sky
And hear its engine steaming.

My heart is warm with the friends I make,
And better friends I'll not be knowing,
Yet there isn't a train I wouldn't take,
No matter where it's going.

—Edna St. Vincent Millay

146

TRAV'LER

Music by Mark Wilson
Words by Jane Foster Knox

1. Would you like to be a trav' - ler sail - ing far___ a - cross the
2. We will sure - ly find en - chant - ment, in a land___ so far a -

sea? I can take you on a jour - ney, to a place where you have longed to
way. But we fail to see the splen - dor that sur - rounds us ev' - ry

Part 1

be, For oth - er lands seem so much more ex - ci - ting!___ Our spir - its
day. For beau - ty blooms where it is plan - ted!___ It

Part 2

soar with ev' - ry pass - ing mile; and won - d'rous beau - ty
shines in cor - ners we ig - nore, and waits for us to

calls to us, "Come pause___ and rest a - while." } So close your
slow our step; to pause___ and to ex - plore.

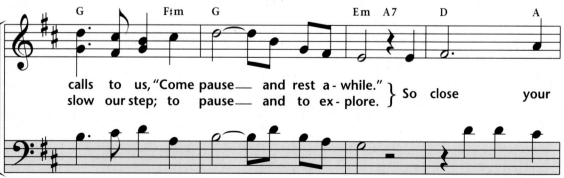

So close your

A MAJOR JOURNEY

The melody of "Trav'ler" is in D major. Notice that the key signature has two sharps.

In major keys with sharps in their key signatures, the last sharp is *ti*. A half step up from this sharp is the pitch that gives the key its name. The last sharp in this key signature is C♯; this tells you that the name of the key is D major.

The sharps in a key signature always fall in the same order. Remember the order of sharps by saying:

Father **C**harles **G**oes **D**own **A**nd **E**nds **B**attle

What is the sequence of the whole and half steps in the D major scale?

A **motive** is a short fragment of a melody or a rhythm that can be easily recognized. How many times is this melodic motive used in the melody of "Trav'ler"?

A MINOR DIVERSION

The melody of "Dance for the Nations" uses the D minor scale. Compare the sequence of whole and half steps in the first five pitches of this scale to that in the D major scale of "Trav'ler." Which scale step is different?

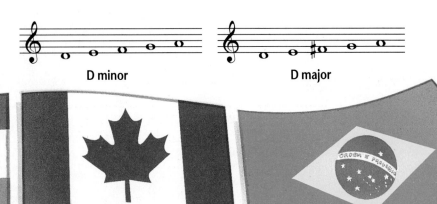

D minor   D major

DANCE FOR THE NATIONS

Words and Music by John Krumm

'Round and 'round we go! We hold—— each oth-er's hands and

weave our-selves in a cir - cle. The

time is gone, the dance goes—— on!

"American Dream" expresses the composer's vision of this country's future. It has one section in B♭ major and one section in G minor.

B♭ major   G minor

Is the first phrase of the A section major or minor? The first phrase of the B section?

AMERICAN DREAM

Words and Music by Ed Harris

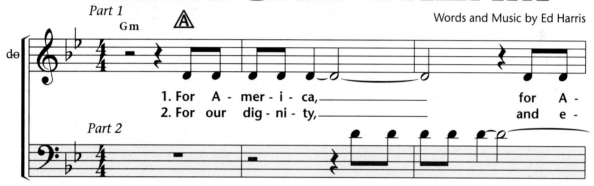

1. For A-mer-i-ca,_____ for A-
2. For our dig-ni-ty,_____ and e-

1. For A-mer-i-ca,_____
2. And our lib-er-ty,_____

mer-i-ca,___ for A-mer-i-ca___ I dream. In my mind I have a
qual-i-ty,___ This and more I dare___ to dream. No more dan-ger or sus-

___ for A-mer-i-ca___ I dream.
___ This and more I dare___ to dream.

Part 1 only

vi-sion of what A-mer-i-ca can be, and we're faced with a de-
pi-cion, and no more fight-ing, no more pain, no more self-ish con-dem-

ci - sion _____ to shape our des - ti - ny.
na - tion, _____ for fool - ish pride is vain.

Part 2 only

Look with me in - to the fu - ture. Come look as far as you can see.
No more hun - ger, no more sor - row, and no more wor-ry, no more fear.

Try to see a new to-mor - row.___ Come and dare to dream with me.
No more doubt a-bout to-mor - row,___ for the dream is ve - ry clear.

Come and dare to dream with me.
for the dream is ve - ry clear.

Dream _____ the A- mer - i - can dream with me. See it ___ and re - joice.

Dream _____ the A- mer - i - can dream with me. See it ___ and re - joice.

Dream ___ of A- mer - i - ca yet to be, a land of hope ___ and ___

Dream ___ of A- mer - i - ca yet to be, a land of hope and

Rhythmic Explorations

"Yonder Come Day" is an African American folk song from the Georgia Sea Islands off the Georgia coast. When tied notes appear in the music, you hear **syncopation**. Syncopation results from placing stresses on weak beats or parts of beats that are normally unstressed.

YONDER COME DAY

Georgia Sea Islands Folk Song
Additional Words and Arrangement
by Judith Cook Tucker
Arrangement Adapted by Michael Jothen

154

Taiwan is a large island off the east coast of the Chinese mainland. The Republic of China is governed from this island. Residents of Taiwan include native Taiwanese and immigrants from China and their descendants. In the past thirty years, many people have come to the United States from Taiwan.

Tsing Chun U Chü

YOUTH DANCE SONG

Taiwanese Folk Song
Collected and Transcribed
by Kathy B. Sorensen

Chinese: 太 陽 下 山 明 朝 依 舊 爬 上 來
Pronunciation: tai yang sia shan ming jau yi jiu pa shang lai
English: **Though the sun has dis - ap - peared in - to the___ west,**

花 兒 謝 了 明 年 還 是 一 樣 的 開
hua ər sie liau ming niɛn hai shi yi yang di kai
still the sun will rise a - gain each morn - ing at dawn.

美 麗 小 鳥 一 去 無 踪 影 我 的 青 春 小 鳥 一 樣
me li shiau niau yi tsü wu ying jung wɔ di tsing chun shiau niau yi yang
Though the flow - ers wilt and___ die in___ fall, there will be new blos- soms when the

READ and pat these rhythms.

SING the verse, then pat these rhythms to accompany the interlude and the repeat of the verse.

PLAY the rhythms on unpitched percussion instruments.

Meter Matters

"Greensleeves" was
written in Renaissance England.
Early American colonists knew and sang this song.

PAT-CLAP as you listen to the song and decide if the
beats are divided into twos $\left(\frac{2}{4}\right)$ or threes $\left(\frac{6}{8}\right)$.

GREENSLEEVES

16th Century
English Song

A - las, my love— you do me wrong— to cast me off— dis -

cour - teous - ly; And I have loved—— you so long,— de -

light - ing in—— your com - pa - ny. Green - sleeves— was

all my joy,—— Green - sleeves— was my de - light. Green - sleeves was my

heart of gold,— and who but my la - dy Green - sleeves.

PLAY this melodic accompaniment for "Greensleeves" on recorder, keyboard, or bells.

Fantasia on Greensleeves
by Ralph Vaughan Williams

In 1934, the British composer Ralph Vaughan Williams used "Greensleeves" and another Renaissance tune called "Lovely Joan" to create his Fantasia on Greensleeves.

LISTENING MAP   *Listen for the form of this piece as you follow the map. What meter do you hear in the A section? In the B section?*

Introduction: Violin and Harp

a

a'

b

b'

Fine

three times

c

d

Interlude: Violin and Harp

D. S. al Fine

ROOTS and RHYTHM

Rhythmic and harmonic accompaniments add color and excitement to music. Accompany "El tambor" with chord roots based on the first and fifth steps of the scale (*do* and *so*). In accompaniments, the fifth step often is used as a low pitch as well as a high pitch.

SING the lower version of the fifth step for this accompaniment.

- Transfer the accompaniment to keyboard, bells, or recorder.
- Stamp this rhythm with your feet and then transfer it to a conga drum.

- Pat the rhythm below. Pat down-stemmed notes on your left leg and up-stemmed notes on your right leg. Notice the syncopated rhythm (♪♩♪) in the second measure. Once you have learned the pattern, transfer it to bongos.

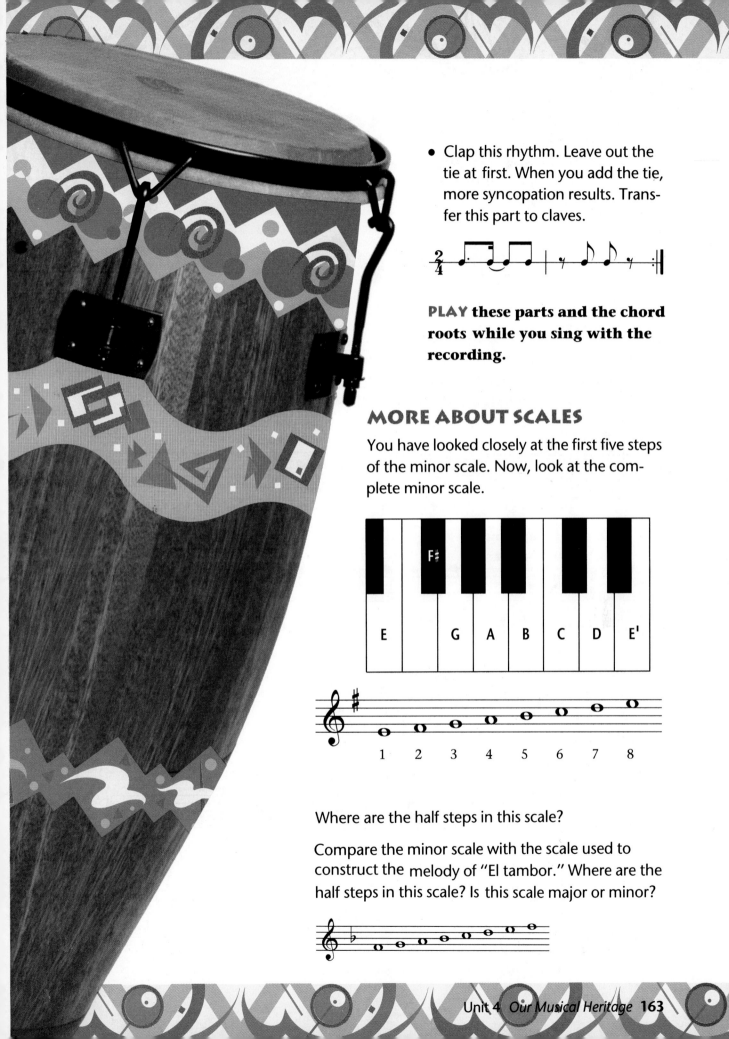

- Clap this rhythm. Leave out the tie at first. When you add the tie, more syncopation results. Transfer this part to claves.

PLAY these parts and the chord roots while you sing with the recording.

MORE ABOUT SCALES

You have looked closely at the first five steps of the minor scale. Now, look at the complete minor scale.

Where are the half steps in this scale?

Compare the minor scale with the scale used to construct the melody of "El tambor." Where are the half steps in this scale? Is this scale major or minor?

A SONG FROM THE SOUTH PACIFIC

LISTEN for the instrument that accompanies the singing in "Hoe Ana," a folk song from Tahiti. Then sing the song.

Hoe Ana

Tahitian Folk Song
Collected and Transcribed
by Kathy B. Sorensen
Cambiata Part by Robert J. de Frece

Melody

Tahitian: Ho-e a-na, ho-e a-na, ho-e na te va-ka te va-ka nei.
Pronunciation: ho e a na ho e a na ho e na te va ka te va ka nei

Descant

Ho-e a-na, ho-e a-na, ho-e na te va-ka te va-ka nei.

Cambiata (optional)

Ho-e a-na, ho-e a-na, ho-e na te va-ka te va-ka nei.

Hae-re mai na, hae-re mai na, hae-re mai e i-ne ma-e.
hae re mai na hae re mai na hae re mai e i ne ma e

Hae-re mai na, hae-re mai na, hae-re mai e i-ne ma-e.

Hae-re mai na, hae-re mai na, hae-re mai e i-ne ma-e.

The **ukulele** played the accompaniment to "Hoe Ana." It is a four-stringed instrument that originated in Hawaii. The ukulele is widely used to accompany songs in the South Pacific islands. It developed from two other instruments, the ukeke and the bragha. The ukeke is a native Hawaiian stringed instrument. The Portuguese brought the bragha, a small guitar, to Hawaii in the 1870s.

The melody of "Hoe Ana" uses pitches from this scale.

Look at the key signature and figure out the name of the key. Where are the half steps in this scale? Is it a major or minor scale?

SING the roots of the I and V chords to accompany "Hoe Ana." Use this chart. Each shell represents one ♩. beat. Sing D for I and A for V. Then play the roots on keyboard or bells.

ADD these rhythmic patterns. First pat them, then transfer them to unpitched percussion instruments.

Pattern 1

Pattern 2

The Original American Music

You have learned that music from many parts of the world has contributed to the rich heritage of American music. But before all of this music arrived, the music of American Indians was already here.

There are still hundreds of different Indian nations living in the United States today. They represent many different cultures and languages.

LISTENING

Taos Round Dance

The music of the Native Americans has been passed down through the generations by oral tradition. Children have learned songs from their parents and grandparents.

LISTEN to a dancing song from the Taos nation of New Mexico. Does the song sound major or minor? Do you hear a meter?

The Taos people do not think of their music as being major or minor, or having meter. It is important to remember that the same ideas do not always apply to the music of all cultures.

166

LISTENING

Navajo Courtship Song

Sung by Freddy Wheeler

This song comes to us from another Southwest Indian nation, the Navajo. Listen to Freddy Wheeler talk about the importance of music to the Navajo and describe the "Navajo Courtship Song." Find a quiet way to keep the beat as you listen to the song.

Freddy Wheeler

EXPRESSION THROUGH POETRY

READ "Whip Man," a poem by Phil George of the Nez Perce nation. It was written in 1976 to remember many Nez Perce who died in a battle at Big Hole, Montana in 1877. Phil George's great-grandfather, then fourteen years old, was a survivor of this battle.

Whip Man

The old man, with silver braids
Borrowed from the rising sun
Tinges of orange, red, yellow—
And flushed his copper-colored face
In peaceful pastels of a new dawn.

Whip Man, although almost blind,
Had eyes as free, as wild as appaloosas.
100 winters and with visions beyond the moon,
He could see tomorrow's tomorrow.

On his quill-woven willow whip were
Breath plumes, sinew secured.
Whip Man made children dance.
Balanced within the circle—
Disciplined in the ways of generations past.

He departed the dances one night.
In sleep his breath stopped.
They found him in his tepee, cold.
Some say he had died.

Others prepared for Whip Man's return.
With three sets of Seven Drums,
His people sang for three nights, two days.
Then Whip Man arose
In a trance. In tears.

He sang slow and easy—like the sound of
High Mountain flowing waters.
Chanting—telling of the Next World
Where our ancestors now live in utopian freedom
  of long ago.

Drummers gathered—Dancers moved,
Old ones reclined in the shade to watch.
In classic elegance people appeared in clouds.
Whip Man's whip touched the knees of
Wide-eyed, open-mouthed children:

Take care of your past.
Take care.
Your past, take care.
You, you take care of your past.
Your past.
Our past.
Their past.
Take care of your past.
Take care of your past,
Take care, take care.

—Phil George

The Nez Perce have long occupied what is now
north central Idaho and northeastern Oregon. They
once lived on local wildlife and edible plants, as well
as on buffalo and antelope that they hunted on the
plains of what is now Montana. They were known
for raising superior horses.

THINK IT THROUGH

What are some ways in which you can "take
care of your past"?

Big Hole Valley, Montana

EXPRESSION THROUGH DANCE

Some time before the arrival of the Europeans in North America, several northeast Indian nations joined together to form a strong spiritual, political, military, and economic union known as the Iroquois Confederacy. This confederacy had a democratic system of government that later became a model for the government of the United States.

LISTENING

Tekanionton'néha'

Centuries ago, the Iroquois people would invite other nations to make peace agreements. Each nation would teach the other a song or dance as a record of their friendship. "Tekanionton'néha' (Alligator Dance)" was given to the Iroquois long ago, as the result of a peace agreement probably reached with either the Seminole or Creek people. Both these nations lived further south, where alligators were found.

LISTEN to performers from the Mohawk nation tell the story of the "Alligator Dance." Then do the dance. Join the singers on the response. When you hear "yo ho," sing "wi ye." When you hear "yo-o ya," sing "he."

171

People of many different cultures can live together in harmony in the United States. By singing and playing chords, you can create rich musical harmony.

You have sung chords and played chord roots. You can also play complete chords on pitched instruments. The most frequently used chords in a major key are the chords built on the first, fourth, and fifth steps of the major scale. To build each chord, begin with the scale step.

A G major chord is built on the first step of the G major scale. Because this scale step is on a line, the other two notes in the chord will be on the two lines above it.

The IV chord will be built on the fourth scale step, which, in G major, is C.

IV

This is a C major chord. Because the scale step is in a space, the other two notes in the IV chord will be in the two spaces above it.

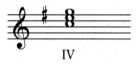

IV

What is the fifth step of the G major scale? What pitches will be in the chord?

PLAY these chords on keyboard or bells.

Use the I, IV, and V chords to accompany "Movin' On."
Play a chord on the first beat of each measure.

Movin' On

Words and Music by
Raymond R. Hannisian

1. There is a voice____ that has no name;_____
2. The night has mu - sic that calls to me____
3. Speak to me soft - ly but tell me no lies;_____

It comes with eve - ning_____ or be - hind the rain:_____
A - cross the can - yons_____ of an end - less sea._____
I see to - mor - row_____ shin - ing in your eyes._____

"I have no time__ now to stop and ex - plain;_____
I seek the shad - ows of yes - ter - day;_____
"I have no time__ now to stop and ex - plain;_____

I just keep mov - in'_____ 'cause it helps to
To - day can't hold me,_____ and I must be
I just keep mov - in'_____ 'cause it helps to

ease _____ the pain."_____
on_____ my way._____
ease_____ the pain."_____

HARMONY WITH NATURE

Many centuries ago, the Anasazi people built these cliff
dwellings, now in Mesa Verde National Park, Colorado. The
natural rock formations protected them from the weather.

Our Heritage of Harmony

Our musical heritage includes many varieties of music. For some people, music represents important connections to their family history. Is there any music that is special to your family?

PLAYING A COMPLETE HARMONIC ACCOMPANIMENT

You used a team approach to play the harmonic accompaniment for "Movin' On." Now play the complete accompaniment for this song by using **inverted chords.** When you invert something, you turn it upside down. When you invert a chord, the note from the bottom of the chord becomes the top note. For example:

root position	first inversion	second inversion

In the first inversion, G moves from the bottom to the top. In the second inversion, B, which was the bottom note of the first inversion, is moved to the top.

Inversions make it easier to move from one chord to another on a keyboard. The less distance your fingers have to move, the easier it is to play the right notes. To play the I, IV, and V chords, invert the IV and V chords like this:

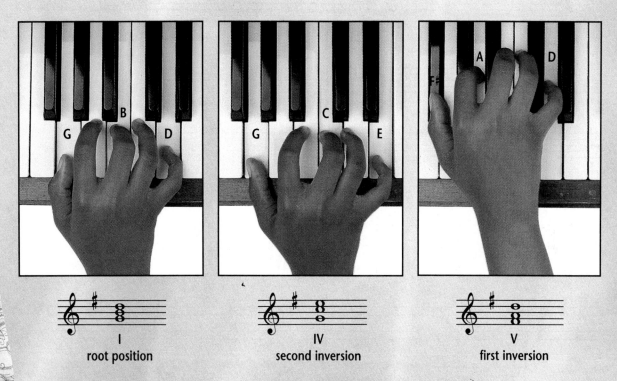

| I | IV | V |
| root position | second inversion | first inversion |

PLAY the harmonic accompaniment to "Movin' On" following the chords that appear with the notation on page 174. Use inverted IV and V chords.

FROM HARMONY TO ANOTHER MELODY

Composers often use inverted chords to make the bass line into a smoother melody with steps instead of leaps. Lee Holdridge, the composer of "An American Hymn," page 178, inverted chords to create a melodic bass line in the form of a descending scale.

SING the melodic bass line and then play it on keyboard or bells. Is this melody major or minor?

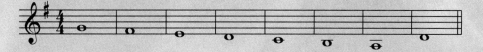

PLAY this melodic bass line as an accompaniment to
"An American Hymn."

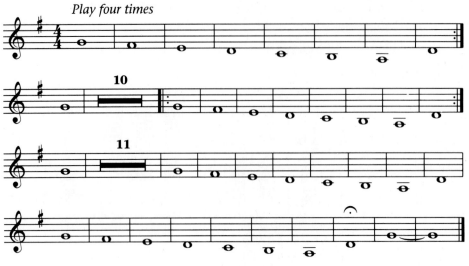

AN AMERICAN HYMN

Music by Lee Holdridge
Words by Molly-Ann Leikin

1. I_____ have seen a sum-mer day_____ that
2. I_____ have stum-bled through the night_____ a -
(3.) seen_____ the sil - ver moun-tain-tops_____ and
(4.) dreamed_____ of E - den all my life,_____ I

slow - ly o - pens like a rose_____ A -
lone as an - y man can be,_____ then
gold - en prai - ries on my way._____ } Now
find it more and more each day._____

long ___ a qui - et road that wan - ders by, and
found ___ a si - lent can - yon full of stars and
ev' - ry - where I go a - cross the land, I

I have smiled and won - dered where it goes.
in my heart I heard them tell - ing
stand so proud - ly in the sun and

me I was home. ___ The gen - tle winds, The rains that fall,

The tall - est trees, I'm part of it all. ___ 3. I've

say, "I am home." 4. I've say, "I am home." ___

REVIEW

CELEBRATING AMERICAN MUSIC

We celebrate the music that has come together in the United States to create our heritage in sound. From the music of the Native Americans who have lived here for thousands of years to the music of the many people who have come to this land and made it their home, we have built our great musical heritage. Over the years, people have been drawn "Away to America."

We celebrate with the music that makes our feet dance and our spirits soar. Sing and dance to "Dance for the Nations."

We celebrate the meeting of the music of different cultures in this great land. For example, "El tambor" comes to us from Panama, in Central America. "Hoe Ana" comes to us from Tahiti, an island in the South Pacific Ocean.

When we celebrate the "American Dream," we celebrate with music, our heritage in sound.

CHECK IT OUT

1. Do you hear the first five steps of a minor scale?

   a. Yes   **b.** No

2. Do you hear the first five steps of a minor scale?

   a. Yes   **b.** No

3. Which rhythm do you hear?

   a.
   b.
   c.
   d.

4. Which rhythm do you hear?

   a.
   b.
   c.
   d.

CREATE

A Musical Celebration

CLAP the rhythm shown by the notation below. Read the poem in the rhythm shown.

Words by H. Wilburr

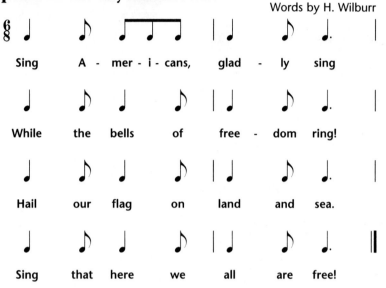

Sing A - mer - i - cans, glad - ly sing

While the bells of free - dom ring!

Hail our flag on land and sea.

Sing that here we all are free!

CREATE your own melody, following these directions.

• Use pitches from the C major scale.

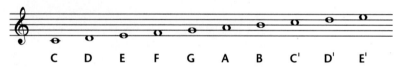

C   D   E   F   G   A   B   C'   D'   E'

• Avoid large leaps. If you do choose a leap, follow it with step-wise motion.
• In measure 4 use pitches D' E' D'. In measure 8 use pitches E D C.

SING the melody you have created. Your composition is now another part of America's sound heritage.

Write

In this unit, we have explored many contributions to the musical heritage of the United States. Choose four or five pieces of music that represent your family's heritage. Name each piece and briefly explain why you chose it.

ENCORE

DANCES
OF OUR
WORLD

LISTENING

Sumer Is Icumen In
Late Medieval (c. 1310)

The farandole *is the oldest European folk dance still in existence today. Popular in France and Italy during medieval times, it was a simple dance that was often accompanied by song. As time went on, the farandole became more and more complicated. Performers had to master a difficult series of steps, turns, and twists. Many Mediterranean and South American dances are similar to the farandole.*

LISTEN to a song which may have accompanied the farandole.

Do you remember some of the first song-and-dance games you played? Perhaps you danced to "Skip to My Lou" or played "London Bridge Is Falling Down." These songs and dances are part of a long folk tradition.

Folk songs and dances grew out of daily activities and rituals. At one time, important events, such as a birth or marriage, were celebrated with dances. Other songs refer to historical events or natural disasters. For example, the line "Ashes, ashes, all fall down" in "Ring Around the Rosy" may refer to the devastating effect of the plague over 600 years ago. Today, the original meaning of many dances is lost. Most folk dances that still exist today are performed for recreation.

LISTENING

Yagi Bushi

Japanese Folk Song

The Yagi Bushi *is performed in the summer at the Bon Odori festival, a three-day celebration honoring one's ancestors. At that time, people gather at the local temple, where they build a high platform. The musicians perform from the top of the platform while the people dance and join in the chorus.*

LISTEN to the song. Create your own dance steps. Then learn the traditional dance. Are any of the steps you created actually in the dance?

Red River Valley *American Folk Dance*

Square dancing *is popular in many parts of the United States. Many of the steps came from European folk dances. Each group of four couples forms a square. The caller, who gives the steps, can use a known version of a dance or combine steps to create a new one.*

You may be familiar with some of the square-dance calls—do si do or promenade. Try some of them with a partner.

LISTEN to "Red River Valley," a popular folk dance.

Amores hallarás *Ecuadorian Folk Dance*

In Ecuador and throughout the Andes, festivals are a time to visit with friends and neighbors. People come to the festivals to buy and sell products during the day and to sing and dance at night. The amores hallarás describes the courtship, in earlier times, of young people in some parts of the Andean region.

The steps used in this folk dance are very traditional. Listen to the guitar or the drum ostinato at the beginning of the dance. How would you move to the rhythm ♩ ♩ ♩?

LISTENING

Pata Pata *by Miriam Makeba*

When Miriam Makeba, a famous South African singer, wrote "Pata Pata," she was thinking of a dance done in her homeland. The recording of the song was very successful in the United States in the late 1960s. The dance became popular as well.

LISTEN to "Pata Pata." *Pata* means "touch" in Zulu and Zhosa. The basic motion in this dance is touch, step.

from

There's No Business Like Show Business

There's no bus'ness like show bus'ness
    like no bus'ness I know.
Trav'ling thru the country will be thrilling,
Standing out in front on opening nights,
Smiling as you watch the theatre filling,
And there's your billing out there in lights.
There's no people like show people,
They smile when they are low.
Yesterday they told you you would not go far,
That night you open and there you are,
Next day on your dressing room they've hung a star
Let's go on with the show.

—*Irving Berlin*

ON STAGE

Curtain Up!

Many different combinations of music and drama are found all around the world. These works can include singing, dancing, costumes, scenery, lighting, instruments, and spoken words.

Musicals are plays that contain songs and dances. They developed in the United States around 1900. Many famous musicals were written in the 1940s and 1950s, including *The Sound of Music* by Rodgers and Hammerstein and *My Fair Lady* by Lerner and Loewe.

The musical *Kiss Me, Kate* by American composer Cole Porter opened in 1948 on Broadway, New York City's theater street. Usually composers work with a **lyricist** who writes the words, or **lyrics,** of the songs. Porter, however, wrote his own words. "Another Op'nin'" is the first song in *Kiss Me, Kate*. It expresses the feelings of many performers on opening night.

Some important performance choices are made by the singer. One of these choices has to do with how the pitches are delivered—are they smoothly connected or sharply separated? This is called the **articulation** of a song. "Another Op'nin'" is sung in a very marked, accented way. One term for this manner of articulation is **marcato**. The performer can also choose a smoother, **legato** articulation.

LISTEN for *marcato* articulation and for the different solo voices you hear in "Another Op'nin'." How many soloists are there? How are the female soloists' voices different from one another? The male soloists' voices?

Another Op'nin,' Another Show

Words and Music by Cole Porter

Another op'nin', another show in Philly, Boston, or Baltimoe,
A chance for stage folks to say "hello"; Another op'nin' of
    another show.
Another job that you hope, at last, will make your future
    forget your past,
Another pain where the ulcers grow; Another op'nin' of
    another show!
Four weeks, you rehearse and rehearse,
Three weeks and it couldn't be worse.
One week, will it ever be right?
Then out of the hat, it's that big first night!
The overture is about to start, you cross your fingers and
    hold your heart,
It's curtain time and away we go;
Another op'nin' of another show.

The 1953 movie version of *Kiss Me, Kate*

The *Will Rogers Follies* opened in 1991 at the Palace Theater on Broadway. It tells the story of Will Rogers, an Oklahoma cowboy, whose great popularity as an entertainer extended from the 1910s into the 1930s. "Look Around" expresses Will's concern for the environment. Decide whether a *legato* or a *marcato* style seems more appropriate for expressing the spirit and mood of the words.

Look Around

Music by Cy Coleman
Words by Betty Comden
and Adolph Green

view clear to the ho - ri - zon?

Look a - round, they dis - ap - pear from sight,

Look———————— a - round,   when

And when I re - call what used to be, I'm

I re - call what used to be, I'm

weep - ing like a weep - ing wil - low tree,———— Just

like a weep - ing wil - low tree,———— Just

look a - round, you'll see a mem - o - ry.——————

If you were to try out for a singing part in a musical, you would be asked, "What voice are you?" Each of the adult voice categories has a different range. The four major adult, or **changed voice**, categories are **soprano, alto, tenor,** and **bass.**

The range of a young voice is usually in about the same range as the adult soprano. This category is called **unchanged voice**. However, the category of a person's voice may change several times during the pre-teen and teen years. One special stage for boys is when their voices first start to change. This type of voice is called **cambiata**, or changing voice.

PORGY AND BESS, A GREAT AMERICAN FOLK OPERA

An **opera** is a musical play in which most—usually all—of the words are sung. American composer George Gershwin wrote the opera *Porgy and Bess* in 1935. Based on a novel about a beggar living in coastal South Carolina, it was the first opera to use blues and jazz. Gershwin called it a folk opera, because he thought of it as a folktale, with music that resembled folk songs.

LISTENING Summertime

from Porgy and Bess
by George and Ira Gershwin

This lullaby is heard at the beginning of the opera. It sets the mood, as well as letting us know the season of the year in which the opera is set.

THE CHOICE IS YOURS!

The term **interpretation** refers to the performance choices made by a singer or other performers. The words and music are already given by the composer and lyricist. Sometimes they will also write suggestions in the music for **dynamics** (the degrees of loud and soft) and **tempo** (the speed of the beat). Often, however, these and other decisions are left up to the singer's judgment. You must determine, for example, whether to sing a song with a *legato* or a *marcato* articulation. You must also decide on the vocal tone color that you will use to best express the idea and spirit of a song. Should it be bright or dark, breathy or full-voiced, floating or full, light or heavy?

The Boy Friend, a 1953 musical by Sandy Wilson, makes fun of British manners and musicals of the 1920s. The story takes place at an elegant girls' school. "Won't You Charleston With Me?" is an invitation to do the Charleston, the dance craze of the time.

Julie Andrews on
stage in *The Boy Friend*

What vocal tone colors would you choose for this song?
Compare your ideas with the recording.

🎵 Won't You CHARLESTON with Me?

Words and Music by Sandy Wilson

Won't you Charleston with me?
Won't you Charleston with me?
And while the band is playing that
Old vo-de-o-do,
Around we will go,
Together we'll show them
How the Charleston is done.
We'll surprise ev'ryone.
Just think what Heaven it's going to be
If you will Charleston, Charleston with me.

YOUR OWN INTERPRETATION

A Funny Thing Happened on the Way to the Forum is a 1962 comic version of life in ancient Rome. Stephen Sondheim, the lyricist for the famous musical *West Side Story,* sets up the show's hilarious atmosphere with this opening song.

Imagine that you are writing a newspaper review of a performance of *A Funny Thing Happened on the Way to the Forum,* in which "Comedy Tonight" is sung. In order to review the interpretation of this song, you will need to decide how you would like it performed. Compare your decisions with those on the recording.

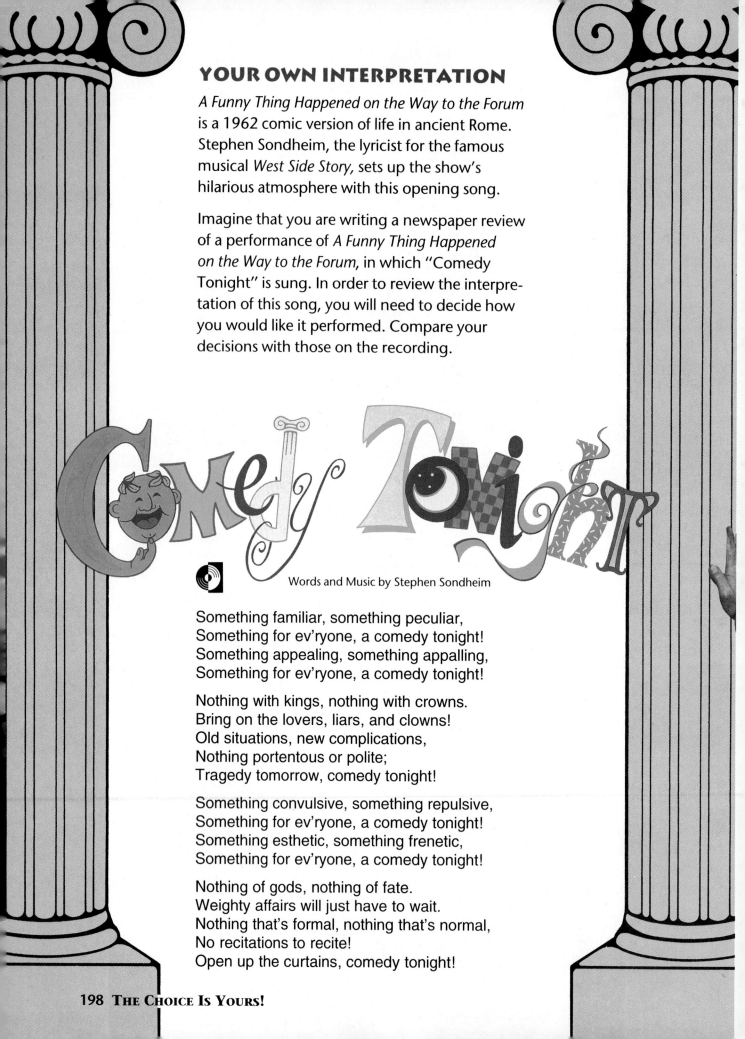

Words and Music by Stephen Sondheim

Something familiar, something peculiar,
Something for ev'ryone, a comedy tonight!
Something appealing, something appalling,
Something for ev'ryone, a comedy tonight!

Nothing with kings, nothing with crowns.
Bring on the lovers, liars, and clowns!
Old situations, new complications,
Nothing portentous or polite;
Tragedy tomorrow, comedy tonight!

Something convulsive, something repulsive,
Something for ev'ryone, a comedy tonight!
Something esthetic, something frenetic,
Something for ev'ryone, a comedy tonight!

Nothing of gods, nothing of fate.
Weighty affairs will just have to wait.
Nothing that's formal, nothing that's normal,
No recitations to recite!
Open up the curtains, comedy tonight!

Zero Mostel (top) and Jack Gilford in the 1966 film of *A Funny Thing Happened on the Way to the Forum*

Marvin Hamlisch wrote the musical *A Chorus Line* in 1975. In the story, a group of dancers are trying out for parts in a Broadway musical. As each performer appears, the audience learns about the sacrifices and frustrations of professional Broadway dancers. At the end of *A Chorus Line*, the dancers who have been chosen for the parts perform in the new musical, which features the song "One."

ONE

Music by Marvin Hamlisch
Words by Edward Kleban

One sin - gu - lar sen - sa - tion, ev' - ry lit - tle step she takes, —

One thrill - ing com - bi - na - tion, ev' - ry move that she makes.

One smile and sud - den - ly no - bod - y else will do.

You know you'll nev - er be lone - ly with you know who.

One moment in her pres-ence and you can for-get the rest,—

For the girl is sec-ond best—— to none, son,

Ooh! Sigh! Give her your at - ten - tion, Do I

real - ly have to men - tion She's the one?————

RHYTHMS FROM BROADWAY

Here are some dotted rhythm patterns heard in two songs from musicals. This rhythm comes from "One."

This rhythm from "Won't You Charleston with Me?" comes from the dance, the Charleston.

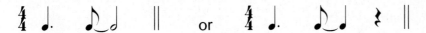

CLAP the melodic rhythm of "Old vo-de-o-do," also from "Won't You Charleston With Me?"

The first three notes shown are a "short-long-short" combination. This is one kind of syncopated rhythm pattern. Syncopation occurs when stressed sounds are heard in unexpected places, such as between beats.

Meet
MARVIN HAMLISCH

When Marvin Hamlisch (b. 1944) was very young, his parents noticed his musical talent. At the age of six, he began taking piano lessons at The Juilliard School of Music in New York City. Hamlisch loved to listen to musicals and rock 'n' roll. At age 7 he began to write his own songs. By the time he reached the sixth grade, Hamlisch could play songs on the piano after hearing them a few times on the radio. Later on, Hamlisch realized how much he loved to write songs and decided to become a composer.

Marvin Hamlisch has written the music for three musicals: A Chorus Line, They're Playing Our Song, and The Goodbye Girl. He has also composed music for more than forty movies. He has won three Academy Awards, or Oscars, for his film music.

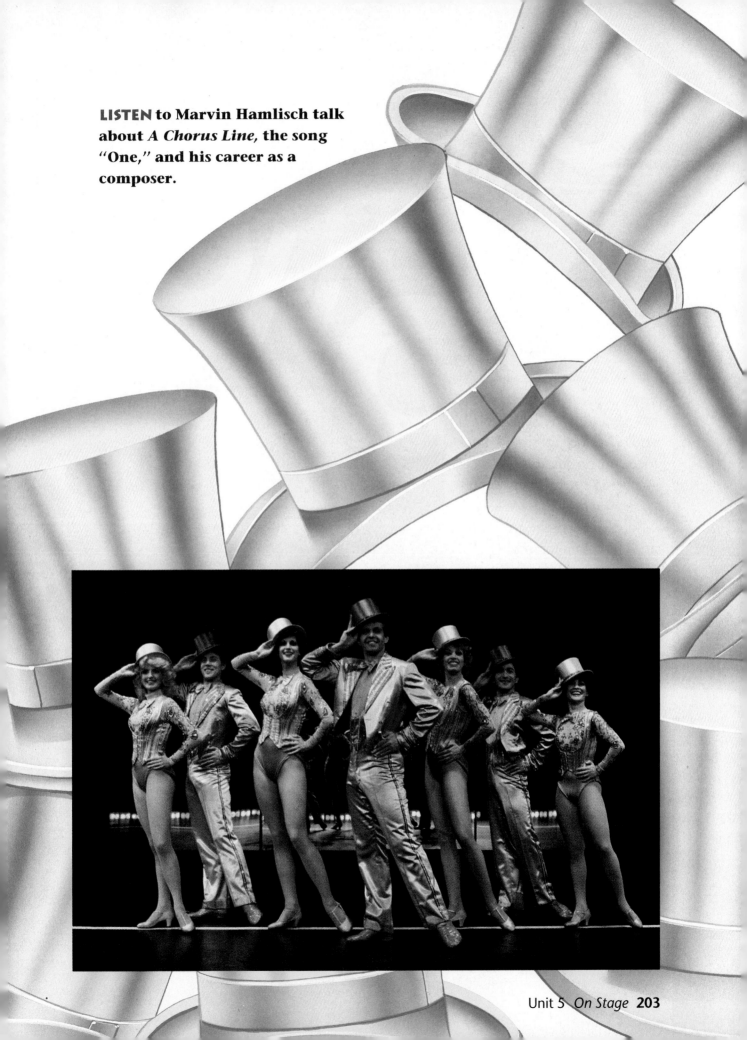

LISTEN to Marvin Hamlisch talk about *A Chorus Line,* the song "One," and his career as a composer.

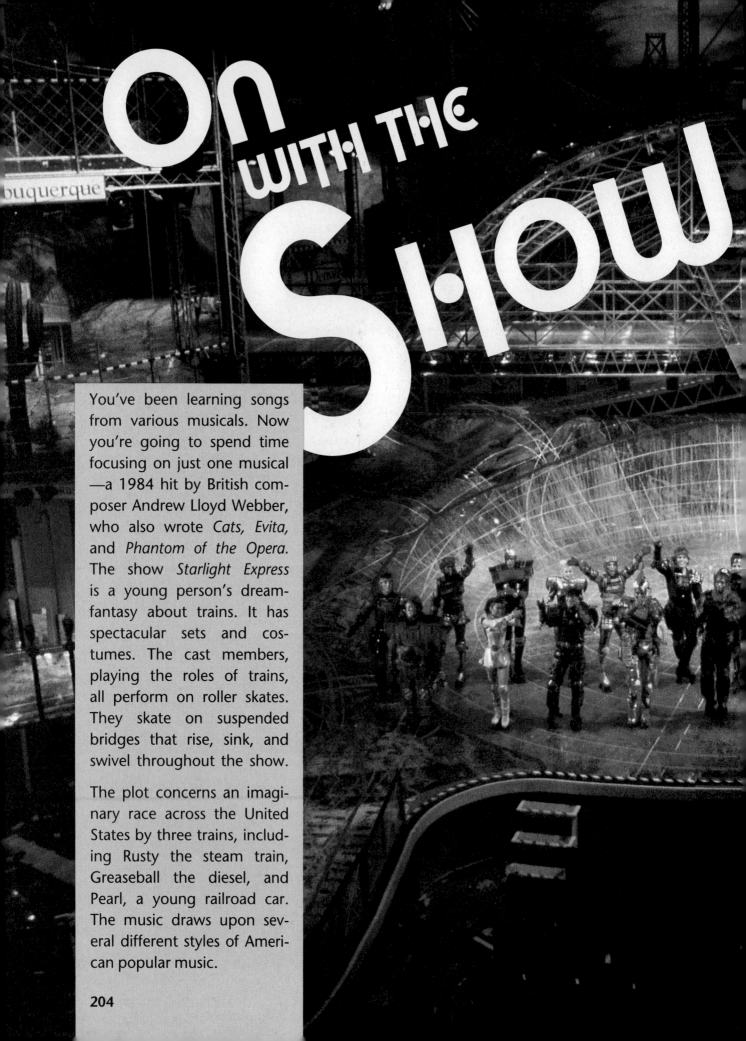

ON WITH THE SHOW

You've been learning songs from various musicals. Now you're going to spend time focusing on just one musical —a 1984 hit by British composer Andrew Lloyd Webber, who also wrote *Cats, Evita,* and *Phantom of the Opera.* The show *Starlight Express* is a young person's dream-fantasy about trains. It has spectacular sets and costumes. The cast members, playing the roles of trains, all perform on roller skates. They skate on suspended bridges that rise, sink, and swivel throughout the show.

The plot concerns an imaginary race across the United States by three trains, including Rusty the steam train, Greaseball the diesel, and Pearl, a young railroad car. The music draws upon several different styles of American popular music.

Pumping Iron

by Richard Stilgoe and Andrew Lloyd Webber

In "Pumping Iron," Greaseball, the defending cross-country race champion, describes his great diesel power.

Greaseball

DESCRIBE **the attitude that Greaseball portrays in the song. List several words that describe the quality of Greaseball's voice.**

PERFORM this accompaniment to "Pumping Iron."

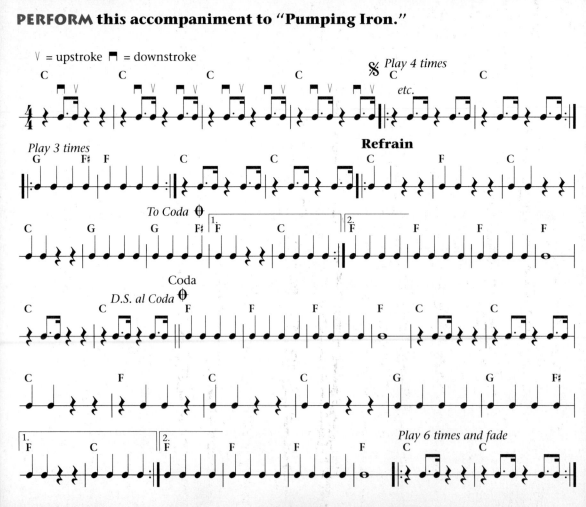

THE STORY CONTINUES...

LISTENING

Starlight Express

by Richard Stilgoe and Andrew Lloyd Webber

The underdog in the cross-country race is Rusty, an old-fashioned steam loco-motive. In the first stage of the race, Rusty loses because Greaseball has used dirty tricks. Discouraged, Rusty decides not to enter the next stage. Rusty's love interest, the young rail-road car named Pearl, doesn't under-stand the real reason why he lost and deserts him. Poppa, an old steam en-gine, tells Rusty about the Starlight Express, a mysterious force that can help him win. Rusty is inspired to re-enter the race.

WRITE **down some words that describe Rusty's vocal tone color.**

Rusty

WHAT'S THE MOTIVE?

In music dramas like musicals and operas, a motive is sometimes used to represent an important character or idea. The musical motive can be sung or played by the orchestra. Each time the motive returns, we are reminded of the other times we heard it. In *Starlight Express,* for example, this motive becomes the musical symbol for the mysterious force, the Starlight Express. Listen for it in the song "Starlight Express."

DETERMINE the pitch letter names of this musical motive.

LISTENING

I Am the Starlight

by Richard Stilgoe and Andrew Lloyd Webber

In "I Am the Starlight," the voice of the Starlight Express tells Rusty about the true source of its power.

COUNT the repetitions of the Starlight Express motive. How many times is it sung in this song?

THE STORY CONTINUES...

Pearl, now aware that Greaseball used dirty tricks to win the first stage of the race, returns to be Rusty's coach in the final stage.

THE PERFECT ENDING

LISTENING

The Light at the End of the Tunnel

by Richard Stilgoe and Andrew Lloyd Webber

The race is run and Rusty, with the help of Pearl, is the winner. There is great rejoicing as Poppa leads the celebration, singing in gospel style.

CLAP this syncopated
pattern each time you hear it
in "The Light at the End of the Tunnel."

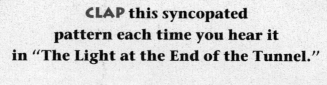

DESCRIBE the mood expressed in this song. Identify
the musical characteristics that project this mood.

OPERA
A Grand Tradition

Operas were first written around 1600. Many operas heard today were written in the 1700s and 1800s by composers such as Mozart, Wagner, and Verdi. Most operas are plays in which all the words are sung. A few, like *Porgy and Bess*, have spoken text. Operas contain solo songs, called **arias**, vocal groups, sung text, and sections for the orchestra alone. Some include dances. The singers must train for years in order to develop the beautiful, strong sound needed to fill a large opera house, where no electronic equipment is used to make the voices louder.

Many operas end tragically, but some are funny and end quite happily. The short comic opera *Gianni Schicchi* was written by the Italian composer Giacomo Puccini. It had its first performance in New York in 1918. Puccini's operas, such as *La Bohème, Tosca,* and *Madama Butterfly,* are known for their beautiful melodies and dramatic plots.

Giacomo Puccini

212

Buoso and his family in the opening scene of *Gianni Schicchi*

LISTENING

Gianni Schicchi Opening Scene
by Giacomo Puccini

The story takes place hundreds of years ago in Florence, Italy. An elderly, wealthy man, Buoso, has just died moments before. Members of his scheming, greedy family are gathered round, pretending to mourn.

THINK IT THROUGH

How does the music played by the orchestra give the impression that the relatives are not sincere?

The family's weeping soon gives way to worrying about Buoso's will. One of them has heard that Buoso left most of his estate to a nearby monastery. They find the will and discover that what they feared is true. They are to receive only small inheritances, rather than larger shares of Buoso's vast wealth !

The family reads Buoso's will.

Firenze è come un albero fiorito

from *Gianni Schicchi*
by Giacomo Puccini

One of the less greedy relatives, Rinuccio, is in love with Lauretta. His family has forbidden him to marry her because she is too poor to have a dowry—money given by a bride's father to her bridegroom. Rinuccio tells the family that he has sent for the only person who can help them get Buoso's money—Gianni Schicchi, Lauretta's father. The family does not like the idea of asking for help from a lowly peasant, but Rinuccio sings an aria in which he convinces them that Schicchi is quite clever, always playing tricks and practical jokes. Then Lauretta and Schicchi arrive and the family tries to get Schicchi's help.

LISTEN to this aria. What type of voice does Rinuccio have? Describe the tempo, dynamics, tone color, and articulation in Rinuccio's aria.

Lauretta and Rinuccio

LISTENING

O mio babbino caro

from *Gianni Schicchi*
by *Giacomo Puccini*

Schicchi does not want to help the family because he is disgusted by their greed and their treatment of Lauretta. Lauretta begs him to do so, however, so she can have the money for a dowry and marry Rinuccio.

DESCRIBE the tempo, dynamics, tone color, and articulation you hear in Lauretta's aria.

Schicchi finally agrees to help and devises a scheme. Since no one else knows that Buoso has died, he will impersonate him and dictate a new will. When the doctor comes, Schicchi jumps into the bed and pretends to be Buoso. Having fooled the doctor, Schicchi sends for the lawyer and dictates a new will. However, instead of making sure that the relatives get the money, he tells the lawyer that the choicest property is to go to Gianni Schicchi! The family can say nothing lest they get into trouble for assisting in the plot.

LISTENING

Ladro! Ladro!

from *Gianni Schicchi*
by *Giacomo Puccini*

After the lawyer leaves, the relatives explode in fury, calling Schicchi a thief. Schicchi kicks them out of the house. Now Lauretta and Rinuccio will have the money to get married.

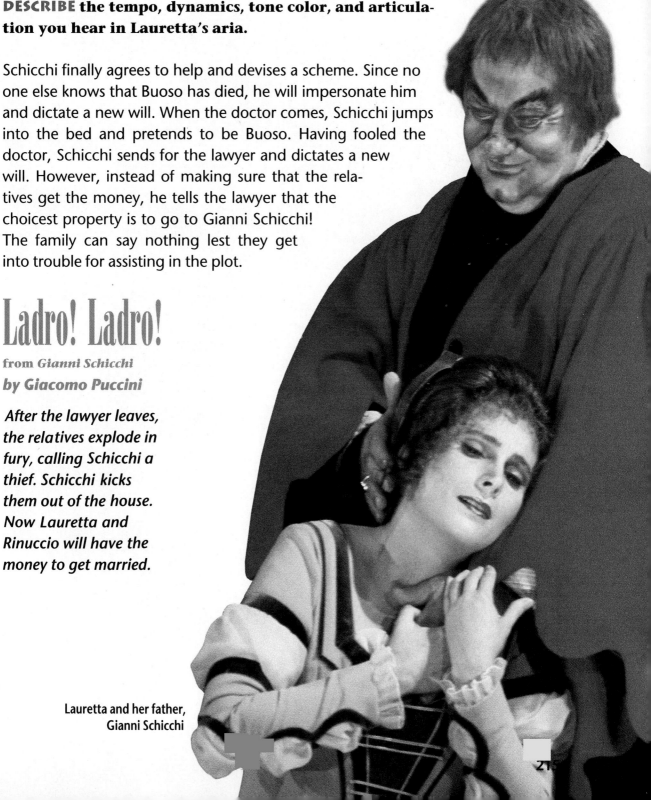

Lauretta and her father,
Gianni Schicchi

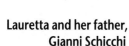

Theatrical Traditions

Long before anyone ever thought of Broadway musicals or opera, other kinds of musical theater were enjoyed in different parts of the world.

LISTENING

Eka Tala *(Excerpt)*
South Indian Theater Music

Kudiyattam is the oldest kind of musical drama that is still in existence today. It comes from South India and is said to be over 1,000 years old. Kudiyattam is associated with the Hindu religion. The lines are chanted, rather than sung.

Four instrumentalists accompany the movement in Kudiyattam. Two performers play pot-shaped drums, while one plays an hourglass-shaped drum. The fourth person plays a small pair of cymbals. Listen for the instruments in "Eka Tala." Once you hear a regular rhythm, tap your fingers together on each stressed beat. In Indian music, a rhythm pattern is called a **tala.**

LISTEN for four beats in each group of the "Eka Tala."

216

Kathakali is a newer form of South Indian musical drama, but it is closely patterned after Kudiyattam. The rhythms are more complex than those of Kudiyattam.

PLAY a rhythm from the Kathakali tradition.

ta ki ka ta ta ki na ta ki ta ki ta kyam

The Hindu god Shiva is holding an hourglass drum in his top right hand. Hindus believe that Shiva's dancing preserves the world.

INDONESIAN SHADOW PUPPET THEATER

The *wayang kulit* theater, or shadow puppet theater, is very popular in Indonesia. A storyteller, called the *dalang*, recites ancient Indian and Indonesian stories as he manipulates puppets behind a screen. A light behind the screen causes the puppets to cast shadows. The audience sees only the shadows of the puppets, moving as if by themselves. Some people are allowed to sit in special seats where they can see the puppets and the dalang in action behind the screen. Instrumentalists and a singer accompany the show. The dalang also plays percussion instruments with his foot and conducts the musicians as well. He is highly respected for these abilities. Many different puppets are used. They are made of beautifully decorated, painted, and elaborately cut leather.

The music for the wayang kulit theater is provided by an instrumental group called *gender wayang.* The gender wayang consists of four metallophones.

LISTENING

Prologue to *Mahabarata* (Excerpt)

Traditional Indonesian Music

Listen to the gender wayang as it opens a shadow puppet performance in Bali, one of the islands of Indonesia. Listen carefully and you will hear the crickets in the background of this outdoor performance, recorded live.

PLAY patterns on metallophones or other barred instruments to create a sound like that of the gender wayang.

These performers come from Java. Java is a neighbor of Bali and the two islands have related shadow puppet theater traditions.

ZARZUELA: THE OPERA OF SPAIN

Zarzuela is a type of Spanish opera that combines spoken dialogue with music. It takes its name from the Palace of La Zarzuela near Madrid. Lively and exciting festivals that included these musical productions took place at La Zarzuela as early as 1629. Zarzuelas remain popular today.

LISTENING

De este apacible rincón *from Luisa Fernanda*
by Federico Moreno Torroba

Listen for Spanish rhythms in this brilliant aria, sung by the famous Spanish tenor Placido Domingo. In the aria, a well-to-do man named Javier—now far away from home—remembers the peaceful corner of Madrid where he spent his childhood dreaming of success and wealth.

What choices in interpretation did Placido Domingo make in order to project the feeling of the song effectively?

The variety of musical theater productions around the world is almost endless. Here are some scenes from a few more.

A zarzuela performance in Spain

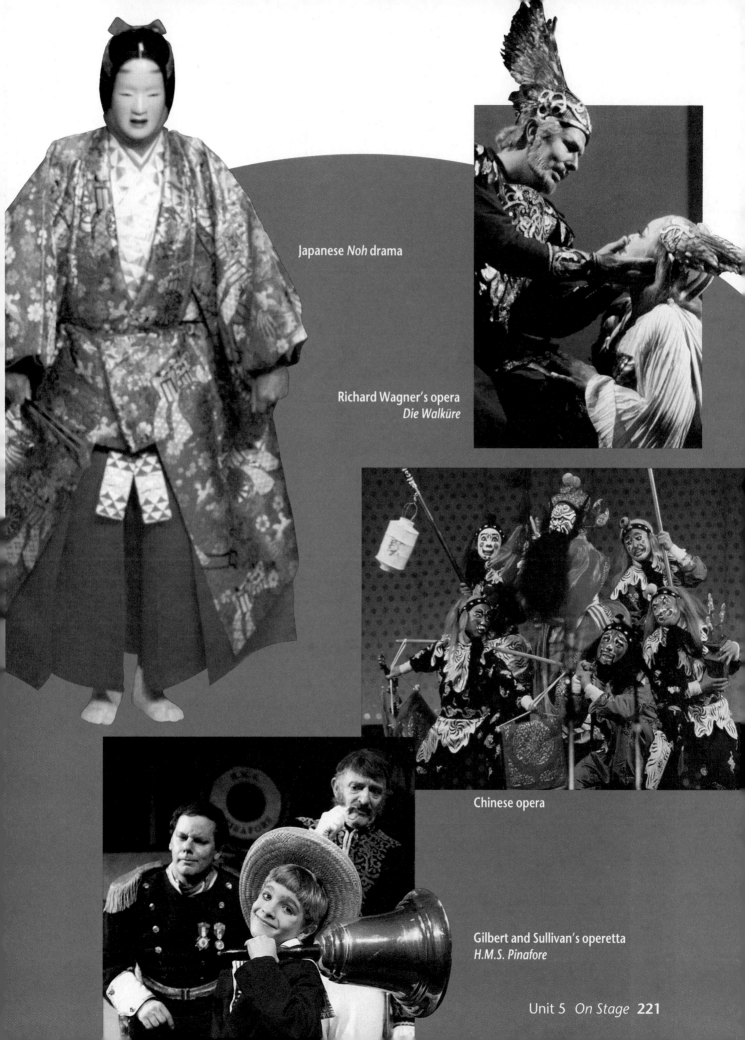

Japanese *Noh* drama

Richard Wagner's opera
Die Walküre

Chinese opera

Gilbert and Sullivan's operetta
H.M.S. Pinafore

CURTAIN CALLS

"Our Time" is from the 1981 musical *Merrily We Roll Along* by Stephen Sondheim. In the song, a group of recent high school graduates look forward to their lives as adults.

LISTEN for the way tempo, dynamics, articulation, and tone color are used to project the feelings and thoughts of the song.

OUR TIME

Words and Music
by Stephen Sondheim

1. Some-thing is stir - ring, shift-ing ground.— It's just be - gun.—
2. Feel how it qui - vers, on the brink,— ev'- ry - thing!—

— Edg - es are blur - ring all a - round,— and
— Gives you the shiv - ers, makes you think— there's

yes - ter - day— is done.— Feel the flow,—
so much stuff— to sing.— And you and me,—

hear what's hap - pen - ing. We're what's hap - pen - ing.
we'll be sing - ing it like the birds,_____ me with mu - sic and

Don't you know?___ We're the mov - ers and we're the shap - ers,
you the words,___

we're the names__ in to - mor - row's pa - pers, up to us___ now to

show 'em.___ It's

our time,___ breathe it in.___ Worlds to change___ and

"Give My Regards to Broadway" is by George M. Cohan, who not only wrote and directed his own shows, but also sang and danced in them.

GIVE MY REGARDS TO BROADWAY

Words and Music by George M. Cohan

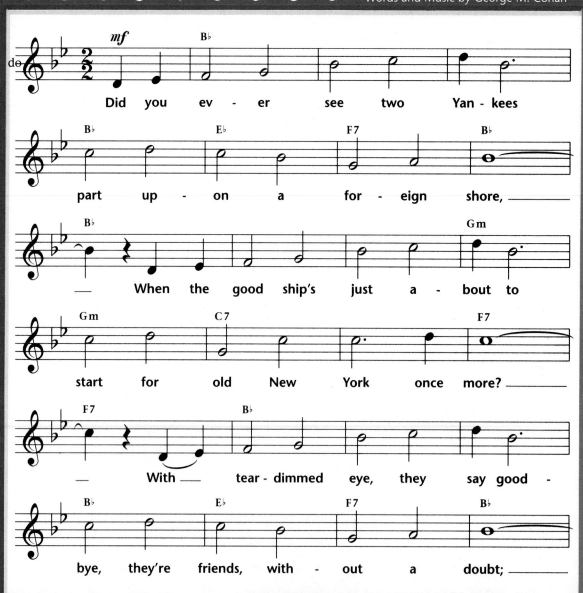

THE STAGE IS YOURS

Musical theater productions have enchanted audiences for thousands of years in many parts of the world. Musicals have been enjoyed in the United States since the beginning of the 1900s. Sing "Another Op'nin', Another Show" to get the feeling of being on stage on opening night.

Musicals can be funny, or they can send a serious message. Sing "Comedy Tonight" and "Look Around," then compare the moods of these two songs.

"I Am the Starlight" tells us that we have the power to make the things that we wish for come true. Listen for the motive that is a musical symbol for the Starlight Express.

It's time to leave the theater for now. Sing "Give My Regards to Broadway" to salute New York's center of theater magic.

Stephen Sondheim

Andrew Lloyd Webber

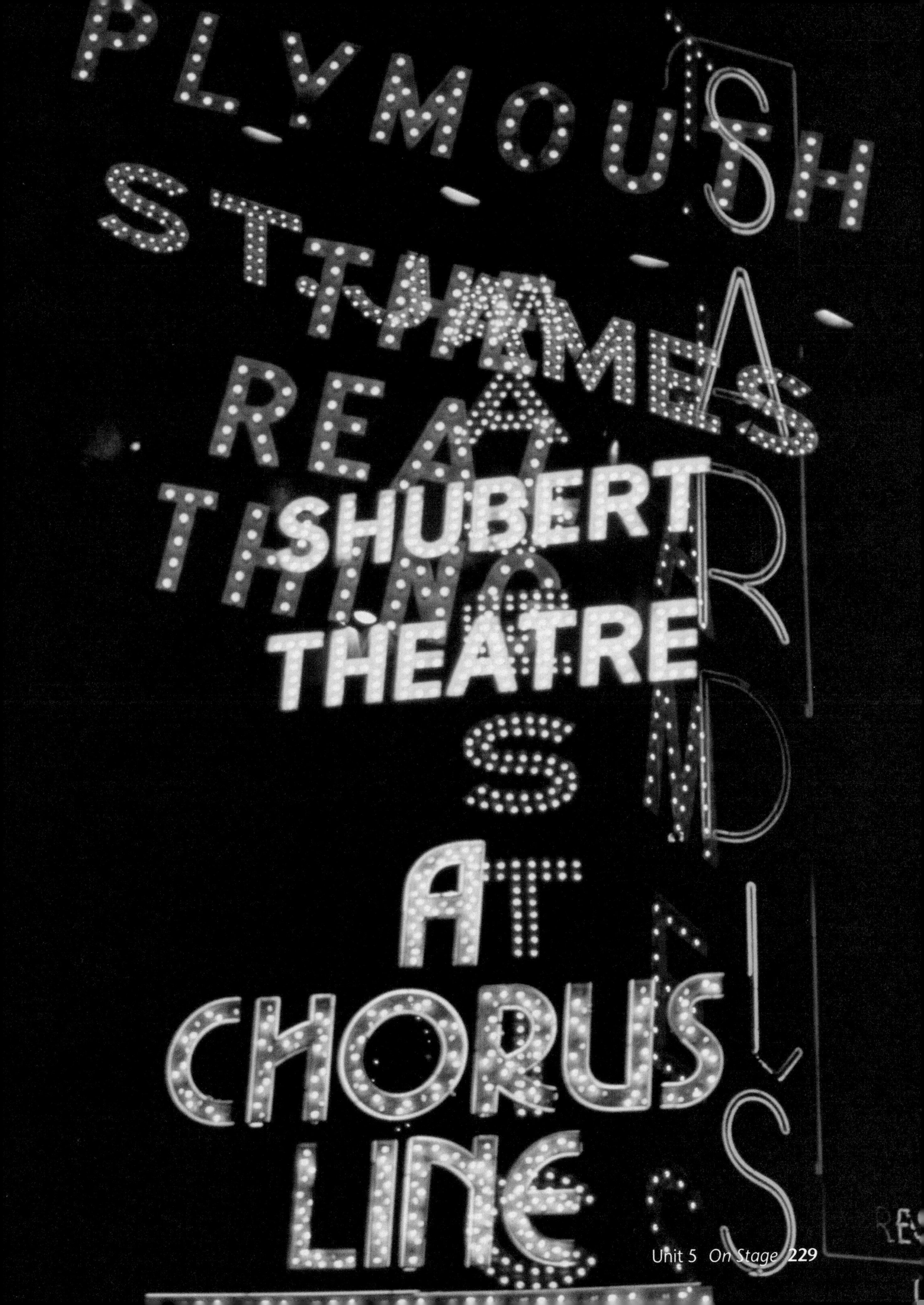
PLYMOUTH
SHUBERT
THEATRE
CHORUS
LINE

1. Which vocal range do you hear?

   a. soprano

   c. tenor

   b. alto

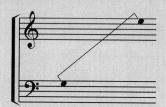

   d. bass

2. Which musical element is changed?

   a. tempo   **c.** vocal tone color
   b. dynamics   **d.** articulation

3. Which vocal tone color do you hear?

   a. heavier voice   **b.** lighter voice

4. Which articulation do you hear?

   a. legato   **b.** marcato   **c.** something else

CREATE

Perform in Your Own Style

Choose a song to perform individually or in small groups. It may be from a Broadway musical or from an opera. If you choose a song that is not from this book, find and bring in the music. You may use a recording as background or a teacher, another student, or a special guest can accompany you.

Use appropriate tone color, articulation, dynamics, and tempo. The interpretation should be a cooperative result of group planning and effort.

PERFORM your selection for the class. Have someone videotape the performance if possible.

Write

Write the story for a musical that you would like to produce on Broadway. The plot can be completely new, or like many musicals, it can be based on a book you have read or a movie or television show you have seen. Include some ideas about the songs in your show and indicate where they would appear in the story.

The Story of Carmen

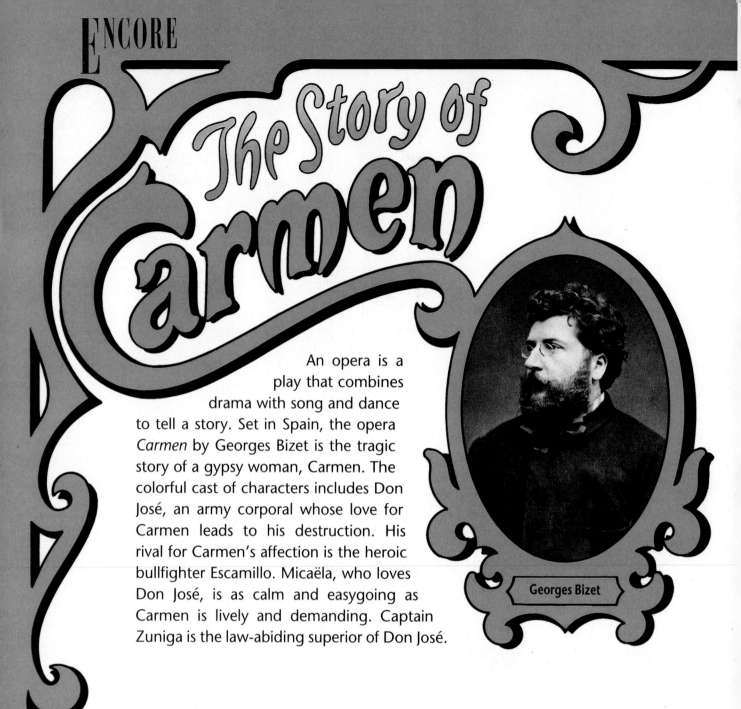

Georges Bizet

An opera is a play that combines drama with song and dance to tell a story. Set in Spain, the opera *Carmen* by Georges Bizet is the tragic story of a gypsy woman, Carmen. The colorful cast of characters includes Don José, an army corporal whose love for Carmen leads to his destruction. His rival for Carmen's affection is the heroic bullfighter Escamillo. Micaëla, who loves Don José, is as calm and easygoing as Carmen is lively and demanding. Captain Zuniga is the law-abiding superior of Don José.

LISTENING

Carmen (excerpts)
by Georges Bizet

A prelude is an introduction the orchestra plays before the curtain goes up and the opera begins. In the Prelude to Act 1 of Carmen, *Bizet uses contrasting rhythm patterns, tempos, and dynamics to create the atmosphere for the story. You will hear one of the musical themes return later in the opera. What instrument families are featured in the prelude?*

CLAP the rhythm patterns on the next page. Which one features the dotted rhythm?

LISTEN to the Prelude and identify the order in which the rhythm patterns appear. The dynamic markings will help you. A rhythm pattern may occur more than once.

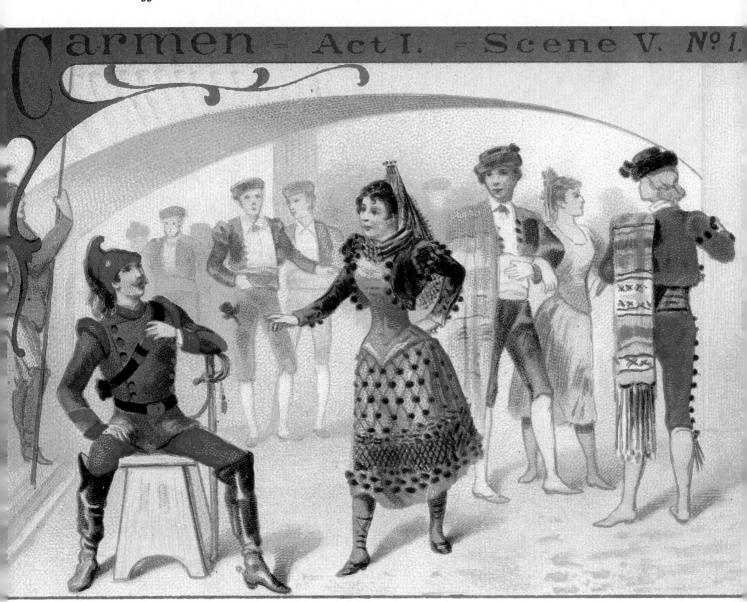

SEGUIDILLA

Carmen is arrested after attacking another woman. Don José is ordered by Captain Zuniga to take her to prison. Left alone with Don José, Carmen tries to persuade him to set her free. In the aria (an extended solo song) "Seguidilla," Carmen succeeds in coaxing Don José to let her go. As Act I ends, Carmen escapes and Don José is arrested for helping her escape.

TOREADOR SONG

Act 2 opens in Lillas Pastia's tavern, where the bullfighter Escamillo is introduced. In the famous "Toreador Song," Escamillo describes the shouting crowds that await him and the fame he will win through his courage. Listen for this rhythm, which you first heard in the prelude.

Refrain

p first time (Escamillo–solo)
ff second time (Chorus joins in)

THE STORY CONCLUDES

When Don José is released from prison, he meets Carmen outside Lillas Pastia's tavern. Charmed by her beauty, he deserts the army to follow her and her friends into the mountains. He stays there until Micaëla persuades him to come to the side of his dying mother.

Meanwhile, Carmen falls in love with the toreador Escamillo. Carmen and Don José meet again outside a bullring where Escamillo is fighting. Despite Don José's pleas, Carmen refuses to go away with him. Carmen, proud and determined, throws a gold ring he once gave her into the dust to confirm the end of their love. Filled with rage, Don José fatally stabs Carmen.

Georges Bizet did not live to see Carmen *become a success. The first performances were poorly received. It was not until the first performance at the Paris Opéra-Comique, three months after Bizet's death, that this great work won public approval.*

FROM RAG

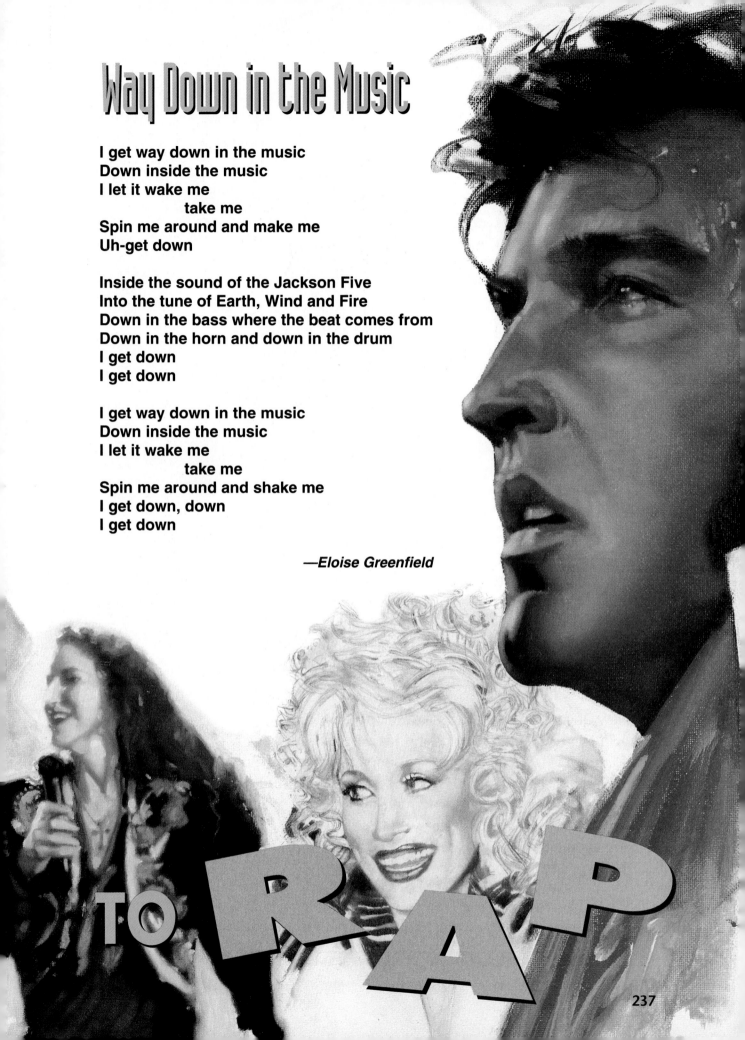

Way Down in the Music

I get way down in the music
Down inside the music
I let it wake me
　　　　take me
Spin me around and make me
Uh-get down

Inside the sound of the Jackson Five
Into the tune of Earth, Wind and Fire
Down in the bass where the beat comes from
Down in the horn and down in the drum
I get down
I get down

I get way down in the music
Down inside the music
I let it wake me
　　　　take me
Spin me around and shake me
I get down, down
I get down

—*Eloise Greenfield*

TO RAP

The 1900s and 1910s

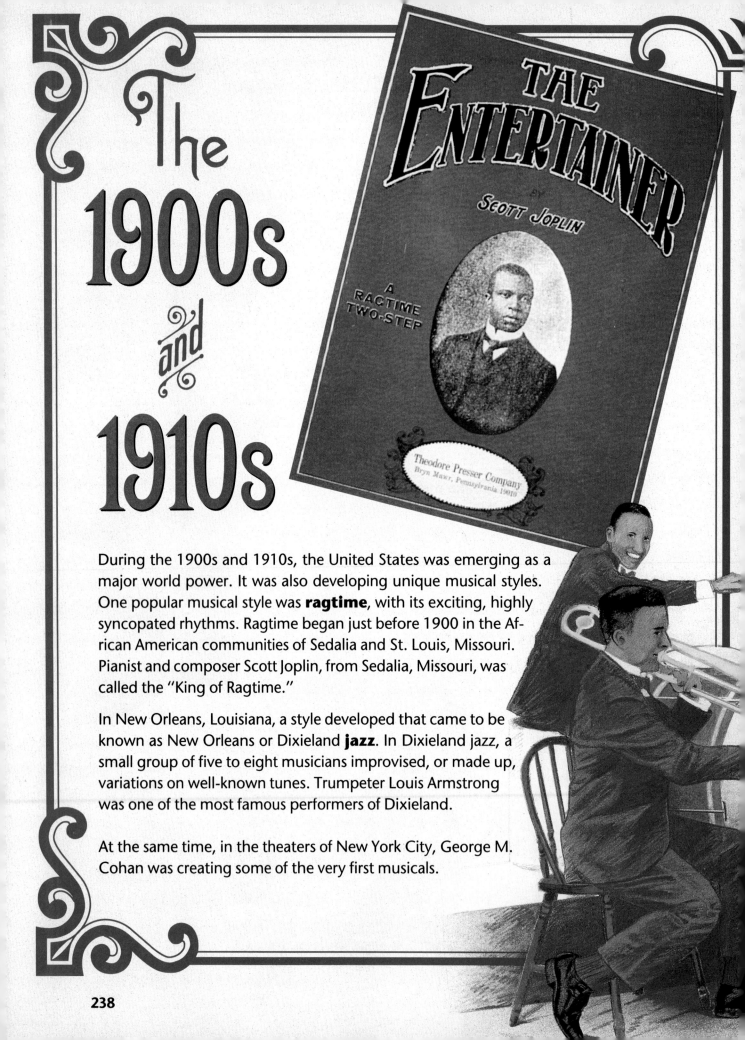

During the 1900s and 1910s, the United States was emerging as a major world power. It was also developing unique musical styles. One popular musical style was **ragtime**, with its exciting, highly syncopated rhythms. Ragtime began just before 1900 in the African American communities of Sedalia and St. Louis, Missouri. Pianist and composer Scott Joplin, from Sedalia, Missouri, was called the "King of Ragtime."

In New Orleans, Louisiana, a style developed that came to be known as New Orleans or Dixieland **jazz**. In Dixieland jazz, a small group of five to eight musicians improvised, or made up, variations on well-known tunes. Trumpeter Louis Armstrong was one of the most famous performers of Dixieland.

At the same time, in the theaters of New York City, George M. Cohan was creating some of the very first musicals.

Alexander's Ragtime Band

Words and Music by Irving Berlin

Oh, ma honey, Oh ma honey, Better hurry and let's meander
Ain't you goin', Ain't you goin', To the leader man, ragged meter man?
Oh, ma honey, Oh ma honey, Let me take you to Alexander's grand stand,
    brass band,
Ain't you comin' along?

Come on and hear, Come on and hear Alexander's Ragtime Band,
Come on and hear, Come on and hear, It's the best band in the land,
They can play a bugle call like you never heard before,
So natural that you want to go to war;
That's just the bestest band what am, honey lamb,
Come on along, Come on along, Let me take you by the hand,
Up to the man, Up to the man, who's the leader of the band,
And if you care to hear the Swanee River played in ragtime,
Come on and hear, Come on and hear Alexander's Ragtime Band.

PERFORM a percussion accompaniment to the "1900s–1910s Medley."

LISTENING

1900s - 1910s MEDLEY

THE 1920s

The 1920s have often been called the Roaring Twenties. World War I, described as "the war to end all wars," was over. People were relieved and lighthearted. The country seemed prosperous, and the world was filled with a sense of optimism: people felt that things would get better and better. Much popular music of the 1920s portrayed this lightheartedness. Dixieland jazz increased in popularity. The Charleston, with its lively music, was the favorite dance of the time.

Not all music of the 1920s was lighthearted, however. The **blues**, a style created by African American musicians, usually expressed sorrow but looked with hope to the future.

Royal Garden Blues

Words and Music by
Clarence Williams and Spencer Williams

Hon, don't you hear that trombone moan?
Just listen to that saxophone.
Gee, hear that clarinet and flute,
Cornet a-jazzin' with a mute.
Makes me just throw myself away
When I hear 'em play.

That weepin' melancholy strain,
Say, but it's soothin' to the brain.
Just wanna get right up and dance,
Don't care, I'll take most any chance.
No other blues I'd care to choose
But Royal Garden Blues.

Singer Gertrude "Ma" Rainey, pictured with her band in 1925, has been called "the mother of the blues."

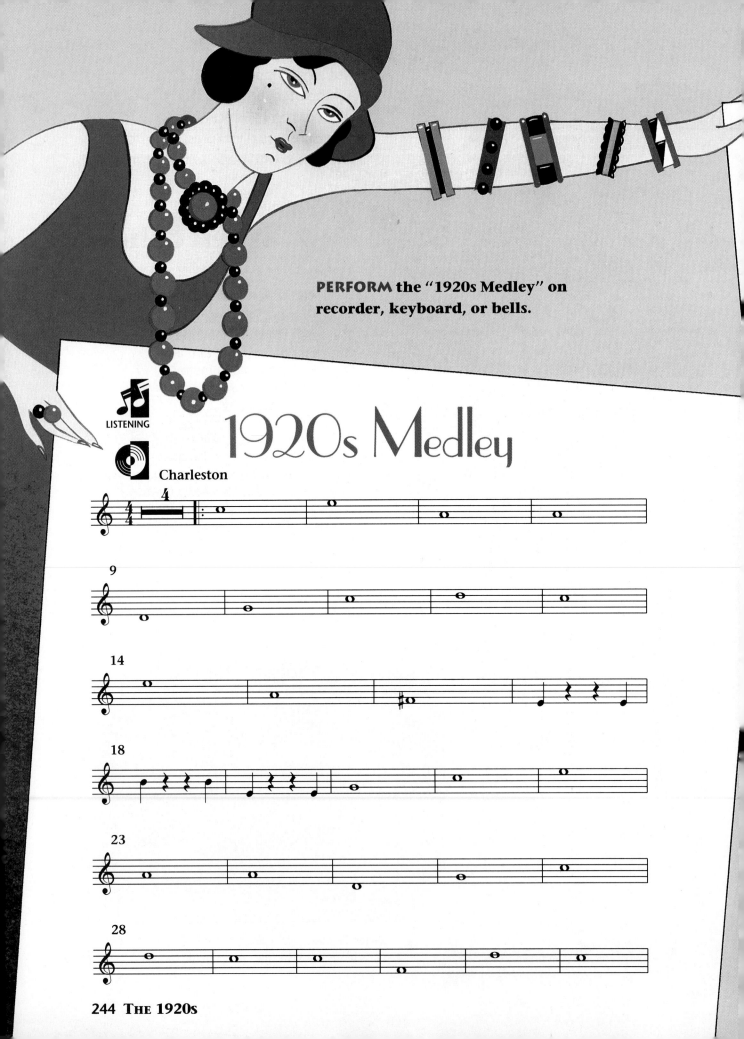

PERFORM the "1920s Medley" on recorder, keyboard, or bells.

LISTENING

1920s Medley

Charleston

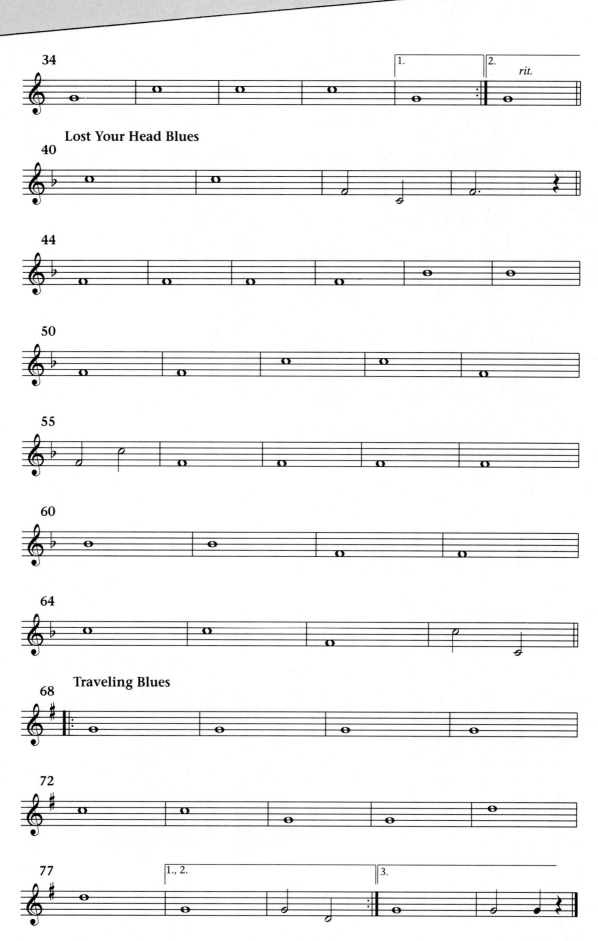

Lost Your Head Blues

Traveling Blues

The 1930s

Woody Guthrie

The 1930s were a time of economic and social difficulties. Many people experienced the severe hardships of the Great Depression. These hardships were reflected in some of the music. Folksingers like Woody Guthrie and blues musicians like Bessie Smith sang of the tough times. But not all music was sad. A new style of jazz developed, called **swing**. Swing was dance music. It was performed by big bands—bigger than the Dixieland groups of the 1920s. With such large bands, swing music had to be carefully composed and arranged. A band leader coordinated the performance. Duke Ellington was one of the most famous band leaders and composers of the time. Clarinetist and bandleader Benny Goodman also helped mold the sounds of the swing era.

Duke Ellington

IT DON'T MEAN A THING
(IF IT AIN'T GOT THAT SWING)

Words and Music by Duke Ellington and Irving Mills

What good is melody, what good is music,
If it ain't possessin' something sweet?
It ain't the melody, it ain't the music.
There's something else that makes the
   tune complete.

It don't mean a thing if it ain't got that swing,
doo wah, doo wah, doo wah, doo wah,
doo wah, doo wah, doo wah, doo wah.
It don't mean a thing, all you got to do is sing,
doo wah, doo wah, doo wah, doo wah,
doo wah, doo wah, doo wah, doo wah.
It makes no diff'rence if it's sweet or hot,
Just give that rhythm ev'rything you got.
Oh, It don't mean a thing if it ain't got
   that swing,
doo wah, doo wah, doo wah, doo wah,
doo wah, doo wah, doo wah, doo wah.

Benny Goodman

PERFORM a percussion part to the swing-style "1930s Medley."

 # 1930s MEDLEY

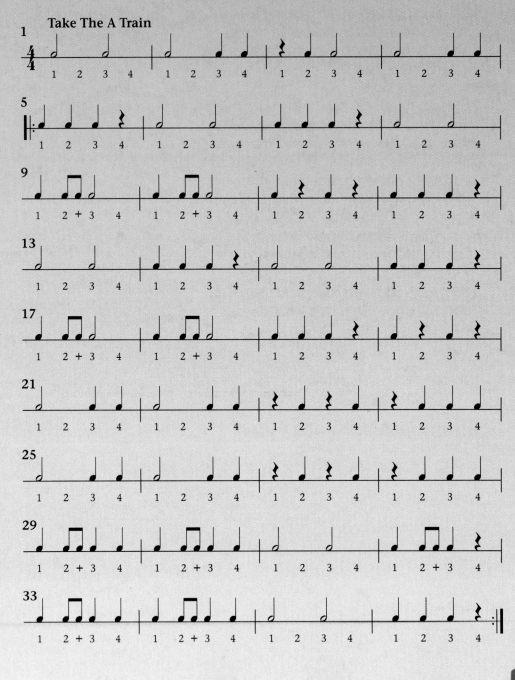

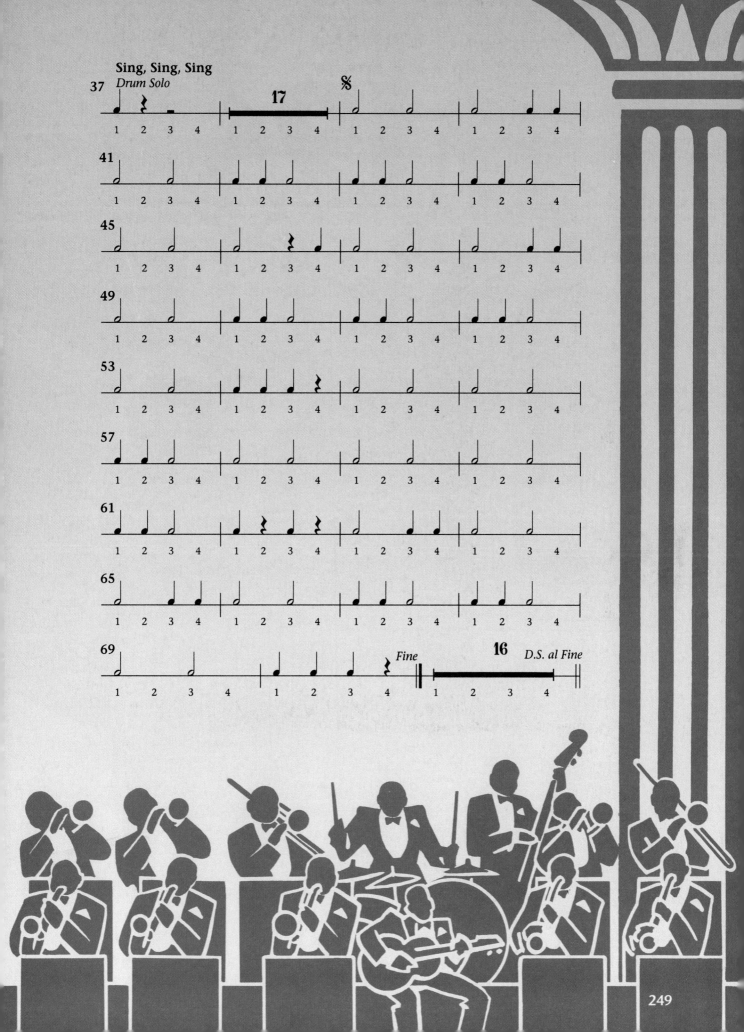

Sing, Sing, Sing

249

THE 1940s

The Andrews Sisters

Popular music in the 1940s allowed people to escape from some of the grim events of World War II. Big band music continued to be popular, led by such famous musicians as Glenn Miller, Count Basie, Stan Kenton, Benny Goodman, Tommy and Jimmy Dorsey, and Duke Ellington. Famous vocalists included the Andrews Sisters, Ella Fitzgerald, and Frank Sinatra.

In the later 1940s, performers like saxophonist Charlie Parker and trumpeter Dizzy Gillespie created a new kind of jazz called **bebop**. Bebop bands had only a few members, and improvisation was an important part of the band's playing style. Bebop harmonies were more complex than those in most swing music.

BOOGIE WOOGIE BUGLE BOY

Words and Music by Don Raye and Hughie Prince

He was a famous trumpet man from out Chicago way,
He had a "boogie" style that no one else could play.
He was the top man of his craft.
But then his number came up, and he was gone with the draft.
He's in the army now a-blowin' reveille,
He's the BOOGIE WOOGIE BUGLE BOY of Company B.

They made him blow a bugle for his Uncle Sam,
It really brought him down because he couldn't jam.
The captain seemed to understand
Because the next day the "cap" went out and drafted a band,
And now the comp'ny jumps when he plays reveille,
He's the BOOGIE WOOGIE BUGLE BOY of Company B.

A toot! A toot! A toot diddle ah-da toot.
He blows it eight to the bar in "boogie" rhythm.
He can't blow a note unless a bass and guitar are playin' with 'im.
He makes the comp'ny jump when he plays reveille,
He's the BOOGIE WOOGIE BUGLE BOY of Company B.

He puts the boys to sleep with "boogie" ev'ry night,
And wakes them up the same way in the early bright.
They clap their hands and stamp their feet
Because they know how he plays when someone gives him a beat,
He really breaks it up when he plays reveille,
He's the BOOGIE WOOGIE BUGLE BOY of Company B.
A toot! A toot! (etc.)

PERFORM the "1940s Medley" on guitar.

Hold the guitar as shown. The fingers of your left hand should be above the open strings.

PLAY the D, G, and A chords.

Notice where to place your fingers on the strings. The fingers are numbered from the index finger (1) to the little finger (4).

The X at the top of the chord diagram indicates that the string is not to be played. A string marked with an O should be played open.

1940s MEDLEY

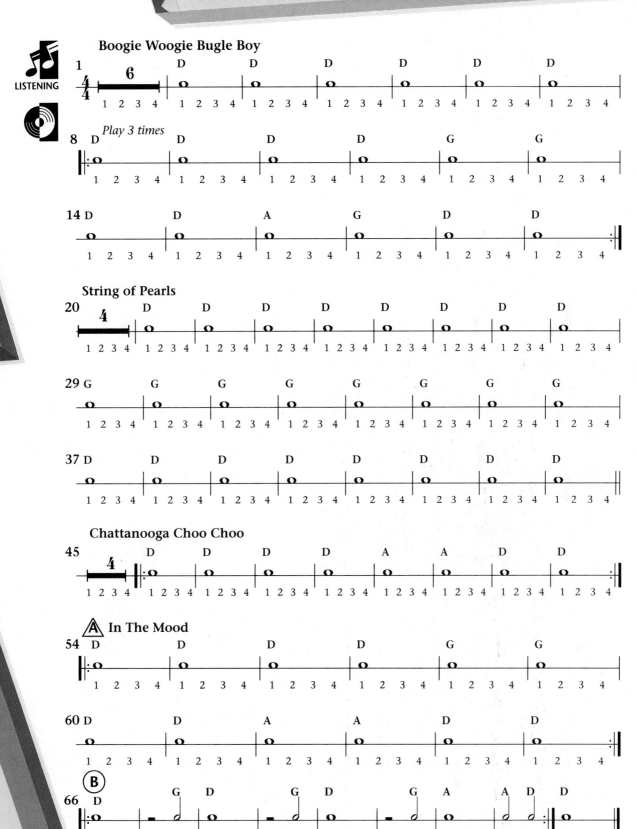

Boogie Woogie Bugle Boy

String of Pearls

Chattanooga Choo Choo

In The Mood

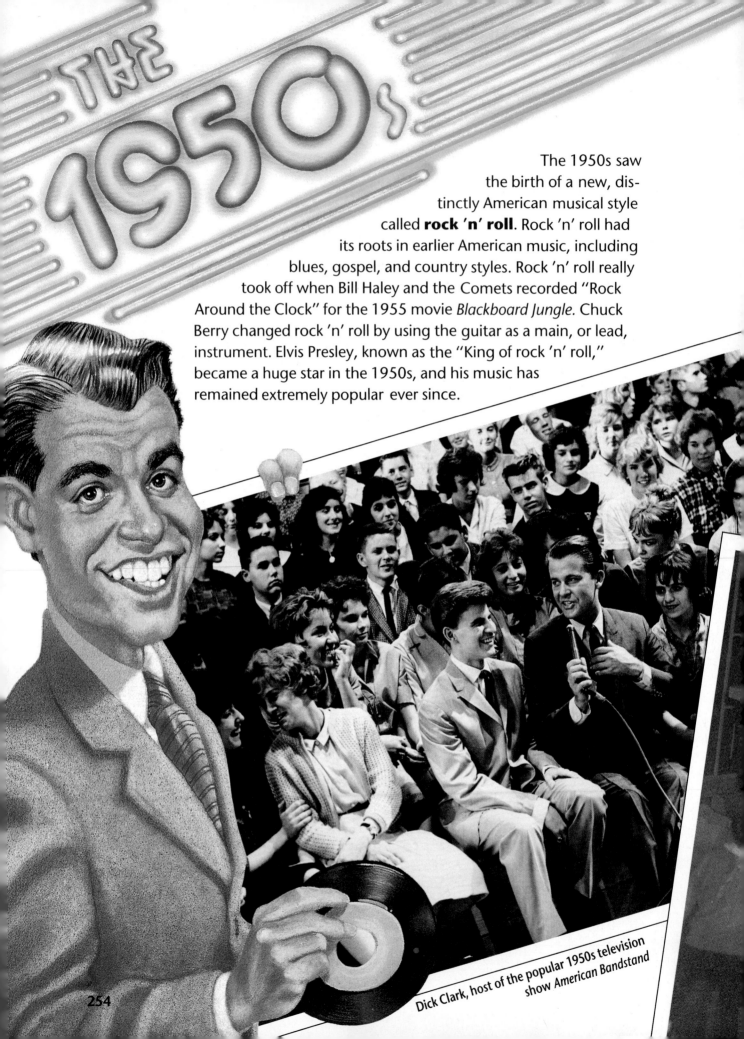

THE 1950s

The 1950s saw the birth of a new, distinctly American musical style called **rock 'n' roll**. Rock 'n' roll had its roots in earlier American music, including blues, gospel, and country styles. Rock 'n' roll really took off when Bill Haley and the Comets recorded "Rock Around the Clock" for the 1955 movie *Blackboard Jungle.* Chuck Berry changed rock 'n' roll by using the guitar as a main, or lead, instrument. Elvis Presley, known as the "King of rock 'n' roll," became a huge star in the 1950s, and his music has remained extremely popular ever since.

Dick Clark, host of the popular 1950s television show *American Bandstand*

Bandstand Boogie

Words by Barry Manilow
and Bruce Sussman
Music by Charles Albertine

Refrain

We're goin' hoppin', we're goin' hoppin' today,
where things are poppin', the Philadelphia way;
we're gonna drop in on all the music they play on
the Bandstand. (Bandstand.)

And I'll jump and, hey, I may even show 'em my handstand,
because I'm on, because I'm on the American Bandstand.
When we dance real slow I'll show all the guys in the grandstand
what a swinger I am; I am on American Bandstand.

Refrain

Whatdaya know, here on the show ready to go, what a pro!
Hey! I'm makin' my mark; Gee, this joint is jumpin'.
They made such a fuss just to see us arrive.
Hey! It's Mister Dick Clark; what a place you've got here,
swell spot, the music's hot here.
Best in the East, give it at least a seventy-five!

And now we're hoppin', and we'll be hoppin' all day
where things are poppin' the Philadelphia way,
And you can drop in on all the music they play on the Bandstand.
And we'll rock and roll and
Stroll on American, Lindy Hop and Slop, it's American.
Tune in , I'm on, turn on, I'm in, I'm on! Today, Bandstand.

PERFORM a harmonic accompaniment to the "1950s Medley" on guitar.

Play the C chord so that you can use it with the G and D chords. Remember that your fingers are numbered from the index finger (1) to the little finger (4).

Easy C

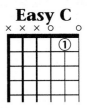

LISTENING

1950s MEDLEY

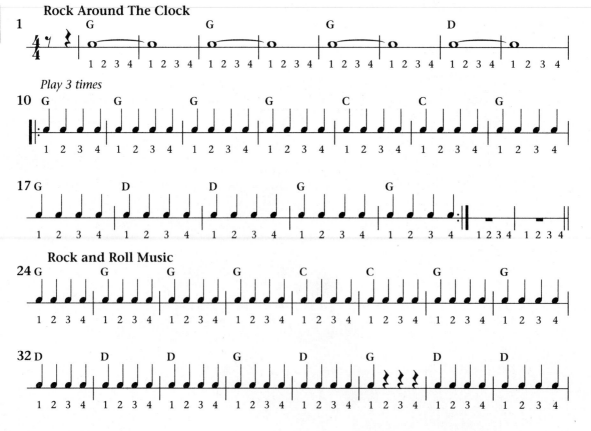

THE 1960s

In the early part of the 1960s, folk music by singer-songwriters such as Bob Dylan, Joan Baez, and Peter, Paul, and Mary addressed social and political issues. To focus on their lyrics, these performers used little accompaniment, often just guitar.

Not all of the 1960s music was serious, however. The Twist emerged as the dance craze of the early 1960s when Chubby Checker performed it on national television. Surf music, with themes of fun in the sun, became popular as played by groups like the Beach Boys. This group specialized in smooth vocal harmonies.

Toward the end of the 1960s, peace and friendship were celebrated when up to 500,000 young people came together for huge rock 'n' roll concerts in Monterey, California; Woodstock, New York, and other locations.

"Ask not what your country can do for you..."

THE TWIST ON STAGE IN PERSON TV REVUE

"I have a dream..."

WE MARCH FOR JOBS FOR ALL NOW!

"The answer is blowin' in the wind."

Blowin' in the Wind

Words and Music by Bob Dylan

How many roads must a man walk down
Before you call him a man?
Yes, 'n' how many seas must a white dove sail
Before she sleeps in the sand?
Yes, 'n' how many times must the cannonballs fly
Before they're forever banned?
The answer, my friend, is blowin' in the wind,
The answer is blowin' in the wind.

How many times must a man look up
Before he can see the sky?
Yes, 'n' how many ears must one man have
Before he can hear people cry?
Yes, 'n' how many deaths will it take 'till he knows
That too many people have died?
The answer, my friend, is blowin' in the wind,
The answer is blowin' in the wind.

How many years can a mountain exist
Before it's washed to the sea?
Yes, 'n' how many years can some people exist
Before they're allowed to be free?
Yes, 'n' how many times can a man turn his head
Pretending he just doesn't see?
The answer, my friend, is blowin' in the wind,
The answer is blowin' in the wind.

PERFORM the contrasting styles of the "1960s Medley" on guitar.

Learn the A7 chord so that you can use it with the G, C, and D chords. Remember that your fingers are numbered from the index finger (1) to the little finger (4).

A7

LISTENING

1960s Medley

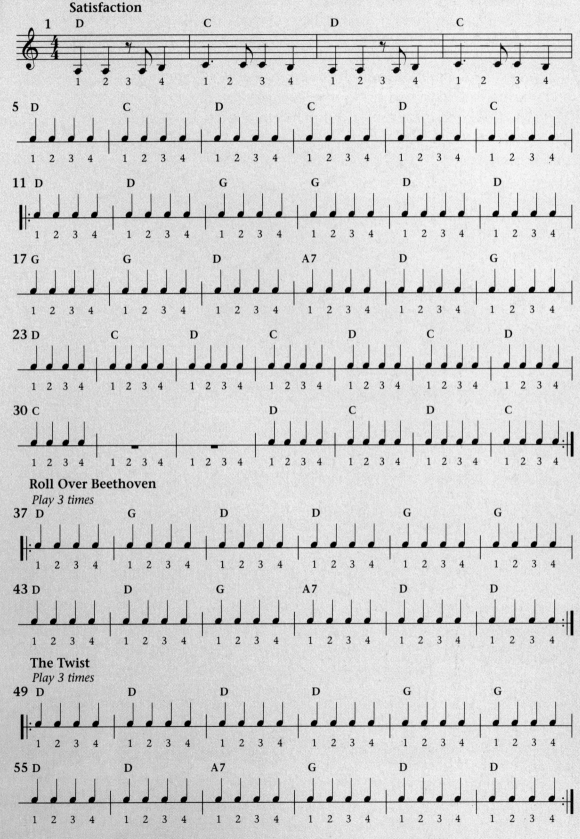

THE BEATLES: THE BRITISH INVASION

In the 1960s, British rock groups such as the Rolling Stones, the Animals, and the Who began to give concerts in the United States. These groups became extremely popular. The most influential and famous of these groups, however, was the Beatles.

The Beatles changed rock 'n' roll in the 1960s by accompanying their songs with orchestral instruments, instruments from India, and unusual electronic sounds. Their initial American tour in 1964 was a phenomenal success. In less than a decade, the Beatles sold 125 million single records and 85 million albums.

The Beatles

FOLLOW the text and figure out the musical form of "Birthday." The song contains three musical sections, which have different words, shown below.

LISTENING

Birthday

Words and Music by John Lennon and Paul McCartney

You say it's your birthday, it's my birthday too, yeah.
You say it's your birthday, we're gonna have a good time.
I'm glad it's your birthday, Happy Birthday to you!

Yes, we're goin' to a party, party.
Yes, we're goin' to a party, party.
Yes, we're goin' to a party, party.

I would like you to dance (Birthday)
Take a cha-cha-cha-chance (Birthday)
I would like you to dance (Birthday)
Dance.

"Birthday" has a form in which the refrain, or A section, returns. This repetition of a musical section serves as a familiar landmark for the listener.

1970s

The 1970s saw advances in music technology. Amplifiers made music louder and electronic devices changed guitar and keyboard tone colors. This enabled rock bands like Led Zeppelin to create new sounds. They helped start a new style called **heavy metal.** Later in the 1970s, a style called **disco** emerged with performers such as Donna Summer. Disco's strong, steady beat made it easy to dance to. Another style popular in the 1970s was **country and western**. This music, which grew out of earlier country music styles, features the banjo, fiddle, and pedal-steel guitar. The harmonies stay simple so that listeners can focus on the expressive vocal styles of the singers. Singers such as Dolly Parton, Randy Travis, and Garth Brooks have kept country music popular into the 1990s.

SING this popular song from the mid-1970s.

 Fly Like an Eagle   Words and Music
by Steve Miller

(*Tip top tip.* Doot doot doo doo.)
Time keeps on slippin', slippin', slippin', into the future.
Time keeps on slippin', slippin', slippin', into the future.
I wanna fly like an eagle to the sea:
fly like an eagle, let my spirit carry me.
I want to fly like an eagle till I'm free, right through the
  revolution.

Feed the babies who don't have enough to eat.
Shoe the children with no shoes on their feet.
House the people livin' in the street.
Oh, there's a solution.
Doo doot-n doo doot. Doo doot-n doo doot.

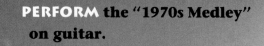

PERFORM the "1970s Medley" on guitar.

Learn to play the the E minor chord so that you can use it with the G, C, A, and D chords. Remember that your fingers are numbered from the index finger (1) to the little finger (4).

1970s MEDLEY

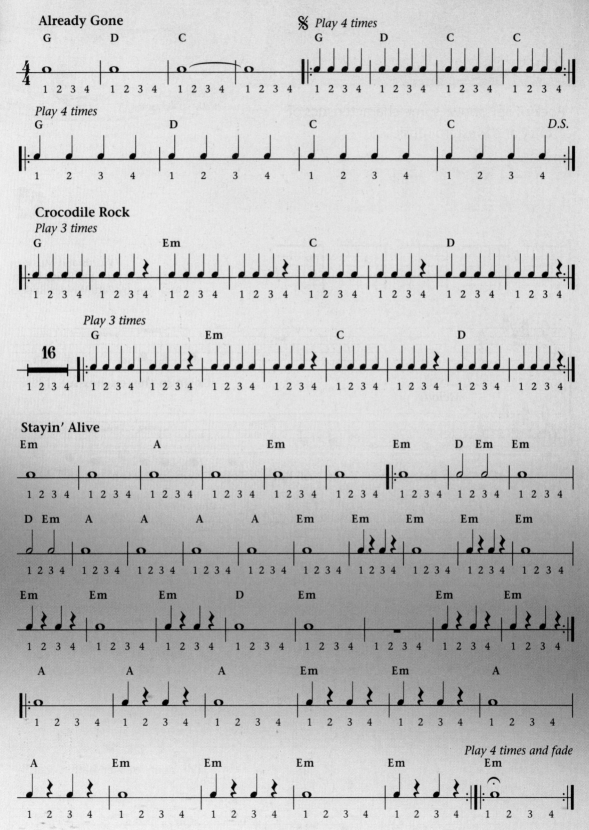

"Rocky Top" shows some characteristics of country and western music.

ROCKY TOP

Words and Music by
Boudleaux Bryant and Felice Bryant
Arranged by Patti Windes-Bridges

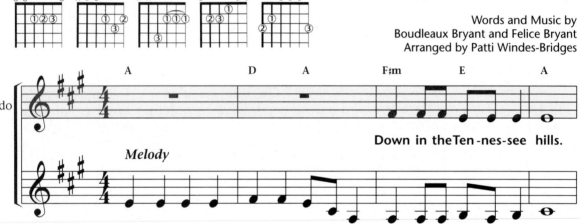

Down in theTen -nes-see hills.

Melody

Wish that I was on ol' Rock-y Top, Down in theTen-nes-see hills.

Ain't no tel - e - phone bills.

Ain't no smog-gy smoke on Rock-y Top, Ain't no tel - e - phone_ bills.

Half bear, oth-er half cat.

Once I knew a girl on Rock-y Top, Half bear, oth-er half cat.

The 1980s

New Wave was one style popular at the beginning of the 1980s. Groups like Blondie and Talking Heads played music that had simple harmonies and odd, sometimes humorous lyrics. They were reacting against some of the complicated and serious heavy-metal songs of the late 1970s.

In the early 1980s, computer technology became widely used by pop musicians. The Musical Instrument Digital Interface, or MIDI, allowed performers and producers to control and play musical instruments like electronic drums, guitars, and keyboards with a computer. Not only did superstar performers like Michael Jackson and Madonna use this modern technology, but so could anyone with a personal computer and a synthesizer at home. Rap and dance music performers also took advantage of this new technology.

David Byrne of the
band Talking Heads

SING this song, made popular by Whitney Houston in the 1980s.

The Greatest Love of All

Words by Linda Creed
Music by Michael Masser

I believe that children are our future;
teach them well and let them lead the way.
Show them all the beauty they possess inside.
Give them a sense of pride, to make it easier;
let the children's laughter remind us how we used
    to be.

Ev'rybody's searching for a hero;
people need someone to look up to.
Never found anyone who fulfilled my need.
A lonely place to be, and so I learned to depend
    on me.

I decided long ago never to walk in anyone's
    shadow.
If I fail, if I succeed, at least I lived as I believe.
No matter what they take from me, they can't take
    away my dignity.

Because the greatest love of all is happening
    to me.
I found the greatest love of all inside of me.
The greatest love of all is easy to achieve.
Learning to love yourself is the greatest love of all.
And if by chance that special place that you've
    been dreaming of
leads you to a lonely place, find your strength
    in love.

PERFORM the "1980s Medley."

Learn to play the the A minor chord so that you can use it with the G, C, D, A major and E minor chords. The A minor chord is formed by placing your fingers on the fingerboard like this:

LISTENING

Am

1980s MEDLEY

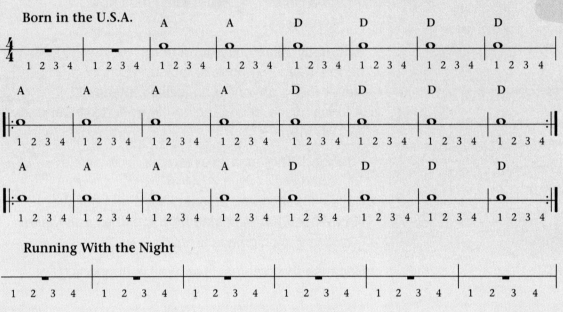

Born in the U.S.A.

Running With the Night

Play 4 times

Play 3 times

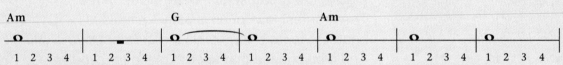

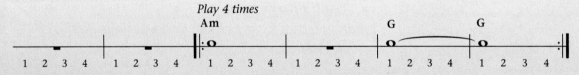

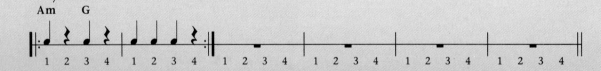

Head Over Heels

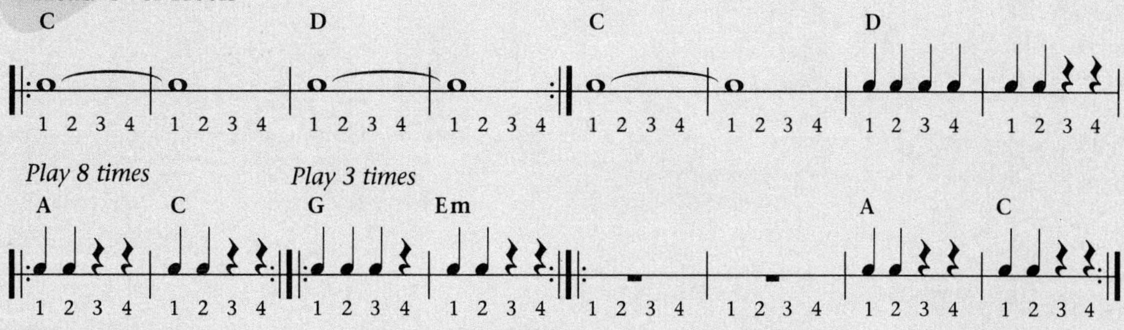

Shake It Up

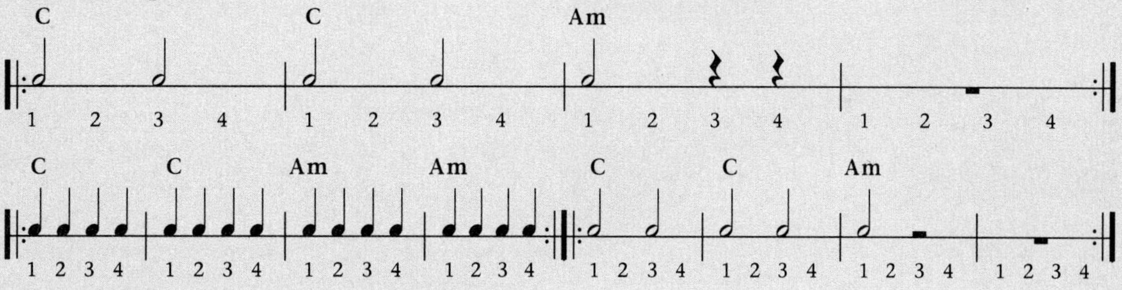

Born in the U.S.A.

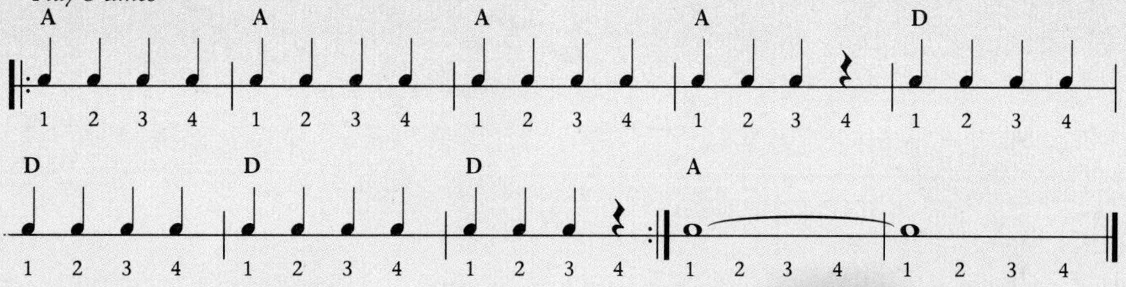

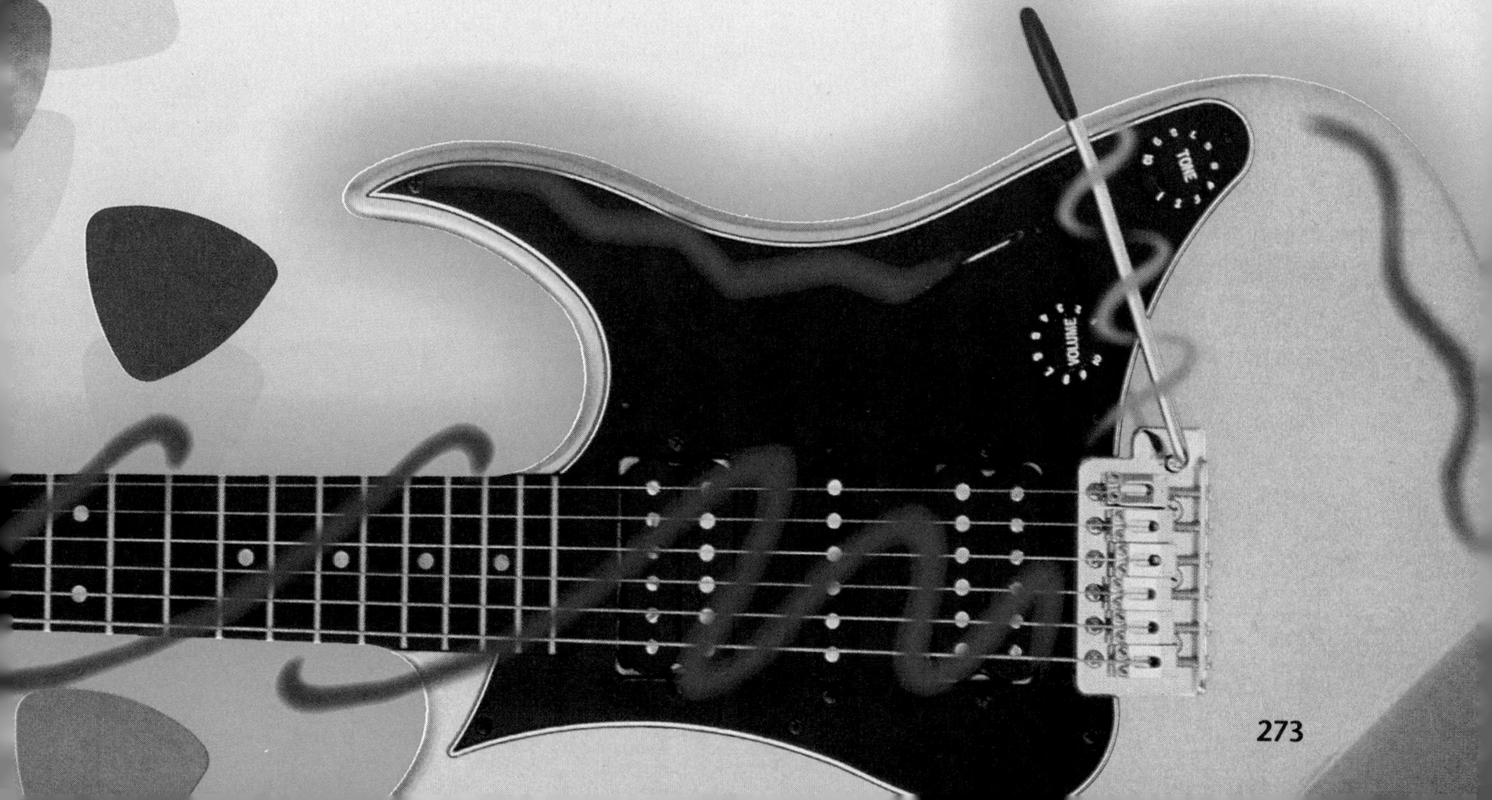

THE 1990s

Satellites and other new devices help the people of the 1990s to communicate faster than ever before. In the 1990s, music reflects this ability to be in touch with people everywhere. Many opportunities exist to learn musical styles from all over the world. The next time you go to your local music store, look over the variety of music from other countries.

Rap music, sometimes called *hip-hop*, gained in popularity in the 1990s. It began in the 1970s with young African Americans who would improvise spoken rhymes to the beat of their favorite records. Rap concerts usually involve rappers performing live to a pre-recorded musical background. The music ranges from a simple drum pattern to an entire rock band.

Rap artist Salt (Cheryl James) of the group Salt-n-Pepa

At the beginning of the 1990s many people felt
a renewed commitment to world peace and
understanding. This song expresses
that view.

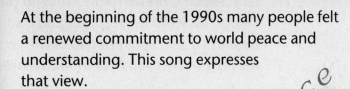

Words and Music by Julie Gold

From a distance, the world looks blue and green,
and the snow-capped mountains white.
From a distance, the ocean meets the stream,
and the eagle takes to flight.
From a distance there is harmony, and it echoes through the land.
It's the voice of hope, it's the voice of peace. It's the voice of everyone.

From a distance, we all have enough,
And no one is in need.
There are no guns, no bombs, and no disease,
No hungry mouths to feed.
From a distance, we are instruments
Marching in a common band;
Playing songs of hope, playing songs of peace,
They're the songs of everyone.
God is watching us, God is watching us,
God is watching us, from a distance.

From a distance, you look like my friend
Even though we are at war.
From a distance I just cannot comprehend
What all this fighting is for.
From a distance there is harmony and it echoes through the land.
It's the hope of hopes, it's the love of loves. It's the heart of everyone.
God is watching us...

Uirapurú Do Amazonas (excerpt)

by Gaudencio Thiago de Mello

In the 1990s many composers and performers combine musical elements of different world cultures. In this recording you will hear musical styles from Brazil and the United States. The Brazilian composer Gaudencio Thiago de Mello, who has roots in the Maue Indian nation of the Amazon, worked together with American saxophonist and composer Paul Winter to create this composition. Thiago de Mello sings in Portuguese, in his native Indian dialect, and imitates sounds heard in nature.

The recording begins with the intricate song of the uirapurú bird, which is native to the Amazon rain forest of Brazil. Then Thiago de Mello is heard, singing a song he composed. Paul Winter plays a solo between two of the verses. See if you can name the instruments you hear in this recording.

PERFORM this repeated pattern with the song on a pitched instrument.

THINK IT THROUGH

How can this recording help you convince someone that the Amazon rain forest must be saved?

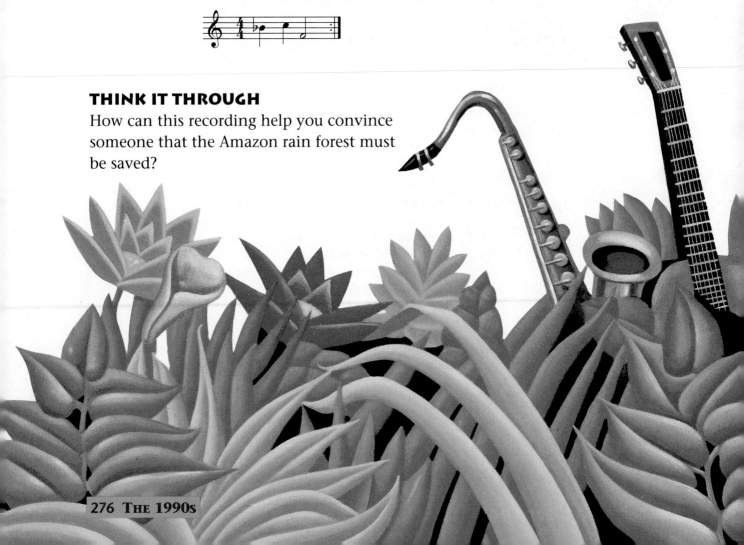

Two-Chord Rock *by James Roberts*

 Listen for the sound of the latest synthesizers in "Two-Chord Rock."

PERFORM this on recorder with "Two-Chord Rock."

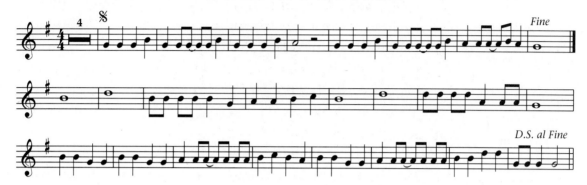

ADD this guitar part.

Strum Pattern 1 for line one and Pattern 2 for lines two and three of the score below.

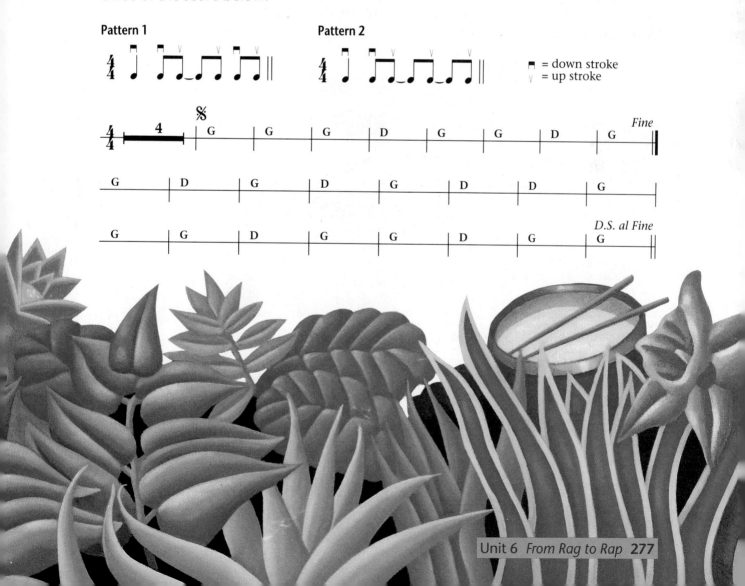

Pattern 1

Pattern 2

◼ = down stroke
V = up stroke

MEET
MALCOLM-JAMAL
WARNER

Many people know Malcolm-Jamal Warner (b. 1967) as the actor who played Theo in television's "The Cosby Show." In addition to acting, Warner now directs and produces films and videos. He first heard rap music as a child, and it still plays an important role in his musical life. Warner even produces rap albums.

LISTEN as Malcolm-Jamal Warner describes his
musical experiences and his involvement
with rap music.

Jump

LISTENING

(excerpt) by Jermaine Dupri
Performed by Kris Kross

The rap group Kris Kross gets its name from members Chris Smith and Chris Kelly. They are known for wearing their clothes backwards and baggy as well as for their music. Their manager Jermaine Dupri writes the songs for Kris Kross to perform. When their hugely successful 1992 album Totally Krossed Out *appeared, Smith and Kelly were 13 years old. Listen for their rap nicknames, "Daddy Mack" and "Mack Daddy," in "Jump," a No. 1 hit.*

Kris Kross

The Rolling Stones

Technology

The audience is already cheering before the concert begins. Green, yellow, and blue lights flicker wildly across the stage. The performers, in unmatched, colorful costumes, enter through smoky clouds. As the singer approaches the microphone with a glittering electric guitar, popping sounds, like firecrackers, can be heard. The smoke clears. There is one quiet moment as the band members wave to their fans. Then the first, vibrant sounds of music can be heard over the claps and cheers of the audience.

Attending a rock concert can be an exciting visual and musical adventure. If you have attended one, you know that. But do you know how it is all put together?

Many types of equipment play a role in producing the sights and sounds of a rock performance. Some of these devices use sophisticated technology.

The electric guitar, electronic keyboards, and drums are the basic instruments in rock bands. To allow the sounds to be heard throughout a huge auditorium, they are changed electronically in a variety of ways.

The band U2 in concert

Microphones change sounds into electric signals. Signal processors modify electric signals. Processors can be used to add echo to a voice, which creates a richer sound, or to change the sounds of the guitar. The amplifier boosts the signals. Then the speakers turn the electric signals back into sound.

The P.A., or public-address system, mixes together all the sounds that are made on the stage and broadcasts them to the audience.

The atmosphere of the stage also relies on special equipment. Lasers use very strong light beams. When moved quickly, they can create lines and shapes. Smoke machines give off a harmless cloud of fog. Used during a performance, they create a dramatic atmosphere. Gels are pieces of colored plastic that are placed in front of lights to change their color. The person who controls the lighting on stage can use a variety of colors to reflect the mood of different songs. The split-second timing of various effects, so important in creating a dramatic mood, can be controlled by computers.

Haiku Calendar

Leaf, brown in the wind
Taps like a bird on the pane
Presaging Autumn.

Leaf, sunk in the soil,
Spends winter dying; new life
Mounts from its leaching.

Leaf, loosing its sheath
Into the warm air unfurls
Green in Spring's morning.

Leaf drinks air and light,
Channels rain, feeds its parent
Great tree of Summer.

Leaf, brown in the wind
Taps like a bird on the pane
Presaging Autumn.

—Pamela Gillilan

HANDS ACROSS THE

Every nation has songs to express patriotism. Besides celebrating our country and its achievements, we sing and listen to music that honors other countries as well.

WATER

The words to "America" were first used at a Fourth of July picnic in Boston. The music is the same as the British national anthem "God Save the Queen."

America

Music by Henry Carey
Words by Samuel F. Smith

Puerto Rico is a special political unit. It is not officially a state, yet its people are citizens of the United States. This song about Puerto Rico shows the pride that Puerto Ricans feel for the flag of their land. Unlike many patriotic songs that sound like marches or hymns, this music reflects the syncopated rhythms of Puerto Rican music.

The flag of Puerto Rico was designed about 100 years ago.

Flaming red flowers adorn the tropical trees of Puerto Rico.

QUÉ BONITA BANDERA

What a Beautiful Flag

Puerto Rican Folk Song
English Version by MMH

Spanish: A - zul, blan - ca y___ co - lo - ra - da, y'en el
Pronunciation: a sul βlan ka i ko lo ɾa ða yen el
English: See our flag of blue,___ white and red.___ In the

me - dio tie - ne u - na es - tre - lla. Bo - ni - ta, se -
me ðio tye neu naes tre ya bo ni ta se
mid - dle, there___ is a star.___ A beau - ti - ful

ñor - es, es la ban - de - ra Puer - to - ri - que - ña.
nyoɾ es es la βan de ɾa pweɾ to ɾi ke nya
ban - ner, my friend, the flag___ of___ Puer - to Ri - co.

Refrain

que - ña. Qué bo - ni - ta ban - de - ra,
ke nya ke βo ni ta βan de ɾa
Ri - co. *Qué bo - ni - ta ban - de - ra,*

Qué bo - ni - ta ban - de - ra, Qué bo - ni - ta ban -
ke βo ni ta βan de ɾa ke βo ni ta βan
Qué bo - ni - ta ban - de - ra, Qué bo - ni - ta ban -

de - ra es la ban - de - ra Puer - to - ri - que - ña.
de ɾa es la βan de ɾa pweɾ to ɾi ke nya
de - ra, the beau - ti - ful flag___ of___ Puer - to Ri - co.

Canada, our neighbor to the north, has two official languages—French and English. Although "O Canada" was first heard in French in 1880, it was not sung in English for another 20 years. This patriotic song became the national anthem of Canada in 1980.

O CANADA

Music by Calixa Lavallée
French Words by Adolfe-Basil Routhier
English Words by Robert Stanley Weir
Arranged by Robert J. de Frece

During the War of 1812, Francis Scott Key observed a British attack in Baltimore Harbor. When he saw that the Americans had successfully defended Fort McHenry, he was moved to write a poem. He later set the poem to music, using a popular British tune. The United States Congress adopted the song as the National Anthem in 1931.

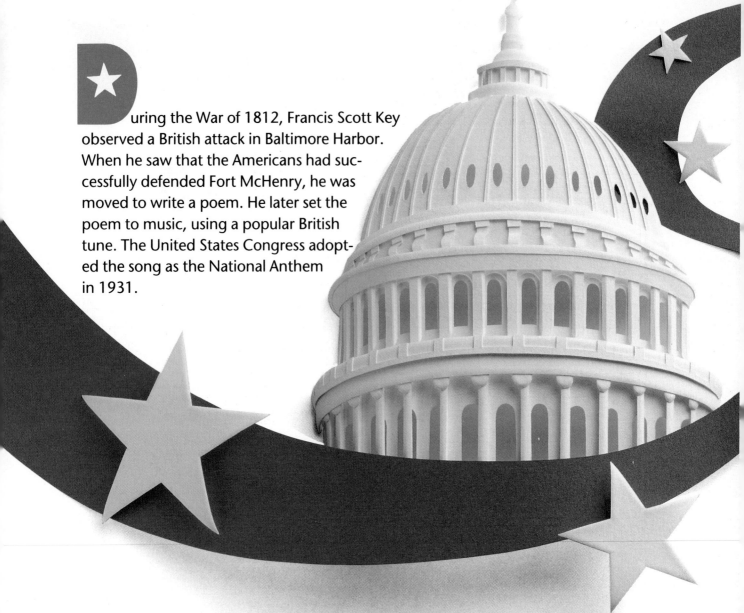

THE STAR-SPANGLED BANNER

Words by
Francis Scott Key
Music attributed to
J. S. Smith

1. Oh! — say, can you see, by the dawn's ear - ly
2. On the shore, dim - ly seen through the mists of the
3. Oh, — thus be it ev - er when — free men shall

light, What so proud - ly we hailed at the twi - light's last
deep, Where the foe's haugh - ty host in dread si - lence re -
stand Be - tween their loved homes and the war's des - o -

♪ **LISTENING**

Battle Hymn of the Republic

played by the Monty Alexander Trio

Monty Alexander is a jazz pianist who was born in Jamaica. His trio first performed this jazz version of "Battle Hymn of the Republic" at the Montreux Jazz Festival in Switzerland. Alexander says that he had very little idea of what he was going to play when he first sat down at the piano. He knew he wanted to feature the "Battle Hymn" in some way. Listen to his improvisation on this well-known patriotic tune.

Julia Ward Howe wrote the poem "Battle Hymn of the Republic" in 1862, during the Civil War. The tune was based on the song "John Brown's Body," also from the Civil War period.

294

BATTLE HYMN
of the Republic

Music by
William Steffe
Words by
Julia Ward Howe

Mine eyes have seen the glo-ry of the com-ing of the Lord;

He is tram-pling out the vin-tage where the grapes of wrath are stored;

He has loosed the fate-ful light-ning of his ter-ri-ble swift sword;

His truth is march-ing on.

Refrain

Glo-ry, Glo-ry, Hal-le-lu-jah! Glo-ry, Glo-ry, Hal-le-lu-jah!

Glo-ry, Glo-ry! Glo-ry, Hal-le-lu-jah.

Glo-ry, Glo-ry, Hal-le-lu-jah! His truth is march-ing on!

Glo-ry, Glo-ry! His truth is march-ing on.

HAUNTED NIGHT

Most people have at least one scary story to tell on the right occasion. This song is the ghostly tale of a haunted ship.

The Ghost Ship

Words and
Music by
Don Besig and
Nancy Price

1. Now lis-ten well as a tale I tell of a night I
(2.) then I spied off the star-board side a— strange, mys-

shook with fear.___ We were sail-ing west on the o-pen sea,
ter-ious sight.___ I___ froze with fear as it drift-ed near

head-in' home from a long,— long year.___ I was stand-ing
like a ghost in the dark— of night.___ I could see a

watch all a - lone that night when I heard a wail - ing cry.___
sail on a bro - ken mast and de - sert - ed decks be - low.___

As I strained to see what the sound could be,
From___ all a - round came a mourn - ful sound,

some - thing flashed and caught_ my eye.___ } And the cold wind
but I saw not a liv - ing soul!___

f   *p*

blew,___

1.
___ and the cold wind blew.___   2. 'Twas

mf

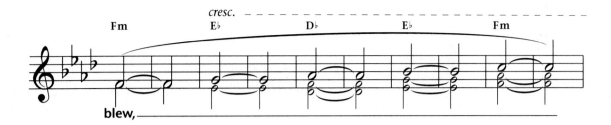

blew,

and the cold wind blew! _____

and the cold wind blew! _____

OLD ABRAM BROWN

Music by Benjamin Britten
Words by Walter de la Mare

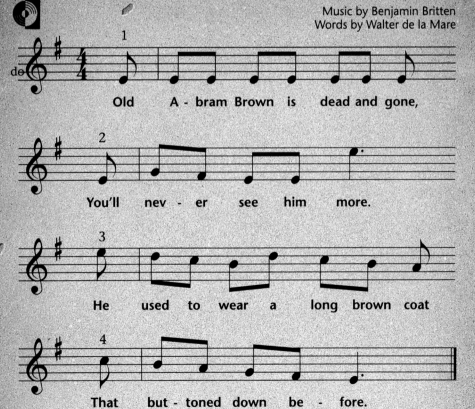

1 Old A - bram Brown is dead and gone,

2 You'll nev - er see him more.

3 He used to wear a long brown coat

4 That but - toned down be - fore.

Happy Holidays

Some winter holiday customs are quite old, having passed from one generation to the next. Both Christmas and Hanukkah have been celebrated for many hundreds of years. The customs of Kwanzaa, a newer holiday, are becoming more widely observed each year.

Although the celebrations of winter vary, one thing is the same. The joyful spirit of family, friendship, hope, and peace is an important part of each celebration.

DESCRIBE special customs that you or someone you know observe for the winter holidays.

Holiday Sing-Along

Traditional Holiday Songs

Singing songs, or caroling, has been part of winter celebrations for centuries. Carols are generally simple yet festive tunes. Many carols, such as "Joy to the World" and "Angels We Have Heard on High," tell of the Christmas story. Others, such as "Deck the Hall," describe holiday customs.

SING along with these holiday favorites.

Holidays are not the only reason to celebrate in winter. The beauty of snow and other seasonal elements often inspire poetry and music.

WINTER POEM

once a snowflake fell
on my brow and i loved
it so much and i kissed
it and it was happy and called its cousins
and brothers and a web
of snow engulfed me then
i reached to love them all
and i squeezed them and they became
a spring rain and i stood perfectly
still and was a flower

—Nikki Giovanni

The words of this Hanukkah song are in Ladino. This is a language that blends ancient Hebrew, medieval Spanish, and Arabic with Slavic, Greek, French, and Turkish words.

OCHO KANDELIKAS
EIGHT CANDLES

Words and Music by Flory Jagoda
English Version by MMH

Ladino: Ha - nu - kah lin - da 'sta a - ki
Pronunciation: xa nu ka lin da sta a ki
English: 1. Han - uk - kah time be - gins to - night.
2. So man - y par - ties we can share,
3. De - li - cious pies for us to eat.

— o - cho kan - del - as par - a mi. mi. Ah.
o cho kan del as pa ɾa mi mi a
— Eight can - dles here for me to light. light.
— With joy and glad - ness in the air. air. } Ah.
— Al - monds and hon - ey for a treat. treat.

U - na kan - del - li - ka, dos kan - del - i - kas, tres kan - del - i - kas,
u na kan de li ka dos kan de li kas tres kan de li kas
One — kan - de - li - ka, Two kan - de - li - kas, Three kan - de - li - kas,

kua - tro kan - del - i - kas, sin - ko kan - del - i - kas, seysh kan - del - i - kas,
kwa tɾo kan de li kas sing ko kan de li kas sesh kan de li kas
Four — kan - de - li - kas, Five — kan - de - li - kas, Six kan - de - li - kas,

sie - te kan - dle - i - kas, o - cho kan - del - as par - a mi.
sie te kan de li kas o cho kan de las pa ɾa mi
Sev - en kan - de - li - kas, Eight can - dles here for me to light.

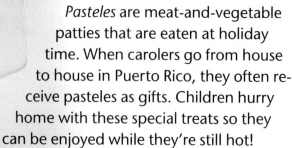

Pasteles are meat-and-vegetable patties that are eaten at holiday time. When carolers go from house to house in Puerto Rico, they often receive pasteles as gifts. Children hurry home with these special treats so they can be enjoyed while they're still hot!

SI ME DAN PASTELES
WHEN YOU BRING PASTELES

Puerto Rican Folk Song
Arranged by
Alejandro Jiménez

Spanish: Si me dan pas-te-les,— dén-me-los ca-lien-tes,—
Pronunciation: si me ðan pas te les dem e los ka lyen tes
English: When you bring *pas-te-les,*— give me on-ly hot ones,—

Le lo lai, le lo lai,
le lo lai le lo lai

que pas-te-les frí-os,— em-pa-chan a la gen-te.—
ke pas te les fri os em pa chan a la xen te
peo-ple who eat cold ones,— all have in-di-ges-tion.—

le lo lai, le lo lai.
le lo lai le lo lai

Si me dan a - rroz___ no me den cu - cha - ra,___
si me ðan a ͞ıos no me ðeng ku cha ɾa
If you give me rice ones,___ don't give me *cu - cha - ra,*

Le lo lai, le lo lai,
le lo lai le lo lai

que ma - má me di - jo___ que se lo lle - va - ra.___
ke ma ma me ði xo ke se lo ye βa ɾa
My *ma - má* has told me___ "Bring them straight home to me!"___

le lo lai, le lo lai.
le lo lai le lo lai

Interlude

Le lo lai, le lo lai. Le lo lai, le lo lai.
le lo lai le lo lai le lo lai le lo lai

Le lo lai, le lo lai. Le lo lai, le lo lai.
le lo lai le lo lai le lo lai le lo lai

On Christmas Eve of 1818, Joseph Mohr wrote the words to "Silent Night" and asked his friend to write the music. The church organ wasn't working, so Franz Gruber wrote a simple setting and used a guitar to accompany the voices. From its modest beginnings, "Silent Night" spread throughout the world.

Silent Night
Stille Nacht

Music by Franz Gruber
Words by Joseph Mohr

Andante *pp*

German: Stil - le Nacht, hei - li - ge Nacht, al - les schläft,
Pronunciation: shtɪ lə naxt haɪ li gə naxt a ləs shleft
English: Si - lent night, ho - ly night, All is calm,

ein - sam wacht nur das trau - te hoch - hei - li - ge Paar,
aɪn zam vaxt nur das trɑʊ tə hox haɪ li gə pɑr
all is bright Round yon Vir - gin Moth - er and Child.

hol - der Kna - be im lok - ki - gen Haar, schlaf in himm - li - scher
hol dər kna bə ɪm lɔ ki gən har shlaf ɪn hɪm lɪ shər
Ho - ly In - fant so ten - der and mild, Sleep in heav - en - ly

Ruh,_____ schlaf____ in himm - li - scher Ruh.
ru shlaf ɪn hɪm lɪ shər ru
peace,_____ Sleep____ in heav - en - ly peace.

Carol from an Irish Cabin

Music by Dale Wood
Words Anonymous

1. The cold wind blows o - ver the heath-er,
2. The clean snow falls soft - ly, falls soft - ly,
3. So let there be no fear of dark-ness,

The salt wind blows o - ver the sea, The
The snow crys - tals cov - er the moor. Let
And let there be no fear of sea; Let the

harsh wind blows down from the moun-tains, And
wan - der - ers lost and grown wea - ry, Find
star guide the lost and for - sak - en, Safe

blows a white Christ - mas to me.
wel - come at my cab - in door.
o - ver the moor - lands to me.

The lilting quality of Irish folk music is heard in "Carol from an Irish Cabin" with its dotted rhythms and $\frac{6}{8}$ meter. The spirit of the Christmas season expressed in the song offers a warm welcome to the weary traveler.

Kwanzaa is a seven-day holiday, between December 26 and January 1, which celebrates the values of African American families, communities, and culture. Candles are lit each day of Kwanzaa to symbolize the seven basic principles of the holiday. The song "Siyahamba" celebrates the first two principles—Unity and Self-Determination. It is a traditional Zulu song that has been used as a South African freedom song.

ADD this solo part.

SIYAHAMBA

We Are Marching

African Folk Song
Arranged by
Robert J. de Frece

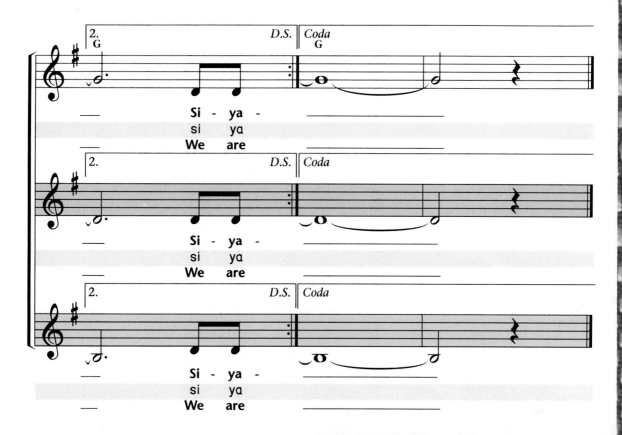

Si - ya -
si ya
We are

Si - ya -
si ya
We are

Si - ya -
si ya
We are

FAMILY

Charles Alston worked in many different styles. His painting *Family* is an abstract representation of mother, father, and children. As an adult, Alston returned to the South, where he grew up, to photograph African Americans at work and at home. These pictures of southern life in the 1930s became the basis of his "family" paintings. Alston felt closest to his works that protested the discrimination against African Americans, yet celebrated their culture.

Family by Charles H. Alston, 1955   Collection of WHITNEY MUSEUM OF AMERICAN ART, NEW YORK, Purchase, with funds from the Artists and Students Assistance Fund, photography by Bill Jacobson, NY

Ring in the New

The new year is celebrated at different times around the world. The Jewish New Year, Rosh Hashanah, and Diwali, the Hindu New Year, are in autumn. The Noruz festival of Iran is on the first day of spring. In China, Scotland, and the United States, the new year begins in winter.

A Chinese orchestra such as the one which plays "Bo Hai Huan Ten" includes woodwinds similar to flute and oboe; plucked, bowed, and hammered strings; and a variety of unpitched percussion instruments.

The Chinese Music Society of North America

LISTENING

Bo Hai Huan Ten

Traditional Chinese New Year Music

You will hear the instruments of the Chinese orchestra played with energy and a sense of festivity in this piece that celebrates the new year. The title means "Jubilation All Around" in English.

PLAY this rhythm along with the recording.

*Cymbals and
   medium
 hand drums*

साल मुबारक

Diwali is the first day of the new year in India. Also called the Festival of Lights, it is an autumn festival that many people of the Hindu religion celebrate. Families fill clay saucers with oil, light them, and place them in windows and along roads and streams. The lights guide Lakshmi, the Hindu goddess of prosperity, to each home.

Batik print of Lakshmi.

سال نو مبارك

In Iran, the first day of spring begins the new year. It is called Noruz, which means "new day." Preparations for Noruz begin about two weeks earlier, when everyone plants a *sabzeh.* Seeds of wheat, barley, or lentils are sprouted in a small container.

The 13 days of Noruz are a time of great celebration—songs, dances, games, gifts, and visiting. Families and friends gather for picnics, where they are entertained by clowns, folk singers, dancers, comic actors, and acrobats. The final day of Noruz is time to throw the sabzeh into the water to send bad luck away.

An Iranian American family celebrates Noruz in Verona Park, New Jersey.

Haji Firuz is one of the entertainers of Noruz. He wears a baggy red shirt and pants with a cone-shaped hat, and, he usually plays a tambourine.

Haji Firuz

As Collected and Sung by
Hooshang Bagheri
English Version by MMH

Pronunciation: ha ji fi ɾuz æm mæn   sɔ li yɛ ɾuz æm mæn
English: Ha - ji Fi - ruz I am!   Ev'- ry year I come 'round.

Instrumental

ha ji fi ɾuz æm mæn   sɔ li yɛ ɾuz æm mæn
Ha - ji Fi - ruz I am!   Ev'- ry year I come 'round.

sɔl e no vi ni ɔ mæd e di ke xɔs ti ɔ mæd
Cel - e-brate a   fine new year,   Cel - e - brate, the time is here.

sha di ko nid pa be ku bid dæst bə zæ nid ke ɔ mæd
Stamp your feet, and clap your hands and Cel - e - brate the fine new year.

Persian:

حاجی فیروزم من   سالی یه روزم من

حاجی فیروزم من   سالی یه روزم من

سال نو و عید آمده   عیدی که خواستی آمده

شادی کنید   پا بکوبید   دست بزنید که عید آمده

שָׁנָה טוֹבָה וּמְאוּשֶׁרֶת

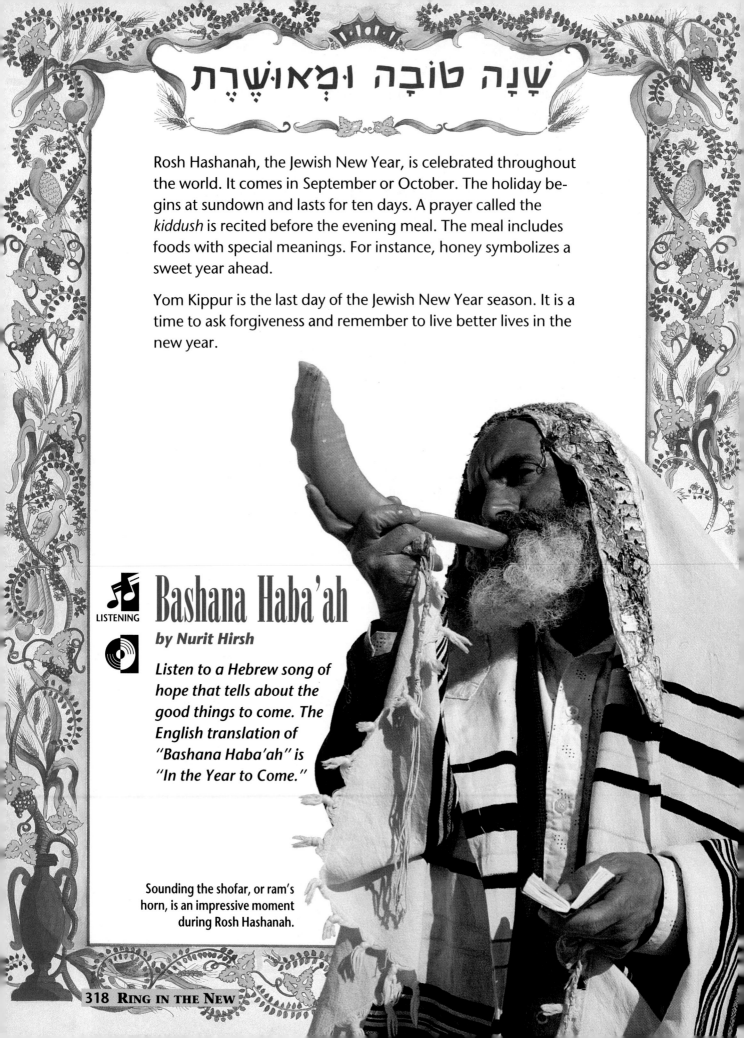

Rosh Hashanah, the Jewish New Year, is celebrated throughout the world. It comes in September or October. The holiday begins at sundown and lasts for ten days. A prayer called the *kiddush* is recited before the evening meal. The meal includes foods with special meanings. For instance, honey symbolizes a sweet year ahead.

Yom Kippur is the last day of the Jewish New Year season. It is a time to ask forgiveness and remember to live better lives in the new year.

LISTENING

Bashana Haba'ah

by Nurit Hirsh

Listen to a Hebrew song of hope that tells about the good things to come. The English translation of "Bashana Haba'ah" is "In the Year to Come."

Sounding the shofar, or ram's horn, is an impressive moment during Rosh Hashanah.

Happy New Year

New Year's Eve in Scotland is known as Hogmanay. At midnight, the front door is opened to send out the old year and bring in the new year. Friends and family join in good wishes, sing "Auld Lang Syne," and hang up the new calendar.

Auld Lang Syne

Scotch Air
Words by Robert Burns

Verse

1. Should auld ac-quain-tance be for-got, And
2. And here's a hand, my trust-y frien', And

nev-er brought to mind? Should auld ac-quain-tance
gie's a hand o' thine; We'll tak' a cup o'

be for-got, And days of auld lang syne?
kind-ness yet, For auld lang syne.

Refrain

For auld lang syne, my dear, For auld lang syne;

We'll tak' a cup o' kind-ness yet For auld lang syne.

A **Dream** of

In the summer of 1963, Dr. Martin Luther King, Jr., delivered his "I Have a Dream" speech to over 200,000 Americans in Washington, D.C. The speech defined the basis of the civil rights movement. Dr. King's words still carry deep meaning for all people.

I Have a Dream

Words and Music
by Teresa Jennings

1. There was a man— in A-mer-i-ca— who
   when he spoke— to the gath-ered crowds,— his

   had a dream, they say, that all the peo-ples of the earth— could
   heart and soul would sing. This gra-cious man,— this gen-tle man.— This

   live in peace some-day. 2. And King.
   Mar-tin Luth-er

   "I have a dream," this
   King.

   great man used to say. "I have a dream." His

   words would light the way. 1. The

Freedom

with growing intensity

time he lived— was a trou-bled time— when peo-ple could not
so he tried——— to tell us all;— his words with peace would

see in spite of all—— our diff-'ren-ces,— we have the right to
ring. This hon-est man,— this no-ble man.— This Mar-tin Luth-er

be. 2. And King. "I have a dream," this great man used to say.
dream," to live in har-mon-y.

"I have a dream." His words would light the way. "I have a
"I have a dream" that

molto rit.   *a tempo*

all of us are free! Are free!

John Denver is one of many musicians bringing attention to the environment through their songs. What is the primary message of Denver's song?

Earth Day Every Day
(CELEBRATE)

Words and Music
by John Denver

Cel- e- brate morn- ing, the cry of a loon on a lake in the night,

dreams that are born in the dawn's ear- ly light,— cel- e- brate morn- ing.

Cel-e-brate liv- ing, the laugh- ter that sings in the heart of a child,

free- dom that flies to the call of the wild,— cel- e- brate liv- ing.

LISTENING

Garden of the Earth

Paul Winter Consort and the Pokrovsky Singers

Paul Winter took his group on tour to Russia in 1986. There he met a popular group dedicated to singing ancient Russian village music. The two groups of musicians from different nations worked together to create a new style. They developed a unique sound, combining Western harmonies with ancient Russian songs. Making music together was a way of expressing friendship and getting to know each other.

Garden of the Earth

Traditional
Russian Folk Song
Words by Paul Winter
and Paul Halley

Russian: Ой ты сад, ты мой сад, Сад зе-
Pronunciation: ui tı sat tı mɔı sat sat zi

English:
1. There's a gar — den 'round the Earth, There's a
(2.) voi — ces, ma — ny tongues, from the
(3.) glo — ry of the Earth, for the

лё — нень — кий, Ты за — чем ра — но цве-
lyɔn nyɛn ki tı za chɛm ɾa nə tsvı

home be — neath the sun; In the beau — ty of this
moun — tains to the sea; Sing of beau — ty all a-
glo — ry of the sun; We will sing of life to-

тёшь, О — сы — па — ешь — ся.
tyɔsh a sı pa yɛsh sya

gar — den, We will hear___ a thou- sand songs. 2.Ma — ny one.
round___ us, in this an — cient har — mo — ny. 3.For the
ge — ther, and for — ev — er live as

THE FIFTH OF MAY

Cinco de Mayo means "fifth of May." This national holiday of Mexico honors the day, more than 100 years ago, when the Mexicans won a major battle against the French.

Celebrations of Cinco de Mayo take place in the United States as well as in Mexico. The holiday is a festive springtime event in New York, Los Angeles, El Paso, and anywhere there are communities of Mexican-Americans.

LISTENING

Música indígena *by Manuel Maria Ponce*

Manuel Maria Ponce, who is often called the "father of modern Mexican music," drew on the folk music of his native country for his compositions. The title of this piece means "indigenous music." You will hear the sound of music that originates or occurs naturally in Mexico—music that is indigenous to Mexico.

Jarabe tapatío

LISTENING

Mexican Folk Melody

The jarabe is the national dance of Mexico. Jarabe means "mixture." The dance features several melodies and tells the story of a courtship. Toward the end of the dance, the man throws down his sombrero and the woman dances on it. Then she picks up the sombrero and puts it on to symbolize her acceptance of the man's proposal.

In the 1970s "De colores" became a theme song for Mexican Americans who were striving for fair treatment in this country. Why would a song about the beauty of different colors be used in a struggle for equal rights?

DE COLORES
MANY COLORS

Spanish Folk Song
English Version
by MMH

do

Spanish:	1. De___ co - lo - res,___ de co - lo - res se vis - ten los
Pronunciation:	de ko lo ɾes ðe ko lo ɾe se βis ten los
English:	1. Oh,___ the col - ors!___ Oh, the col - ors we see in the
	2. Hear___ the roost - er,___ hear the roost - er who sings, "qui - ri,

cam- pos en la pri - ma - ve - ra.___ De___ co -
kam pos en la pɾi ma βe ɾa de ko
blos- som- ing fields in the spring - time.___ All___ the
qui - ri, qui - ri, qui - ri, qui - ri."___ Now___ the

lo - res,—— de co - lo - res son los pa - ja - ri - llos que vie - nen de a-
lo ɾes ðe ko lo ɾe son los pa xa ɾi yos ke βye nen dea
col - ors,—— all the col - ors of bright - fea - thered birds that re - turn from a
hen calls,—now the hen calls back her, "ca - ra, ca - ra, ca - ra, ca - ra,

fue - ra.—— De co - lo - res,—— de co -
fwe ɾa de ko lo ɾes ðe ko
dis - tance.—— Oh,—— the col - ors!—— Oh, the
ca - ra."—— Hear—— the small ones,—— Hear the

lo - res es el ar - co i - ris que ve - mos lu - cir.—— Y por
lo ɾes es el aɾ ko i ɾis ke βe mos lu siɾ i poɾ
col - ors that light up the sky in a beau - ti - ful rain - bow!— And the
small ones cry out, "pí - o, pí - o, pí - o, pí - o, pí - o."—— And the

e - so los gran - des a - mo - res de mu - chos co -
e so los gran des a mo ɾes ðe mu chos ko
col - ors of true love are bright - est, and these are the
col - ors of true love are bright - est, and these are the

1.
lo - res me gus - tan a mí.—— Y por
lo ɾes me gus tan a mi i poɾ
col - ors I love most of all.—— And the
col - ors I love most of all.—— And the

2.
lo - res me gus - tan a mí.
lo ɾes me gus tan a mi
col - ors I love most of all.
col - ors I love most of all.

Summertime

Long ago, many Plains Indians lived in small villages during the winter. When warm weather arrived, several villages gathered together to celebrate. These gatherings were the ancestors of the modern-day event known as the powwow.

Today, people from many different Native American nations participate in powwows. The largest ones take place during the summer months. The powwow is a time to reunite with friends and family and enjoy events such as rodeos, sports, feasts, and dancing contests.

Powwows usually have several categories of dance competition. Two of the most common are the Traditional and Fancy Dance. Traditional dances are based on steps that have been danced for hundreds of years. Fancy Dances feature newer Native American dance styles.

Men's Fancy Dancers competing at a powwow in Wyoming.

Energetic movements are characteristic of both Men's and Women's Fancy Dance.

LISTENING

Grand Entry

Traditional Native American Music

Each powwow begins with the Grand Entry. As special music plays, the dancers enter the arena. The order of their entry depends on the category of dance in which they are participating.

Gary Fields's heritage is Native American. His knowledge of Native American music comes from living on reservations in America and Western Canada. He has learned many Native American songs. Listen as he describes the music and events of the Grand Entry.

THE BOATMAN

African American Folk Song

Oh, the boat - man dance, The boat - man sing, The boat - man up to ev' - ry - thing. When the boat - man come on shore, he spend his mo - ney and he work for more.

Old Ark's A-Moverin'

African American Spiritual
Arranged by Jeff Kriske

Old ark's a - mov - er - in', a - mov - er - in', a - mov - er - in', the old ark's a - mov - er - in' and I thank God!

D.C. al Fine

Old ark she reel, old ark she rock. Old ark she sit - tin' on a moun - tain top.

Hotaru Koi
Come, Firefly

Japanese Folk Song
English Version by MMH

Every Mornin' When I Wake Up

Words and Music by Avon Gillespie

Ev-e-ry morn-in' when I wake__ up I have a new song to sing, my chil-dren,

Ev-e-ry morn-in' when I wake__ up I have a new song to sing.__

Nobody Knows the Trouble I've Seen

African American Spiritual
Arrangement by Vincent Lawrence

No-bod-y knows the trou-ble I've seen, No-bod-y knows my

sor-row. No-bod-y knows the trou-ble I've seen.

Glo-ry hal-le-lu-jah!

334

ESKIMO
Ice Cream Dance

Yupik Song
Collected and Transcribed by Ben Snowball

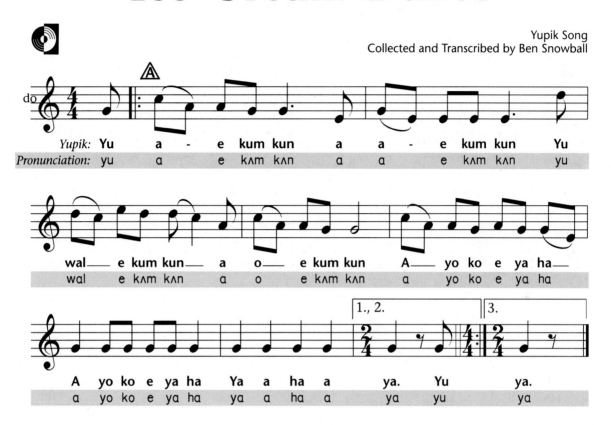

Yupik: **Yu** a - e kum kun a a - e kum kun **Yu**
Pronunciation: yu a e kʌm kʌn a a e kʌm kʌn yu

wal— e kum kun— a o e kum kun A— yo ko e ya ha—
wal e kʌm kʌn a o e kʌm kʌn a yo ko e ya ha

A yo ko e ya ha **Ya** a ha a ya. **Yu** ya.
a yo ko e ya ha ya a ha a ya yu ya

Drum Accompaniment

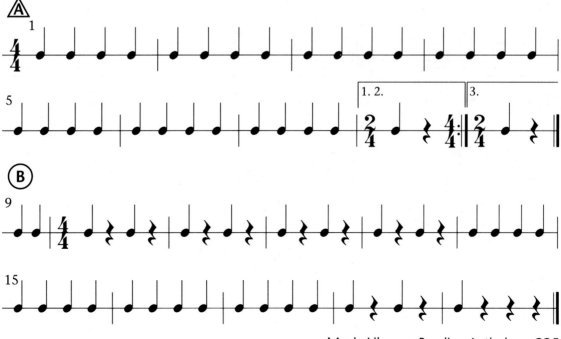

Oh, How Lovely Is the Evening

English Round

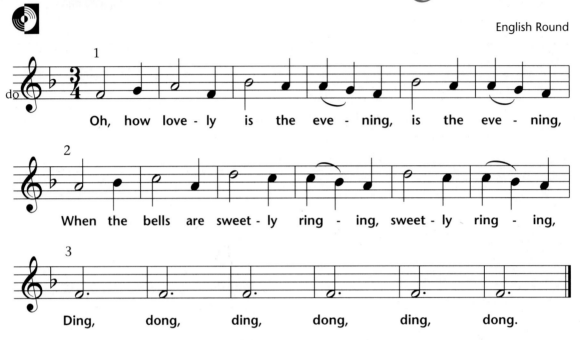

Oh, how love - ly is the eve - ning, is the eve - ning,

When the bells are sweet - ly ring - ing, sweet - ly ring - ing,

Ding, dong, ding, dong, ding, dong.

Jubilate Deo

Music by Michael Praetorius
Text from Psalm 65

Latin: Ju - bi - la - te De - o. Ju - bi - la - te De - o. Al - le - lu - ia!
Pronunciation: yu bi la te dɛ ɔ yu bi la te dɛ ɔ al lɛ lu ya

COME, FOLLOW ME!

Words and Music by John Hilton

1 Come, fol - low, fol - low, fol - low, fol - low, fol - low, fol - low me!

2 Whith - er shall I fol - low, fol - low, fol - low, Whith - er shall I fol - low, fol - low thee?

3 To the green - wood, to the green - wood. To the green - wood green - wood tree.

Dona Nobis Pacem

Latin Hymn

Latin: Do - na no - bis pa - cem, pa - cem.

Pronunciation: dɔ na nɔ bis pa chɛm pa chɛm

Do - na___ no - bis pa - cem.

Do - na no - bis pa - cem.

Do - na no - bis pa - cem.

Do - na no - bis___ pa - cem.

Do - na no - bis pa - cem.

Oh, Sinner Man

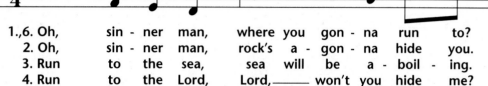

African American Spiritual

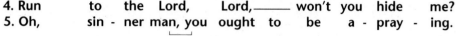

1.,6. Oh,   sin - ner   man,   where you gon - na   run   to?
2. Oh,   sin - ner   man,   rock's a - gon - na   hide   you.
3. Run   to   the   sea,   sea   will   be   a - boil - ing.
4. Run   to   the   Lord,   Lord,——— won't you   hide   me?
5. Oh,   sin - ner man, you   ought   to   be   a - pray - ing.

Oh,   sin - ner   man,   where you gon - na   run   to?
Oh,   sin - ner   man,   rock's a - gon - na   hide   you.
Run   to   the   sea,   sea   will   be   a - boil - ing.
Run   to   the   Lord,   Lord,——— won't you   hide   me?
Oh,   sin - ner man, you   ought   to   be   a - pray - ing.

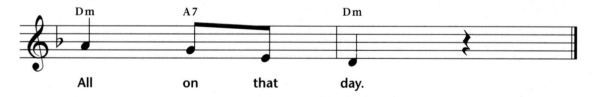

Oh,   sin - ner   man,   where you gon - na   run   to?
Oh,   sin - ner   man,   rock's a - gon - na   hide   you.
Run   to   the   sea,   sea   will   be   a - boil - ing.
Run   to   the   Lord,   Lord,——— won't you   hide   me?
Oh,   sin - ner man, you   ought   to   be   a - pray - ing.

All   on   that   day.

Ostinato

Oh,   sin - ner   man!   Oh,   sin - ner   man!

Oh,   sin - ner   man!   On   that   day.

Bamboo

Words and Music by Dave Van Ronk

1. You take a stick of bam-boo, You take a stick of bam-boo, You
(2.) trav-el on the riv-er, You trav-el on the riv-er, You
(3.) home's a-cross the riv-er, My home's a-cross the riv-er, My

take a stick of bam-boo, You throw it in the wa-ter,
trav-el on the riv-er, You trav-el on the wa-ter, } Oh——
home's a-cross the riv-er, My home's a-cross the wa-ter,

Oh—— Han-nah——— { You take a stick of bam-boo, You
You trav-el on the riv-er, You
My home's a-cross the riv-er, My

take a stick of bam-boo, You take a stick of bam-boo, You
trav-el on the riv-er, You trav-el on the riv-er, You
home's a-cross the riv-er, My home's a-cross the riv-er, My

throw it in the wa-ter,
trav-el on the wa-ter, } Oh—— Oh—— Han-nah!———
home's a-cross the wa-ter,

Refrain

Riv-er,——————— She come down.———————

340

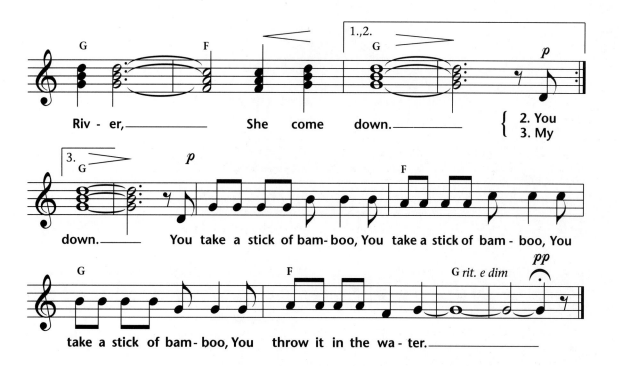

River,_____ She come down._____ { 2. You
                                        3. My

down._____ You take a stick of bam-boo, You take a stick of bam - boo, You

take a stick of bam-boo, You throw it in the wa - ter._____

I Got a Letter

South Carolina Singing Game

1. I got a let- ter this morn - ing,
2. I wrote a let- ter this morn - ing, } Oh, yes;
3. I mailed a let- ter this morn - ing,

I got a let- ter this morn - ing,
I wrote a let- ter this morn - ing, } Oh, yes.
I mailed a let- ter this morn - ing,

De allacito carnavalito
The Carnival Is Coming

Argentine Folk Song
English Version by MMH

Spanish: De a - lla - ci - to, de a - lla - ci - to, ya vie - ne el car - na - va - li - to;

Pronunciation: dea ya si to ðea ya si to ya βye nel kaɾ na βa li to

English: Ev' - ry - one there is— com - ing down to the *car - na - va - li - to*.

To - dos ba - jan en pa - re - ja, yo voy ba - jan - do so - li - to.

to ðos βa xan en pa ɾe xa yo βoi βa xan do so li to

Ev'-ry- one comes down in cou - ples, I am a lone - ly— so - lo.

Fortune

Words and Music
by Ludwig van Beethoven
English Words Traditional

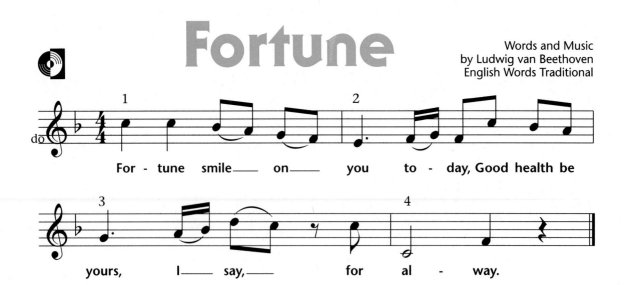

For - tune smile— on— you to - day, Good health be

yours, I— say,— for al - way.

O musique

French Folk Song
English Version by MMH

French: O mu - si - que no - tre a - mie, Sour - ce pure et frai - che.

Pronunciation: o mü zi kə nɔ tɾɑ mi suɾ sə pü ɾe fɾɛ shə

Autumn Canon

Words and Music by Lajos Bárdos
Translated by Sean Deibler

1. Fly, fly, fly,_____ the
2. Cry, cry, cry,_____ the

leaf takes leave of the branch, breez - es are
tears come soft - ly be - hind, turn - ing to

strong, win - ter is com - ing.
frost, touch - ing my heart._____

De Lanterna na Mão
With a Lantern in My Hand

Brazilian Folk Song
English Version by MMH

Portuguese: E - u pro - cu - rei,_____ de lan - ter - na na
Pronunciation: ε u prɔ ku rei ji lan ter na na
English: I___ search for you_____ with a lan - tern in my

mão,_____ pro - cu - rei, pro - cu - rei, e a -
mão prɔ ku rei prɔ ku rei i a
hand._____ Search - ing here, search - ing there and at

chei vo - ce pa - ra o meu cor - a - ção.
shei vɔ se pa ra meu ko ra são
last I find you, and you are my friend._____

E - u pro - cu ção. E a - go - ra, e a - go - ra eu vou jo-
ε u prɔ ku são i a go ra i a go ra εu vo ʒo
I___ look for friend. I have found you,_____ I have found you_____ and now

344

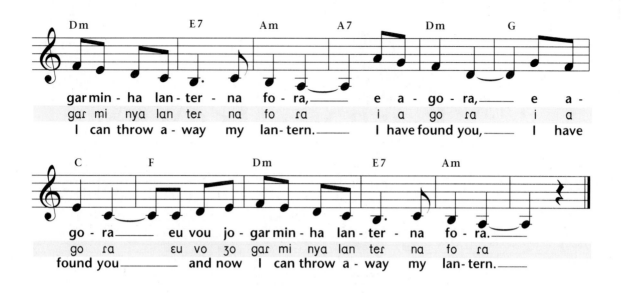

garminha lanterna fora,___ e a‐gora,___ e a‐
garminya lanter na fora i a gora i a
I can throw a‐way my lan‐tern.___ I have found you,___ I have

go‐ra___ eu vou jo‐garminha lan‐ter‐na fo‐ra.
go ra eu vo ʒo garminya lanter na fo ra
found you___ and now I can throw a‐way my lan‐tern.___

Spring Rain

Words and Music by Laura MacGregor
Arranged by Robert J. de Frece

Sung as a round. End when first part has sung lines 1-3 twice.

1

Lis‐ten now; hear the rain, soft‐ly on the hill ‐ side.

2

Slow‐ly the fog comes rol‐ling, cov'‐ring the fields.___

3

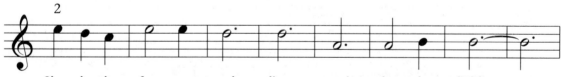

By the trees I sit, list'‐ning to the rain, wait‐ing for the sun.___

Optional ostinato for cambiatas.
Enter as Voice 4.

Rain fal‐ling soft‐ly down, gen ‐ tle rain.___

The Gypsy Rover

Irish Folk Song

Verse

1. The gyp - sy rov - er came o - ver the hill,
2. She left her fa - ther's cas - tle gate.
3. Her fa - ther sad - dled his fast - est steed,
4. "He's no gyp - sy, my fa - ther," said she, "But

Bound through the val - ley so shad - y. He whis - tled and he sang till the
Left her own true lov - er. She left her ser - vants and
Rode by the riv - er Clay - de. Drew near to a man - sion
lord of the free - lands all o - ver, And I will stay till my

green woods rang, And he won the heart of a la - dy.
her es - tate To fol - low the gyp - sy rov - er.
with great speed, Found the gyp - sy and his la - dy.
dy - ing day with my whist - ling gyp - sy rov - er."

Refrain

Ly - de - o, ly - de - o, da - day, Ly - de - o, Ly - de - ay - de; He

whis - tled and he sang till the green woods rang, And

he won the heart of a la - dy.

346

John B. Sails

G   C   D7

Folk Song from the Bahama Islands

1. Oh, we come on the sloop *John B.* My grand-fa-ther and me. A-round Nas-sau Town we did roam. Walk-in' all night, Just see-in' the sights, Well, I feel so break-up, I want to go home.

2. The first mate, he got sad, Feel-in' aw-f'ly bad, Cap-tain come a-board took him a-way. Please let me a-lone, And let me go home, Well, I feel so break-up, I want to go home.

3. The poor cook, he got fits, And throw 'way all the grits, Then he took and eat up all of the corn. Please let me go home, I want to go home. Well, this is the worst trip Since I was born.

Refrain

So hoist up the *John B.* sails, See how the main-s'l set. Send for the Cap-t'n a-shore, Let me go

home. Please let— me go home, I want — to go home.

Well, — I feel so break— up, — I want— to go home.

The Lion Sleeps Tonight

G   C   D

Words and Music by Solomon Linda
Arranged by Robert J. de Frece

Accompaniment

A wim - o - weh a wim - o - weh a wim - o - weh a wim - o - weh a

A wim - o - weh a wim - o - weh a wim - o - weh a wim - o - weh a

A wim - o - weh a wim - o - weh a wim - o - weh a wim - o - weh a

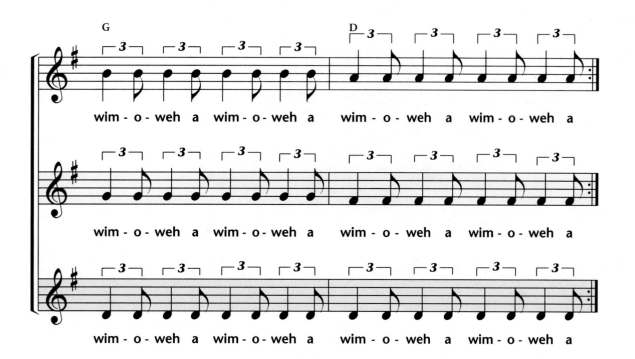

wim - o - weh a wim - o - weh a wim - o - weh a wim - o - weh a

wim - o - weh a wim - o - weh a wim - o - weh a wim - o - weh a

wim - o - weh a wim - o - weh a wim - o - weh a wim - o - weh a

Melody

Verse

1. In the jun - gle, the might - y jun - gle,
2. Near the vil - lage, the peace - ful vil - lage,   }the li - on sleeps   to - night.
3. Hush, my dar - ling, don't fear,   my dar - ling,

In the jun - gle, the might - y jun - gle,
Near the vil - lage, the peace - ful vil - lage,   }the li - on sleeps   to - night.
Hush, my dar - ling, don't fear,   my dar - ling,

Refrain

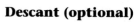

Ee —————————————————— um — mum — a - way ——

Descant (optional)

Ee —————————————————— um — mum — a - way ——

Orion

Words and Music by James Zimmermann

1. O - ri - on is a - ris - ing, You can see his stars a - blaz-
(2.) day is get - ting cold - er, And I real - ly start to won-

ing in the mid - dle of a clear - eyed coun - try
der why they're cloud - ing all the coun - try skies to

sky. And it's nev - er too sur - pris - ing that the
gray. The world is get - ting old - er, You can

sky is still a - maz - ing way out here where noth - ing
hear it in the thun - der and the rain might come and

hides it from my eyes. }
chase it all a - way. }   And sleep - ing out -

side in a bag as a kid, it seems like the

best thing that I ev - er did; And chas - ing the

sha - dows and the tracks in the snow, don't you

know?_____ 2. The know?_____

Coda — The moon is on the wane, And it

looks like it might rain, or may - be snow._____

— And how are we to stay____ here if there's

no room left to play____ here or to

grow. Don't you know? Don't you know?_____

Shenando'

American Sea Chantey

do

1. Oh, Shen - an - do', I long to hear you.
2. Oh, Shen - an - do', I love your daugh - ter.
3. Oh, Shen - an - do', I'm bound to leave you.

A - way, a - way___ you roll - ing riv - er.

Oh, Shen - an - do', I long to hear you.
Oh, Shen - an - do', I love your daugh - ter.
Oh, Shen - an - do', I'll not de - ceive you.

A - way,___ we're bound a - way. 'Cross the

A - way, a - way,

wide___ Mis - sou - ri.

'Cross the wide___ Mis - sou - ri.___

Las mañanitas
The Morning Song

Mexican Folk Song
English Version by MMH

Spanish: És - tas son las ma - ña - ni - tas que can -
Pronunciation: es ta son las ma nya ni tas ke kan
English: Now we sing las ma - ña - ni - tas, as King

ta - ba el Rey Da - vid, a las mu - cha - chas bo -
ta βa el rei ða βið a las mu cha chaz βo
Da - vid long a - go sang a song to greet the

ni - tas se las can - ta - mos a - sí: Des -
ni tas se las kan ta mos a si des
morn - ing, to greet the sun - light's first glow. A -

pier - ta, mi bien, des - pier - ta, mi
pyeɾ ta mi βyen des pyeɾ ta mi
wak - en, dear one, a - wak - en and

ra que ya a - ma - ne - ció, Ya los pa - ja - ri - tos
ɾa ke ya ma ne syo ya los pa xa ɾi tos
wel - come the ros - y dawn. Now the birds are sweet - ly

can - tan, la lu - na ya se me - tió.
kan tan la lu na ya se me tyo
sing - ing, the sil - ver moon - light has gone.

Soon Ah Will Be Done

African American Spiritual
Arranged by Robert J. de Frece

Refrain

Bm   F♯   Bm

Soon ah will be done - a with the trou - bles of the world,

Soon ah will be done - a with the trou - bles of the world,

Bm   Em   Bm

Trou - bles of the world, ____ the trou - bles of the world,

Trou - bles of the world, ____ the trou - bles of the world,

Bm   F♯   Bm

Soon ah will be done - a with the trou - bles of the world,

Soon ah will be done - a with the trou - bles of the world,

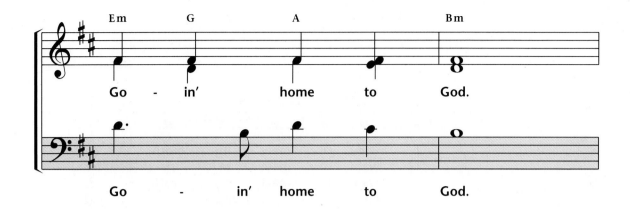

Go - in' home to God.

Go - in' home to God.

Verse

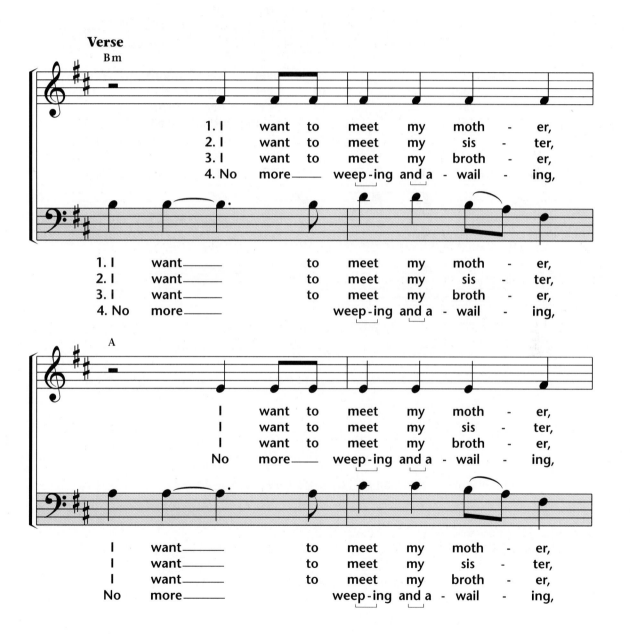

1. I want to meet my moth - er,
2. I want to meet my sis - ter,
3. I want to meet my broth - er,
4. No more weep-ing and a - wail - ing,

1. I want_____ to meet my moth - er,
2. I want_____ to meet my sis - ter,
3. I want_____ to meet my broth - er,
4. No more_____ weep-ing and a - wail - ing,

I want to meet my moth - er,
I want to meet my sis - ter,
I want to meet my broth - er,
No more_____ weep-ing and a - wail - ing,

I want_____ to meet my moth - er,
I want_____ to meet my sis - ter,
I want_____ to meet my broth - er,
No more_____ weep-ing and a - wail - ing,

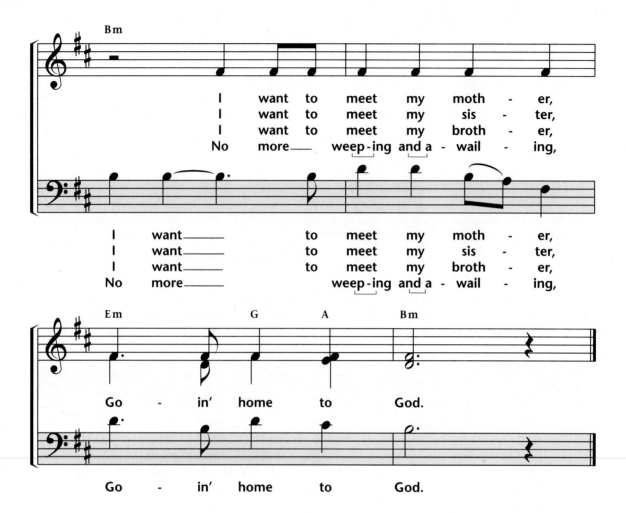

Fussreise
Tramping

Words by Eduard Mörike
Music by Hugo Wolf
English Version by Charles Fonteyn Manney

German: Am frisch-ge-schnitt-en — Wan-der-stab,
Pronunciation: am fɾɪsh gə shnɪ tən van dəɾ shtap
English: With fresh-cut staff at — break of day

wenn ich in der Frü-he so durch—
vɛn ɪç ɪn der fɾü ə zo dʊɾç
To the road I'm tak-ing, Thro' the —

Wäl-der sie-he,— Hü-gel — auf und ab:
vɛl dər zi ə hü gəl aʊf ʊnt ap
woods a-wak-ing, — O'er the— hills a-way.

Dann, — wie's Vög-lein im Lau-be sin-get und sich—
dan vis fög laɪn ɪm laʊ bə zɪng ət ʊnt zɪç
Like — a bird sing-ing glad-ly Where green leaves en-

rührt,— o-der wie die gold'-ne Trau-be
rüɾt o dəɾ vi di gold nə tɾaʊ bə
fold, — Or the rap-ture cours-ing mad-ly

Wie an e - wig neu - en Schö-pfungs - ta - gen,
vi an e vɪç nɔɪ ən ʃœp fʊngs tɑ gən
as on that first day of things cre - at - ed

dei - nen lie - ben Schö - pfer und ___ Er -
dɑɪ nən li bən ʃœp fər ʊnt eʀ
To thy great Cre - a - tor and ___ Pre -

hal - ter. Möcht' es die - ser ___ ge - ben und mein
hal tər mœç tɛs di zəʀ ge bən ʊnt mɑɪn
serv - er. Naught I'd need of ___ heav - en Could this

gan - zes Le - ben wär' im ___ leich - ten Wan - der-schweiss - se
gan tsəs le bən veʀ ɪm lɑɪç tən van dəʀ ʃvɑɪ sə
boon be giv - en: All my ___ life en - tranced to wan - der

ei - ne sol - che Mor - gen - rei - se!
ɑɪ nə sɔl çə mɔʀ gən ʀɑɪ zə
While earth smiles in morn - ing splen - dor!

Chiu, chiu, chiu

Uruguayan Folk Song
English Version by MMH

Spanish: Can - ta, can - ta, pa - ja - ri - to.___ Can - ta, can - ta tu can -
Pronunciation: kan ta kan ta pa xa ɾi to kan ta kan ta tu kan
English: *Can - ta, can - ta pa - ja - ri - to.___* Sing the songs that cheer me

ción, Mi - ra que la vi - da es tris - te y tu can -
syon mi ɾa ke la βi da es tris te i tu kan
so. See, my life is full of sor - row, your mer - ry

tar me a - le - gra el co - ra - zon. Chí - u, chí - u, chí - u,
taɾ mea le gɾa el ko ɾa son chi u chi u chi u
sing - ing sets my heart a - glow. *Chí - u, chí - u, chí - u,*

chí - u,___ chí - u, chí - u, chí - u, chí - u.___ Can - ta, can - ta pa - ja -
chi u chi u chi u chi u chi u kan ta kan ta pa xa
chí - u,___ chí - u, chí - u, chí - u, chí - u.___ Can - ta, can - ta pa - ja -

ri - to. Que tu can - tar me a - le - gra el co - ra - zon.
ɾi to ke tu kan taɾ mea le gɾa el ko ɾa son
ri - to. Your mer - ry sing - ing sets my heart a - glow.

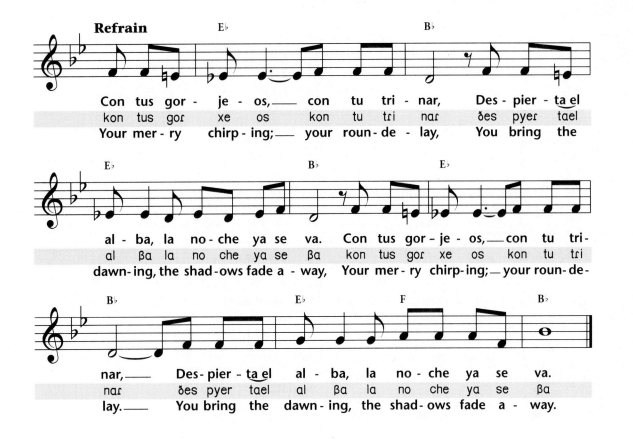

Refrain

Con tus gor - je - os,— con tu tri - nar,
kon tus goɾ xe os kon tu tɾi naɾ
Your mer - ry chirp - ing;— your roun - de - lay,

Des - pier - ta el
ðes pyeɾ tael
You bring the

al - ba, la no - che ya se va.
al βa la no che ya se βa
dawn - ing, the shad - ows fade a - way,

Con tus gor - je - os,— con tu tri -
kon tus goɾ xe os kon tu tɾi
Your mer - ry chirp - ing;— your roun - de -

nar,— Des - pier - ta el al - ba, la no - che ya se va.
naɾ ðes pyeɾ tael al βa la no che ya se βa
lay.— You bring the dawn - ing, the shad - ows fade a - way.

Where'er You Walk

Music by George Friderick Handel
Words by William Congreve

Where'-er you walk, cool gales shall fan the glade; Trees, where you sit, shall

crowd in-to a shade, Trees, where you sit, shall crowd in - to a shade;

Where'-er you walk, cool gales shall fan the glade; Trees, where you sit, shall

crowd in-to a shade, Trees, where you sit,

shall crowd in - to a shade. Where'-er you tread, the

blush-ing flow'rs shall rise, And all things flour - ish, and

all things flour - ish Where' - er you turn your eyes, Where'-

er you turn your eyes, Where'-er you turn your eyes.

Drill, Ye Tarriers

Words and Music by
Thomas Casey and Charles Connolly

Verse

Cm

1. Oh, ev' - ry morn - in' at sev - en o' clock,— There's a
2. Now, our new fore-man was Jer - ry Mc- Cann,— You can
3. Now, next time pay - day come— a - round,— Jim—

Gm

hun - dred tar - ri - ers a - work - in' at the rock, And the
bet that he was sure a blame— mean— man, Last—
Goff a dol - lar— short— was— found, When—

Cm

boss comes a - long and he says, "Keep still! And
week a— pre - ma - ture— blast went off, And a
asked what— for, came— this re - ply, "You were

Gm

come down heav - y on the cast - iron drill," and
mile in the air— went— big Jim Goff, and
docked for the time— you were up in the sky!" So

Refrain

Cm   Gm   Cm   Gm   Cm

Drill, ye tar - ri - ers, drill, Drill, ye tar - ri - ers, drill.

Eb   Cm

Oh, it's work all day for sug - ar in your tay,

Gm   Cm   Gm   Cm

Down be- hind the rail - way, Oh, drill, ye tar - ri - ers, drill!

ISLAND IN THE SUN

Music by Harry Belafonte
Words by Lord Burgess

1. This is my is-land in the sun where my peo-ple have toiled since time be-gun.— Though I may sail on man-y a sea— Her shores will al-ways be home to me.—

Refrain

Oh, is-land in the sun.— Willed to me— by my

Optional Cambiata

fa-ther's hand.— All my days— I will sing in praise— of your

for - ests, wat - ers, your shin - ing sand.

2. I hope the day will nev - er come that I

can't a - wake to the sound of drum.

Nev - er let me miss car - ni - val With ca -

lyp - so songs phil - o - soph - i - cal.

English Folk Song

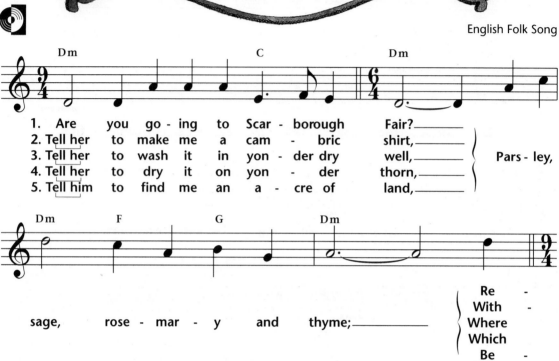

1. Are you go - ing to Scar - borough Fair?_____
2. Tell her to make me a cam - bric shirt,_____
3. Tell her to wash it in yon - der dry well,_____
4. Tell her to dry it on yon - der thorn,_____
5. Tell him to find me an a - cre of land,_____

Pars - ley,

sage, rose - mar - y and thyme;_____

Re -
With -
Where
Which
Be -

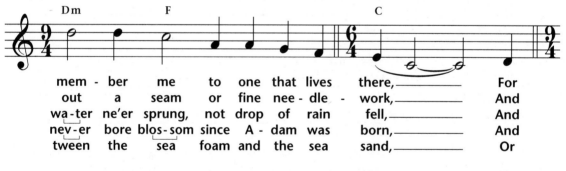

mem - ber me to one that lives there,_____ For
out a seam or fine nee - dle - work,_____ And
wa - ter ne'er sprung, not drop of rain fell,_____ And
nev - er bore blos - som since A - dam was born,_____ And
tween the sea foam and the sea sand,_____ Or

she was once a true love of mine._____
then she'll be a true love of mine._____
then she'll be a true love of mine._____
then she'll be a true love of mine._____
nev - er be a true love of mine._____

6. Tell him to plough it with a lam'd horn
   Parsley, sage, rosemary and thyme;
   And sow it all over with one peppercorn,
   Or never be a true love of mine.

Shady Grove

Southern Appalachian Folk Song

Refrain

Dm | C | Dm | Am

Shad - y Grove, my lit - tle love, Shad - y Grove, I know,

F | C | Dm | C | Dm

Shad - y Grove, my lit - tle love, Bound for Shad - y Grove.

Verse

Dm | C | Dm | Am

1. Cheeks as red as the bloom - ing rose, Eyes of the deep - est brown;
2. Went to see my—— Shad - y Grove, She was stand - ing in the door,
3. Wish I had a—— big fine horse, Corn to—— feed him on,
4. Shad - y Grove,——— my lit - tle love, Shad - y Grove, I say,

F | C | Dm | C | Dm

You are the dar - ling of my heart, Stay till the sun goes down.
Shoes—— and stock - ings in her hand, Lit - tle bare— feet on the floor.
Pret - ty lit - tle girl,—— stay at home, Feed him— when I'm gone.
Shad - y Grove,— my lit - tle love, Don't wait till the Judg - ment Day!

THE KETTLE VALLEY LINE

Dm   Am

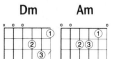

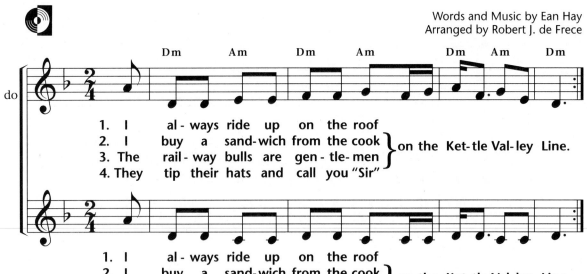

Words and Music by Ean Hay
Arranged by Robert J. de Frece

1. I al-ways ride up on the roof
2. I buy a sand-wich from the cook } on the Ket-tle Val-ley Line.
3. The rail-way bulls are gen-tle-men
4. They tip their hats and call you "Sir"

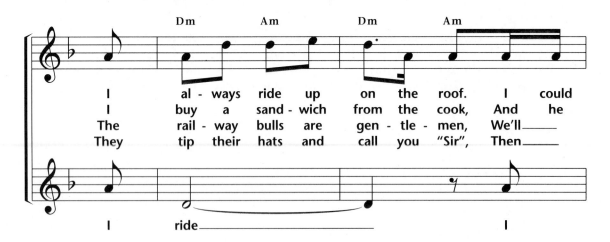

I al-ways ride up on the roof. I could
I buy a sand-wich from the cook, And he
The rail-way bulls are gen-tle-men, We'll___
They tip their hats and call you "Sir", Then___

I ride_____ I

FOLLOW THE DRINKIN' GOURD

Em   G   Am   Easy Bm

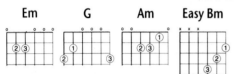

Slowly, but Rhythmically
Verse

African American Spiritual
Adapted by Paul Campbell

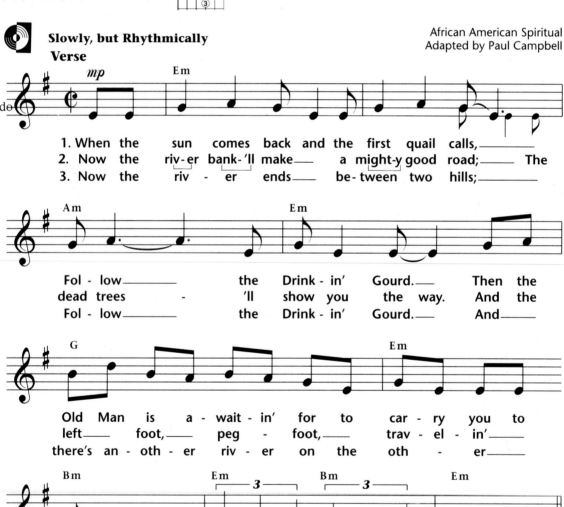

mp   Em

1. When the sun comes back and the first quail calls,_____
2. Now the riv-er bank-'ll make_____ a might-y good road;_____ The
3. Now the riv - er ends_____ be-tween two hills;_____

Am   Em

Fol - low_____ the Drink - in' Gourd.___ Then the
dead trees - 'll show you the way. And the
Fol - low_____ the Drink - in' Gourd.___ And

G   Em

Old Man is a - wait - in' for to car - ry you to
left____ foot,____ peg - foot,____ trav - el - in'_____
there's an - oth - er riv - er on the oth - er

Bm   Em ⌐3⌐   Bm ⌐3⌐   Em

free - dom,_____ Fol - low the Drink - in' Gourd.
on; Just you fol - low the Drink - in' Gourd.
side, Just you fol - low the Drink - in' Gourd.

Refrain

Fol - low _____ the Drink - in' Gourd, _____

Fol - low _____ the Drink - in' Gourd, _____

For the Old Man is a - wait - in' for to

car - ry you to free - dom, Fol - low the Drink - in' Gourd.

Greek Folk Song
English Version by MMH

Verse 1

Greek: M'ά - γα - πᾶς Γα - ρυ - φα - λιά - μου M'ά - γα -
Pronunciation: ma ya pas ga ri fa lya mu ma ya
English: **Tell me now, Ga - ri - fa - lia, do you___ love**

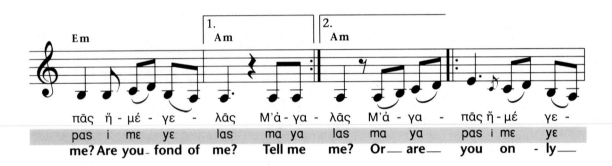

πᾶς ἤ - μέ - γε - λᾶς M'ά - γα - λᾶς M'ά - γα - πᾶς ἤ - μέ γε -
pas i me ye las ma ya las ma ya pas i me ye
me? Are you___ fond of me? Tell me me? Or___ are___ you on - ly

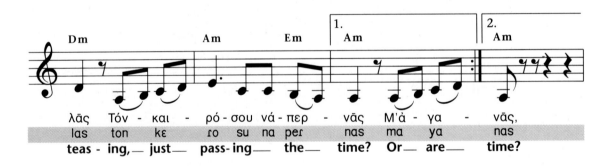

λᾶς Τόν - και - ρό - σου νά - περ - νᾶς M'ά - γα - νᾶς,
las ton ke ro su na per nas ma ya nas
teas - ing,___ just___ pass - ing___ the time? Or___ are___ time?

Verse 2

Σ'ά - γα - πῶ, βα - σι - λι - κέ - μου, Σ'ά - γα -
sa ga po va si li ke mu sa ga
Yes, I love you, my sweet___ Ba - sil, I___ would

372

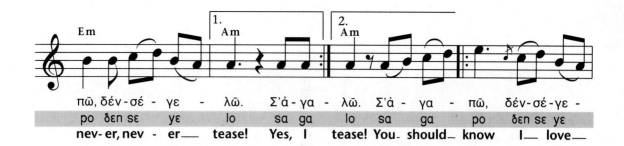

πῶ, δέν-σέ - γε - λῶ. Σ'ἀ - γα - λῶ. Σ'ἀ - γα - πῶ, δέν-σέ-γε -
po δεn sε ye lo sa ga lo sa ga po δεn sε ye
nev- er, nev - er— tease! Yes, I tease! You— should— know I— love—

λῶ, Σάν - τά - μά - τι - α - μου τά - δυό Σ'ἀ - γα - δυό.
lo san ta ma ti a mu ta δyo sa ga δyo
you, I— love— you as my own two eyes! You— should— eyes.

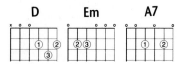

The Haddock

Venezuelan Folk Song
Collected by Francisco Carrero

Spanish: Ya te co-noz-co, Ro-ba-lo por el ca-mi-no que
Pronunciation: ya te ko nos ko ɾo βa lo poɾ el ka mi no ke
English: I rec-og-nize you, Ro-bo-lo, on the high-way where you

vas, con tus za-pa-ti-cos blan-cos y tus
βas kon tus sa pa ti kos βlang kos i tus
go. I see your lit-tle white san-dals and your

me-dias co-lo-rás. Con tus za-pa-ti-cos
me ðyas ko lo ɾas kon tus sa pa ti kos
lit-tle socks of red. I see your lit-tle white

blan-cos y tus me-dias co-lo-rás.
βlang kos i tus me ðyas ko lo ɾas
san-dals and your lit-tle socks of red.

A Voice From A Dream

Words and Music by Joyce Elaine Eilers
Adapted by MMH

When it seems your skies are all gray, and the

When your skies are

trou-bles of the world are here to stay;

gray, And trou-ble's here to stay, Just

376

song, and we'll fly be-yond_ the rain-bow, to that land of en-chant-ment es-

song and we'll fly be-yond_ the rain-bow, to that land of en-chant-ment es-

cape 'til the dawn. And though morn-ing will come and take a-way_ the

cape 'til the dawn. And though morn-ing will come and take a-way_ the

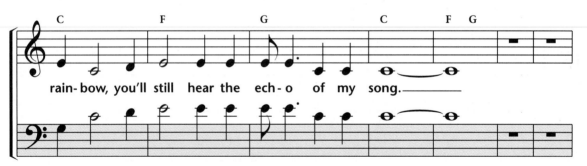

rain-bow, you'll still hear the ech-o of my song.___

rain-bow, you'll still hear the ech-o of my song.___

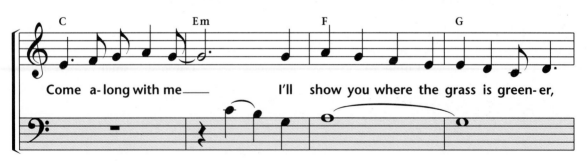

Come a-long with me___ I'll show you where the grass is green-er,

Come_ with me,___

Shall I Dream a Dream?

Words and Music by Julie Knowles

Part 1

Shall I dream a dream; catch a fall - ing star?

Shall I trav - el down the road won-d'ring just how far?

Part 2

Now the time has come, time to think it through.

If we nev - er dream at all, how can they come true?

If you walk be - side me in the days a - head,

If you walk be - side me in the days a - head,

We can climb the high-est hill, we can dream a dream.

We can climb the high-est hill, we can dream a dream.

380

how can they come true?

If we nev - er dream at all, how can they come true?

How can they come true?_____

How can they come true?_____

SOFT SHOE SONG

Words and Music by
Roy Jordan and Sid Bass

Soft Shoe Tempo

Unison

1. Give me that Old Soft Shoe, I said that Old Soft Shoe, Ah-

one, ah-two, ah-doo-dle-dee doo-dle-dee doo, Play me that

Old Soft Shoe and noth-in' else will do, That's the

dance my dar-lin' used to do. We'll sing love's re-

Sing both times

frain,

Dance the whole night through,

Just like a vau-de-ville team.

Do-ing the cut-est rou-tine,

Stroll - ing lov - er's lane,

Just like we're play - ing a scene.

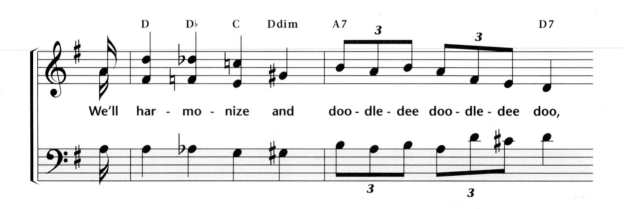

We'll har - mo - nize and doo - dle - dee doo - dle - dee doo,

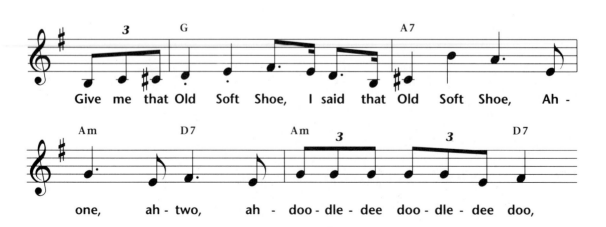

Give me that Old Soft Shoe, I said that Old Soft Shoe, Ah -

one, ah - two, ah - doo - dle - dee doo - dle - dee doo,

384

Play me that Old Soft Shoe and noth-in' else will do, That's the

1.

ch ch ch

2.

dance my dar-lin' used to do. do.

The Wind Beneath My Wings

Words and Music by
Larry Henley and Jeff Silbar

Freely

It must have been cold there in my shad-ow,

to ne-ver have sun-light— on— your face.

You were con-tent to let— me— shine, that's your way,—

you al-ways walked a step— be-hind.

1. So, I was the one with all___ the glo - ry,
2. It might have ap - peared to go___ un - no - ticed,

while you were the one with all___ the strength.
but I've got it all here in___ my heart.

A beau - ti - ful face with - out___ a___ name for so long,___
I want you to know I know___ the___ truth, of course I know___ it,

a beau - ti - ful smile to hide___ the pain.
I would be noth - ing with - out you.

Did you ev - er know___ that you're___ my he - ro,

and ev' - ry - thing I would like to___ be?

I can fly high - er than an ea - gle,

386

'cause you are the wind be-neath my— wings.

wings.   wind————— be-neath— my— wings.

Fly,——— fly,——— fly a-way,— you let— me fly— so—

high.— Oh,— fly,——— fly————— so

high a-gainst— the sky,——— so high— I al-most touch—

— the sky.— Thank— you,   thank— you,   thank

God   for you,—— the wind be-neath— my—— wings.

PREPARING TO SING "HASHIVENU"

"Hashivenu" is a traditional Israeli round. The text is chanted on the Jewish Sabbath, during festivals, and at weekday services when the Torah, a set of scrolls containing the first five books of the Old Testament, is returned to its resting place.

The Hebrew text of "Hashivenu" contains several pure vowels. Can you locate them in the song? Sing the following patterns, focusing on the pure vowels in the word "alleluia" (*ah*, *eh*, and *oo*). Be sure your jaw is open and relaxed.

al ɛ lu ya   al ɛ lu ya   al ɛ lu ya

Hashivenu

Israeli Folk Song
Edited by Doreen Rao
English Version by MMH

Hebrew:
Pronunciation: ha shi ve nu   ha shi ve nu   a do naɪ e ɛ xa
English: **Ha - shi - ven - u,—   Ha - shi - ven - u,— Help us,— Lord, oh— hear— us.**

vǝ na shu va   vǝ na shu va
Cause us   to re - turn,   to re - turn— to you.

xa desh xa desh ya meɪ nu kǝ kɛ dɛm
Days— of old,   days— of old,   re - new— our days of old.

PREPARING TO SING "THE LOBSTER QUADRILLE"

This song is based on a poem by Lewis Carroll, the well-known author of *Alice in Wonderland.* The text describes an invitation for creatures who live on the seashore to join a *quadrille,* a dance for four pairs of partners.

The melody contains several large upward and downward leaps. As you sing the downward leaps, stand on the tips of your toes to help prevent the bottom pitch from sinking into your chest voice. As you sing the upward leaps, bend your knees and pretend to touch the high pitch above your head. This helps prevent straining for the pitch from below.

The Lobster Quadrille

Music by Carolyn Jennings
Words by Lewis Carroll

As though it all made perfectly good sense

"Will you walk a lit-tle fast-er?" said a whit-ing to a snail. "There's a por-poise close be-hind us, and he's tread-ing on my tail. See how ea-ger-ly the lob-sters and the tur-tles all ad-vance! They are wait-ing on the shin-gle, Will you come and join the dance?_____

Will_____ you, won't you, will you, won't you, will you join the dance? Will_____ you, won't you, will you, won't you, won't you join the dance?_____

390

You can real-ly have no no-tion how de-light-ful it will be, When they

3

take us up and throw us, with the lob sters, out to sea!"_____

Part 2

But the snail re-plied, "Too far, too far," and gave a look a-skance, Said he

thanked the whit-ing kind-ly, but he would not join the dance._____

Unison

poco rit   *a tempo*

Would not dance,_____ would not dance._____ Would_____ not, could not,

would not, could not, would not join the dance, Would_____ not, could not,

5

would not, could not, could not join the dance._____

"What mat-ters it how far we go?" his scal-y friend re-plied."There

is an-oth-er shore, you know, up-on the oth-er side.

The fur-ther off from Eng-land the near-er is to France – Then

turn not pale, be-lov-ed snail, but come and join the dance.

Come and dance! Join the dance! Will you, won't you,

will you, won't you, will you join the dance? O, be-lov-ed

snail, won't you come and join the dance. See how ea-ger-ly the

lob-sters and the tur-tles all ad-vance! Turn not pale, be-lov-ed snail, but come and

PREPARING TO SING "THE GYPSY MAN"

The melody of "The Gypsy Man," a Slovakian folk song, contains several repeated melodic patterns. Sing the following melodic patterns and then locate them in the song.

1 do so₁ do re mi re mi so
2 mi re do la₁
3 mi mi fa mi re do
4 so so fa mi fa so

The Gypsy Man

Words and Music by Béla Bartók
from a Slovak Folk Song
Arranged by Benjamin Suchoff
Words Adapted by MMH

(Clap) Who's rid-ing down the street? Some- one I'd like to meet!

(Clap) Who's rid-ing down the street? Some- one I'd like to meet!

Jan - i - šek the gyp - sy man, come catch him if catch you can!

Jan - i - šek the gyp - sy man, come catch him if catch you can!

PREPARING TO SING "OLD JOE CLARK"

"Old Joe Clark" is a familiar American fiddle tune. It was well known in the midwestern and southern parts of the United States in the late 1890s and early 1900s and is still sung today. In this arrangement, Parts 2 and 3 in Verse 3 make sounds that imitate instruments. The "pling pling-a pling" imitates a banjo, and the "pom pom" imitates the plucked strings of a string bass.

This song is in the Mixolydian mode. This means that it has the sound of a major scale, except that the seventh note of the scale is flatted.

Practice the following melodic patterns. They will help you sing "Old Joe Clark" in tune. Can you locate the patterns in the score?

Old Joe Clark

American Folk Song
Arranged by Mary Goetze

Old   Joe—   Clark,   Ain't got long to   stay.

'Round and 'round   Old Joe Clark,   Ain't got long to   stay.

'Round   and 'round,   I   ain't got long to   stay.

Part 3

Joe   Clark's   bed meas-ured eight   by   four. He took his

feath - er   bed   and—   me,   I   got the   floor.

Part 2

Old   Joe   Clark   had   a   feath - er   bed.

Part 3

Joe   Clark's   bed   meas-ured eight   by   four. He got the

He   got   the   bed   and—   I   got   the   floor.

feath - er   bed   and—   me,   I   got the   floor.

Old   Joe——   Clark,   Ain't got long to   stay.

'Round and 'round   Old Joe Clark,   Ain't got long to   stay.

'Round   and 'round   I   ain't got long to   stay.

Part 2

Pling   pling - a   pling   pling - a   pling   pling - a   pling   pling

pling   pling - a   pling   pling - a   pling   pling - a   pling - a   pling - a

pling   pling - a   pling   pling - a   pling   pling - a   pling   pling

Part 2

pling pling-a pling-a pling-a   pling   pling pling- a pling pling- a

Part 3

Pom pom pom   pom   pom

PREPARING TO SING "EL ZAPATERO"

This song was sung in Southern California. How many times are the verse and refrain sung? The words remain the same, but what musical element changes?

Clap the following rhythmic patterns and discover them in the song.

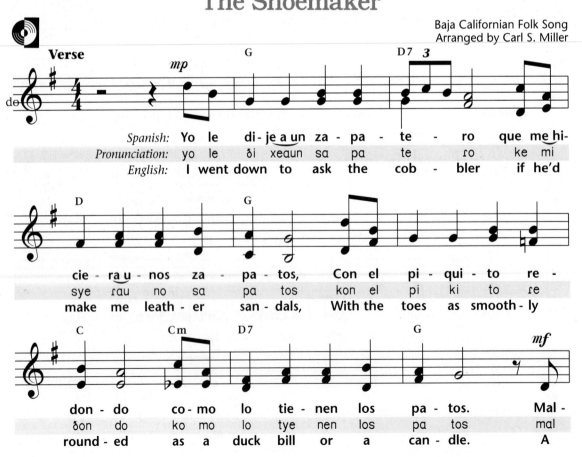

EL ZAPATERO
The Shoemaker

Baja Californian Folk Song
Arranged by Carl S. Miller

Verse

Spanish: Yo le di - je a un za - pa - te - ro que me hi-
Pronunciation: yo le ði xeaun sa pa te ɾo ke mi
English: I went down to ask the cob - bler if he'd

cie - ra u - nos za - pa - tos, Con el pi - qui - to re -
sye ɾau no sa pa tos kon el pi ki to ɾe
make me leath - er san - dals, With the toes as smooth - ly

don - do co - mo lo tie - nen los pa - tos. Mal -
ðon do ko mo lo tye nen los pa tos mal
round - ed as a duck bill or a can - dle. A

PREPARING TO SING "KEEP YOUR LAMPS!"

"Keep Your Lamps!" is a traditional African American spiritual. The text reflects the hope for freedom. The syncopated rhythm patterns are typical of this musical style.

Practice the following rhythm patterns and locate them in the song.

Keep Your Lamps!

African American Spiritual
Arranged by Andre Thomas

Keep your— lamps trimmed and burn - ing, keep your lamps trimmed and burn - ing, keep your— lamps trimmed and burn- - ing,—— the time is draw- ing nigh.— Keep your— — Child-ren

don't get wea - ry, child - ren don't get wea - ry, child - ren

wea - ry

wea - ry wea - ry wea - ry child - ren

1.
Fm

don't get wea - ry 'til your work is— done. Child - ren

wea - ry 'til your work is done.

2. *Unison*
Fm

done. Long, long jour - ney al - most o - ver, long, long

jour - ney al - most o - ver, long, long jour - ney al - most o -

1. 2.

- ver,— the time is draw - ing nigh.— Long, long nigh. Keep your—

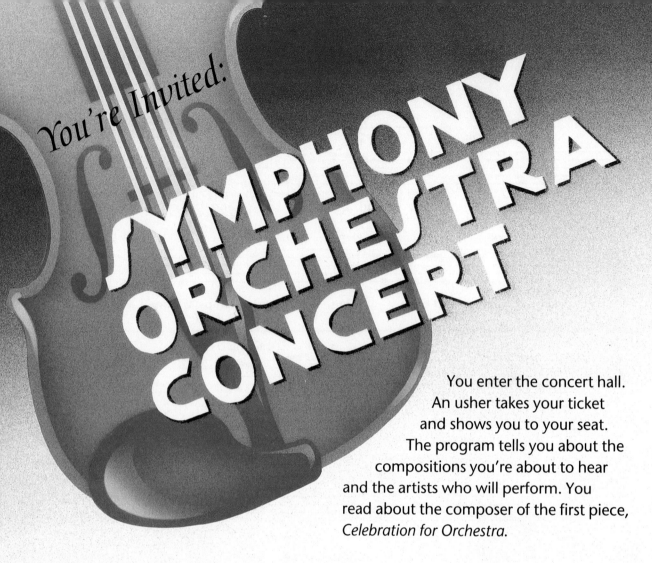

You're Invited: SYMPHONY ORCHESTRA CONCERT

You enter the concert hall.
An usher takes your ticket
and shows you to your seat.
The program tells you about the
compositions you're about to hear
and the artists who will perform. You
read about the composer of the first piece,
Celebration for Orchestra.

Meet Ellen Taaffe Zwilich

Ellen Zwilich began composing when she was ten years old. She also played the piano, violin, and trumpet. Zwilich became a professional violinist. Later she won prizes for several of her compositions, including the first Pulitzer Prize ever awarded to a woman composer.

The audience applauds and the orchestra stands in a gesture of respect as the conductor enters. The conductor steps onto the podium, raises the baton, and the concert begins.

At the end of the composition, Ellen Zwilich is called out to share the applause.

Next is a movement from the Mendelssohn Violin Concerto.
The soloist is Nadja Salerno-Sonnenberg.

♪ Meet Nadja Salerno-Sonnenberg

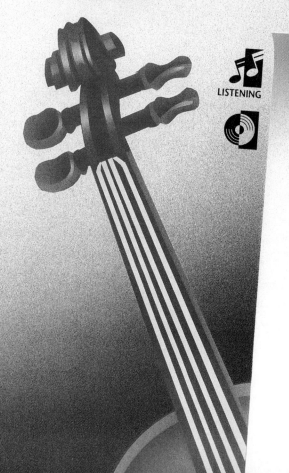

Nadja Salerno-Sonnenberg was born in Rome, Italy. When she was eight, she moved to the United States to study music. She has been a concert violinist for many years and has won awards for her playing.

At the end of the piece, everyone applauds loudly and calls out "Brava" to Nadja Salerno-Sonnenberg in admiration of her playing. Then the conductor waits until the audience is quiet again to begin the next composition. The last piece on the program is a set of variations on "When Johnny Comes Marching Home." When the music ends, the conductor and orchestra take their final bows. You leave the hall, remembering the sounds of the music you heard.

LISTENING

Celebration for Orchestra
Ellen Taaffe Zwilich
(1984)

❧

Violin Concerto in E Minor, Op. 64, Third Movement
Felix Mendelssohn
(1844)

❧

American Salute
Morton Gould
(1944)

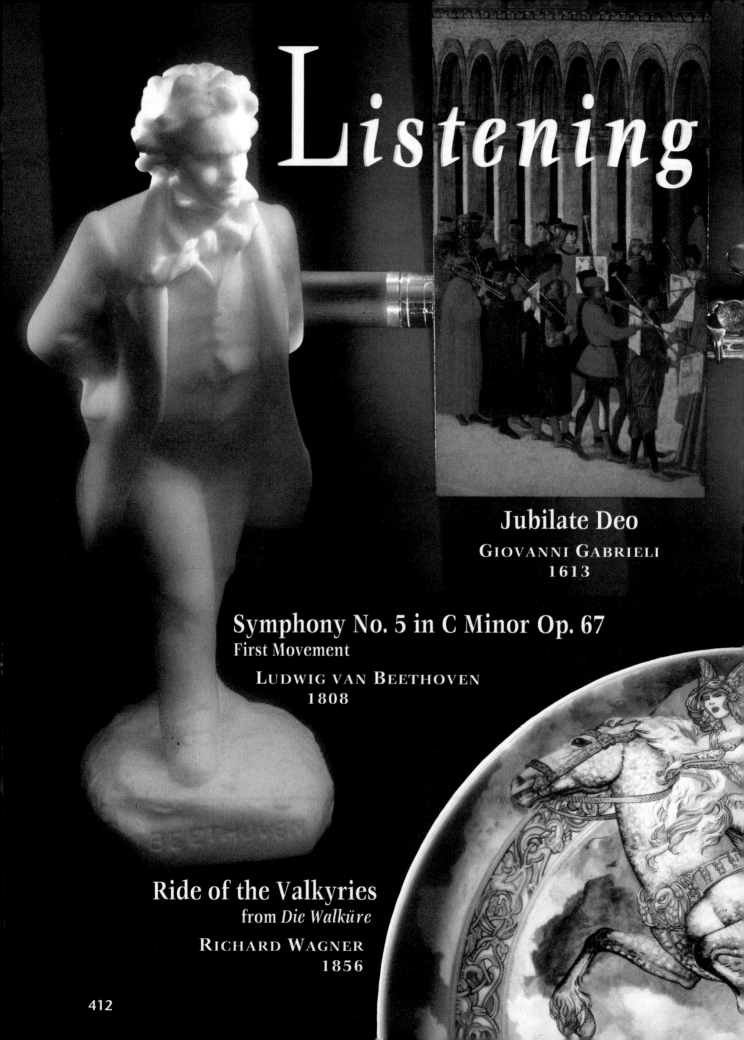

Listening

Jubilate Deo
GIOVANNI GABRIELI
1613

Symphony No. 5 in C Minor Op. 67
First Movement

LUDWIG VAN BEETHOVEN
1808

Ride of the Valkyries
from *Die Walküre*

RICHARD WAGNER
1856

Discoveries

Composers use many different styles to express their musical ideas. Listen to the variety of sounds in the pieces below.

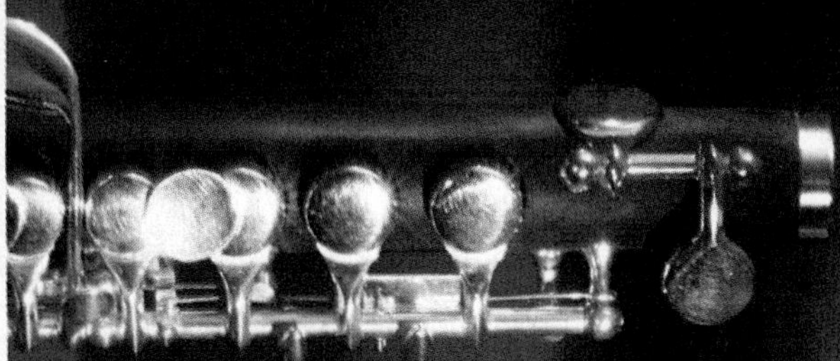

Seventeen Come Sunday
from *English Folk Song Suite*

RALPH VAUGHAN WILLIAMS
1923

Concerto for Orchestra
Second Movement ("Game of Pairs")

BÉLA BARTÓK
1943

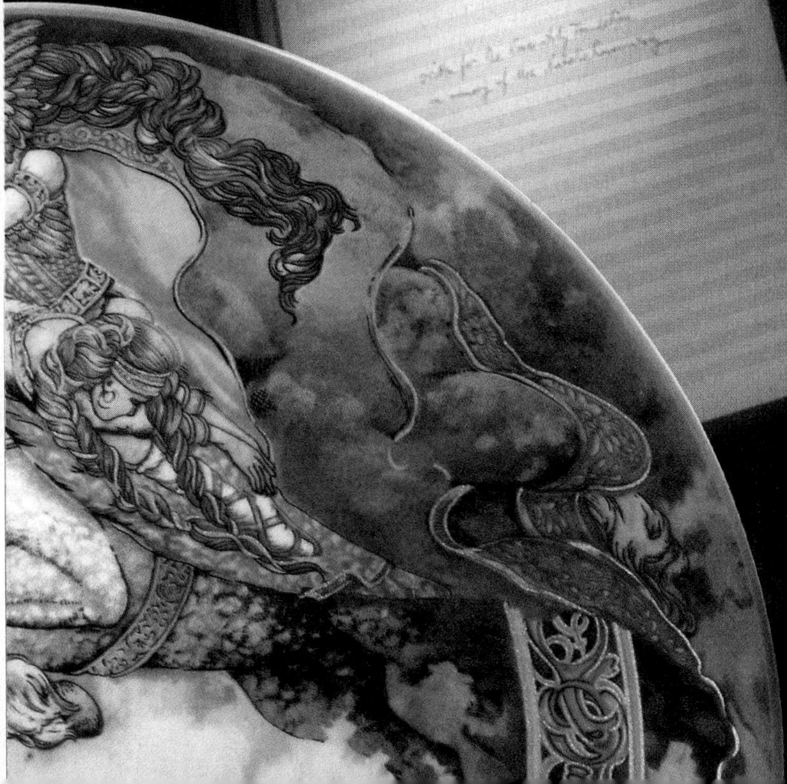

Amoeba

JUDITH E. FICKSMAN
1992

A group of kids hiking through the woods is dismayed to find a terrible change in the forest they love. The Natural Resources look dirty and full of junk.

Among the kids are the Practical Kid, the Idealistic Kid, the Skeptical Kid, the Apathetic Kid, and the Apathetic Kid's Little Sister. The Apathetic Kid says, "We didn't make this mess. There's nothing we can do." The Forest explains how their actions affect everything around them.

Music by Neil Fishman • Book and lyrics by Harvey Edelman •
Story conceived by Harvey and Julie Edelman

WHERE DOES IT COME FROM

Music by Neil Fishman
Words by Harvey Edelman

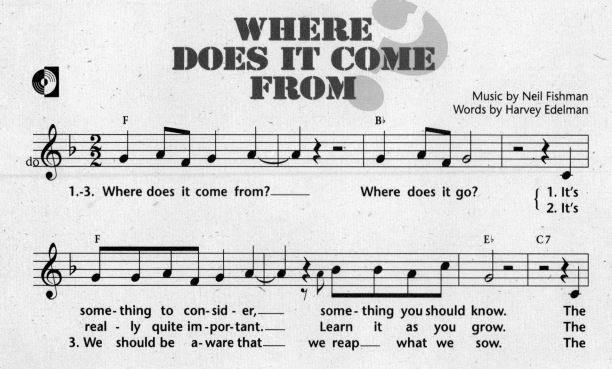

1.-3. Where does it come from?_____ Where does it go?

{ 1. It's
{ 2. It's

some-thing to con-sid-er,_____ some-thing you should know. The
real-ly quite im-por-tant._____ Learn it as you grow. The
3. We should be a-ware that_____ we reap_____ what we sow. The

bag that held your lunch,   the food you did-n't munch,   the
gas in the fa-mi-ly car,   the strings on your gui-tar,   your
for-ests full of trees,   wa-ter in the seas,

plates and cups you left   on your tray.   A piece of o-range
bi-cy-cle___ and your fav'-rite games.   The cloth that makes your
an-i-mals in ev'ry shape and size.   The air that's fresh and

rind,   an ap-ple left be-hind,   the milk you drink,___ the
clothes,   C-Ds and vi-de-os.   Your dad's snow-plow,___ your
clean,   ev'-ry-thing that's green.   Read a book___ or

kit-chen___ sink,___   things you use each day.
pup-py's___ chow,___   more than we could
take a___ look,___   right be-fore your

name.   Things don't just ap-pear___ then va-nish in the air.___

Ev'-ry-thing comes from some-thing and al-ways goes some-where.___

eyes.   Where does it come from?___   Where does it go?

The Natural Resources point out that once
they are gone they can't be replaced.

THERE'S JUST SO MUCH TO GO AROUND

Music by Neil Fishman
Words by Harvey Edelman

1. There's just so much to go a-round,—
2. There's just so much fresh health-y air.—
3. There's just so much of bird and beast.—

in the deep blue sea and un-der-ground.—
You'll find no ex-tra air an-y-where.—
Mo-ther na-ture serves a bal-anced feast.—

You can't as-sume there's more to be found,
Ten bil-lion lungs will just have to share
So you must stop, be-fore she's been fleeced.

there's just so much to go a-round.—
what you've got left of health-y air.—
There's just so much of bird and beast.—

There's just so much clean H-2-O,—
There's just so much of fos-sil fuels,—
There's just so much to go a-round,—

that's health - y wat - er if you did not know.___
you de - pend up - on their mol - e - cules.___
in the deep blue sea and un - der - ground.___

Mixed with pol - lu - tants it will not flow.
When they are gone, it's back to the mules,
You can't as - sume, there's more to be found,

There's just so much clean H - 2 - O.___
so don't you waste our fos - sil fuels.___
there's just so much to go a - round.___

Once there was a ti - ny vil - lage___ with
Once there was a blue - green plan - et,___ a

wa - ter, food, and fuel ga - lore.___ But
won - drous place to work and play.___ Be -

af - ter years of waste and pil - lage___ it's
fore there was a way to ban it,___ pol -

gone like the din - o - saur.
lu - tion turned that plan - et grey.

The kids begin to notice that some of the Natural Resources are indeed missing. Little Sister seems tired. The Air wonders if pollution is affecting her. The kids ask how the disappearance of resources will affect life.

The Forest tells the kids why we need to replace the billions of trees that are cut down each year. While we need trees for building houses and making paper and other materials, the trees keep soil from washing away. They keep the atmosphere supplied with oxygen. In tropical areas, rain forests are home to thousands of species of animals and plants.

PLEASE DON'T CUT DOWN THE TREES

Music by
Neil Fishman
Words by
Harvey Edelman

Please, please don't cut down the trees. They look so pret-ty— sway-ing in the breeze. To save the earth they hold the keys, so please don't cut down the trees.

1. The strength of their roots keeps the earth in place. The
2. A world with-out trees, I-mag-ine the view. If

breadth of their leaves keeps the sun from my face.
we don't take care, well, it just might come true. So

Stand-ing so tall, limbs o-pen wide,
do what you may, do what you must,

D.C. last time to Coda

they seem to call: There's shel-ter in-side.
day af-ter day we hold na-ture's trust.

Coda

Please, please don't cut down the trees.

They look so pret-ty sway-ing in the breeze. To

save the earth they hold the keys, so please,—

— oh please, don't cut down the trees.

When the Skeptical Kid wonders what they can do to help, Little Sister suggests that they become Earth Kids and protect their environment. The Idealistic Kid agrees. The Practical Kid hopes it's not too late, then suggests that they begin by cleaning up the area. The Natural Resources teach the kids about recycling—how to reuse certain products instead of throwing them away.

KEEP THE CIRCLE GOING 'ROUND

Music by Neil Fishman
Words by Harvey Edelman

We must keep the cir-cle go-ing 'round. No-thing's lost that can be found. Find to-mor-row in to-day and the world will be o-kay. We must kay.

1. See the glass glis-ten in the sand.
2. Ev'-ry-thing turns from this to that,

Did you know they go hand in hand?
Like a bird in a ma-gic hat.
Giv-en time and a
But be-ware lest the

lit-tle help, they'll change as planned. We must
bird be-come lunch for the cat! We must

The Resources continue to dwindle. Little Sister dreams of a better future.

I CAN SEE A RAINBOW

Music by
Neil Fishman
Words by
Harvey Edelman

A   **D**   **A**

1. I can see the wilt - ed flow - er— bloom and grow in
2. I can see the dense rain for - ests— free from threat of

D   **A**   **D**

fresh clean air.— In a land— that's parched and dy - ing—
man's ma - chines.— To an end— where all are hap - py—

C#m   **F#**   **B**

I can see— life ev' - ry - where.— I can see— a
I can see— we'll find the means.— I can see— the

E   **B**   **E**

world for - got - ten— grow - ing health - y day by day.—
dis - tant chim - neys— not a puff of smoke in sight.—

B   **C#m**   **D#m**   **G#**

Through the val - ley, 'cross the moun - tains,— I can see there is a way.—
On the fa - ces of the hun - gry— I can see hope tak - ing flight. —

G#   **C#m7**   **B**   **C#m**   **F#7**   **D#m G#m7**

— I can see— a rain - bow light - ing up— the skies.

Show-ing us the way to go,— where to-mor-row— lies.

I can see— a rain-bow_____ like a new— sun-rise.

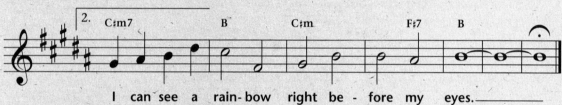

1. I can see a rain-bow right be-fore— my eyes.

2. I can see a rain-bow right be - fore my eyes._____

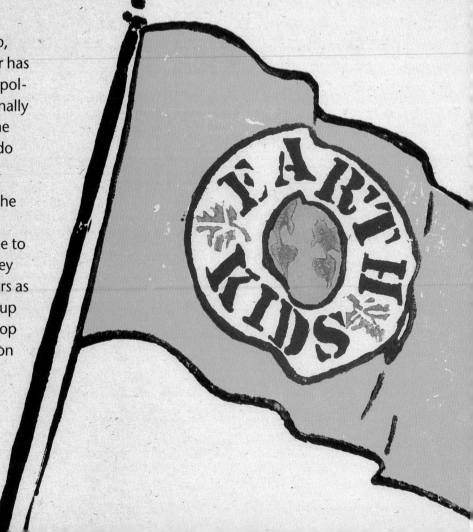

In the course of cleaning up, the kids see that Little Sister has become very sick from the pollution. The Apathetic Kid finally understands how serious the situation is and decides to do something to help.

The Natural Resources tell the kids that they can make a difference. All the kids agree to become Earth Kids, and they talk about convincing others as well. They pledge to clean up the oceans and rivers, to stop pollution and the destruction of the tropical rain forests, and to recycle.

HERE COME THE EARTH KIDS

Music by
Neil Fishman
Words by
Harvey Edelman

Verse

1. From our homes and our schools there's a war to be waged.
2. How we live, work, and play will de-ter-mine our fate.

Moth-er na-ture has rules and we've got-ta be-have.
There are dues we must pay be-fore it's too late.

There's no time to take sides, we must work as a team
Ev'-ry-one must take part so we're sure to suc-ceed.

so the earth will a-bide and be home to our dream.
Search your mind and your heart and then fol-low our lead.

Refrain

Make way, here come the Earth Kids! We've got the pow-er to

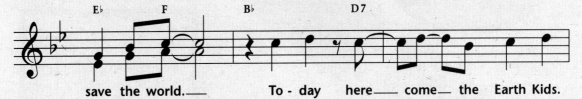

save the world. To-day here come the Earth Kids.

Our shin-ing ho-ur, one flag un-furled. furled. Make way, here

Playing the **R** E

C

F#

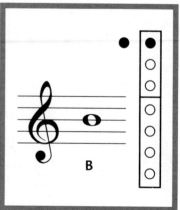

B

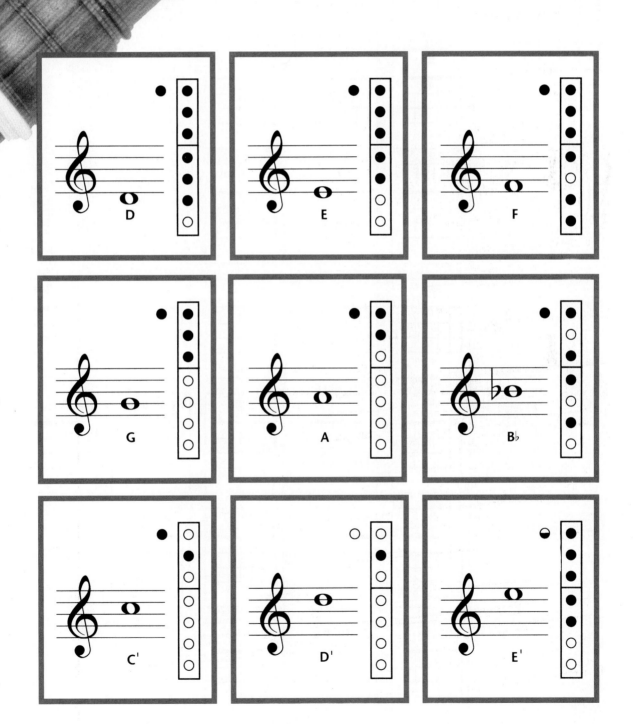

Playing the GUITAR

STANDARD TUNING

E A D G B E

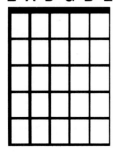

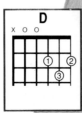 **D**

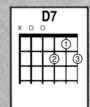 **D7**

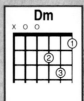 **Dm**

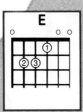 **E**

 E7

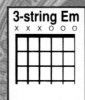 **3-string Em**

 Em

 **Easy F**

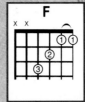 **F**

 Easy F#m

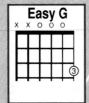 **Easy G**

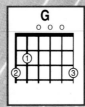 **G**

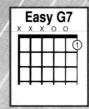 **Easy G7**

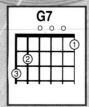 **G7**

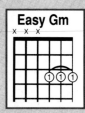 **Easy Gm**

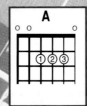 **A**

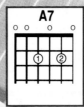 **A7**

 **A7 alt.**

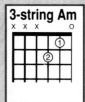 **3-string Am**

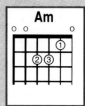 **Am**

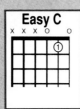 **B**

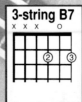 **3-string B7**

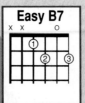 **Easy B7**

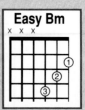 **Easy Bm**

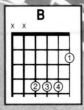 **Easy C**

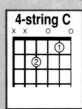 **4-string C**

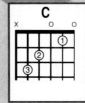 **C**

Baritone ukulele may use standard, D major, or D minor tunings. For fingerings, use first four strings as shown on chord diagrams.

426

ALTERNATE TUNING IN MAJOR AND MINOR

Frets are indicated by the letter *f* and a number (f7 = 7th fret).

D MAJOR TUNING

D A D F# A D

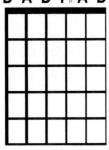

D open

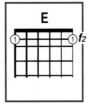
E *f2*

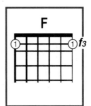
F *f3*

G *f5*

A *f7*

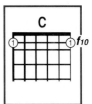
B *f9*

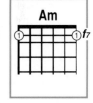
C *f10*

D MINOR TUNING

D A D F A D

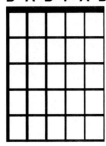

Dm open

Em *f2*

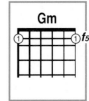
Fm *f3*

Gm *f5*

Am *f7*

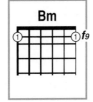
Bm *f9*

Cm *f10*

D

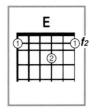
E *f2*

F *f3*

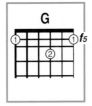
G *f5*

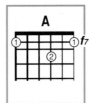
A *f7*

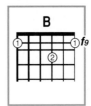
B *f9*

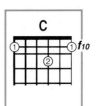
C *f10*

GLOSSARY

A

accent a stress on a given pitch or chord, **108**

accordion a kind of portable organ held by straps over the shoulders, **108**

aria a solo song in an opera, **212**

arranger a person who makes decisions about how style, instrumentation, tempo, harmony, and dynamics can be changed in a piece of music, **36**

articulation the manner in which sounds are performed, for example, smoothly connected or sharply separated, **191**

B

band an instrumental ensemble that usually consists of brass, woodwind, and percussion instruments, **5**

bass clef (𝄢) a clef used to show low pitches, **124**

bebop a style of jazz that developed in the mid-1940s. It is performed by small groups and focuses on improvisation, **251**

big band the ensemble used for swing jazz, usually consisting of woodwinds, brass, and percussion instruments, as well as string bass, **5**

blues a style of music that began in America in the early twentieth century, with roots in African American spirituals and work songs, **243**

C

cambiata the stage when boys' voices first begin to change and they can sing some slightly lower pitches than before, **195**

canon a musical form in which a melody is imitated exactly in one or more parts, similar to a round, **52**

chamber music music played by a small ensemble, **112**

changed voice
changed voice an adult singing voice, usually categorized as soprano, alto, tenor, or bass, **195**

chord three or more pitches sounded together, **30**

coda an ending section to a piece of music, **5**

countermelody a contrasting melody that goes with a melody, **24**

countersubject a melody that is heard with the subject in a fugue, **118**

country and western a style of American music, **264**

D

disco a style of popular dance music that developed in the 1970s, with a strong, steady beat for dancing, **264**

duo-pianists two performers who play music for two pianos, **125**

dynamics the degree of intensity and loudness of sound, **196**

E

envelope the shape of a sound from its beginning to its end, **115**

episode the section of a fugue in which the main melody is not heard, **118**

F

flat (♭) a symbol meaning to lower a tone a half step, **52**

fortepiano an early kind of piano that was smaller and quieter than those used in concerts today, **113**

fugue a composition in which three or more voices enter one after the other and imitate the main melody in various ways according to a set pattern, **118**

G

grand staff the set of two staffs used for piano music that includes very low as well as very high notes, **124**

H

half step the smallest distance between pitches in most western music; the distance between a pitch and the next closest pitch on a keyboard, **51**

harpsichord an early keyboard instrument with strings that are plucked when the keys are pressed, **96**

heavy metal a style of rock 'n' roll music that developed in the 1970s, using loud and distorted electrically produced sounds, **264**

I

instrumentation the choice of instruments in a piece of music, **36**

interpretation choices made by the performer that help make a musical performance more effective, **196**

interval the distance between two pitches, **51**

introduction a section of a piece, **8**

inverted chord a chord played with a note other than the root in the bass, **176**

J

jazz a type of popular American music with roots in African American spirituals, blues, and ragtime, borrowing rhythms from Africa and Latin America and melodies from Europe, **238**

K

key signature sharps or flats placed at the beginning of each staff, **70**

L

ledger lines lines drawn above and/or below a staff to show pitches that are higher and/or lower than those on the staff, **25**

legato a kind of articulation in which pitches are smoothly connected, **191**

lyricist a person who writes the words to songs, **191**

lyrics the words of a song, **191**

M

major scale a scale with *do* as the tonal center, with half steps between steps three and four, and seven and eight, **51**

marcato a kind of articulation in which pitches are sharply separated, **191**

march form a form that usually has sections AABB Trio Trio, **8**

mazurka a Polish dance, always in $\frac{3}{4}$ meter, **108**

melodic contour the upward or downward movement, or shape, of a melody, **18**

minor scale a scale with *la* as its tonal center, with half steps between steps two and three, and five and six, **70**

motive a small building-block of melody or rhythm, **150**

musical a musical theater production featuring a story told with singing and dancing, **190**

N

new wave a style of music popular in the early 1980s, featuring simple harmonies and often humorous lyrics, **270**

O

opera a drama with costumes and scenery, in which all or most of the text is sung, **195**

orchestra a large instrumental ensemble that usually includes members of the string, woodwind, brass, and percussion families, **5**

organ a keyboard instrument whose sound is produced by air forced through pipes, **95**

P

pedal point a single pitch held for a long time under changing chords or scales, **102**

piano a keyboard instrument whose sound is produced by hammers hitting stretched strings, **97**

pitch the highness or lowness of a tone, **18**

player piano a kind of mechanical piano that plays by itself, **110**

prepared piano a way of changing the sound of the piano by placing items such as pieces of paper, coins, spoons, or erasers on or between the strings, **122**

R

ragtime a style of music in which the melody is strongly syncopated while the accompaniment keeps a steady beat, **238**

rap a style of music that developed in the 1970s, involving spoken rhymes usually heard with a background of recorded music, **274**

relative minor a minor key having the same key signature as the major key three half steps higher; for example, A minor is the relative minor of C major, **103**

rock 'n' roll a style of music that developed in the 1950s, based on blues, gospel, and country music styles, **254**

root the pitch on which a chord is built, **31**

S

scale an ordered series of pitches, **51**

sharp (♯) a symbol meaning to raise a pitch a half step, **52**

stretto a technique used in a fugue in which the subject enters quickly in several voices, overlapping with itself, **118**

subject the main melody in a fugue, **118**

swing a kind of jazz that developed in the 1930s, played by big bands, **246**

syncopation a type of rhythm in which stressed sounds occur on weak beats or between beats, **154**

synthesizer an electronic keyboard instrument that can produce new sounds or imitate the sound of any other instrument, **104**

T

tala a rhythm grouping used in music from India, **217**

tempo the speed of the beat, **196**

texture the way melody and harmony combine to create layers of sound, **28**

tie () a musical sign that joins two notes of the same pitch into a single sound equal to their total duration, **28**

tonal center the pitch around which the melody of a piece seems to center; often the last pitch in a melody, **52**

tone color the special sound of each instrument or voice, **5**

treble clef (𝄞) a clef used to show high pitches, **124**

triad a chord with three pitches, each one of which is two steps away from the other, **31**

trio a part of march form and some dance forms that contrasts with earlier sections, **8**

U

unchanged voice the voice of a young person that has not changed to an adult voice, **195**

unison all perform the same part, **66**

V

verse-refrain form a song form in which the words of the verse change following each repetition of the refrain; the verse and refrain usually have different melodies, **12**

W

whole step a distance equal to two half steps, **51**

Z

zarzuela a kind of Spanish opera, **220**

CLASSIFIED INDEX

HOLIDAYS, SEASONAL, PATRIOTIC

MUSICAL

NON-ENGLISH MUSIC

INDEX OF POETRY

INDEX OF LISTENING SELECTIONS

INTERVIEWS

INDEX OF SONGS AND SPEECH PIECES

ACKNOWLEDGMENTS *continued*

ART & PHOTO CREDITS

COVER DESIGN: Designframe Inc., NYC

COVER PHOTOGRAPHY: Jade Albert for MMSD

Cover Set Design by Mark Gagnon
Synthesizer courtesy of Kurzweil Music System/Young Chang America, Inc. Stand courtesy of Ultimate Support System, Inc.

ILLUSTRATION

Steven Adler, 158-159, 190-191; Victoria Allen, 32-33; Don Baker, 180-181; Johanna Bandle, 284-285; George Baquero, 272-275; Andrea Baruffi, 78-79; Karen Bell, 200; Doron Ben-Ami, 84-85, 94-95; Steven Bennett, 64, 90, 176, 313-314, 316, 318-319; Robert Bergin, 212-213; Robert Burger, 226-227, 252-253; Dave Calver, 222-225; Ben Carter, 168-169; Harvey Chan, 140-141; Bradley Clarke, 66-67; Adam Cohen, 34-35; Sally Comport, 188-189; Margaret Cusack, 288-289; Jerry Dadds, 142-143; Tom Daly, 248-249; Jeanne de la Houssay, 86-89, 162-163; Brian Dugan, 172-173, 202-203; Andrea Eberbach, 24-25; Jon Ellis, 268-269; Kerna Erickson, 116-117; Cynthia Fitting, 302-303; Nancy Freeman, 82-83; Barbara Friedman, 36-37; Brad Gaber, 76-77; Chris Gall, 296-297; Linda Gist, 136-137; Joan Greenfield, 304-305; Ken Hamilton, 146-149; Janet Hamlin, 14-15; John Hart, 414-423; Ed Heins, 42-45; Eileen Hine, 164-165; Bill Hobbs, 150-153; Catherine Huerta, 166-167; Neal Hughes, 160-161; Susan Huls, 26-27, 198; Bruce Hutchinson, 206-207; Paul Jermann, 10-13; W.B. Johnston, 298-299; Mark Kaplan, 110-115, 210-211, 228; Greg King, 108-109; Mike Kowalski, 290-291; Elliot Kreloff, 126-127; Lingta Kung, 156-157; Roger Leyonmark, 242-243; Keith Lo Bue, 48-49, 100-101; Roberta Ludlow, 278-279; Fred Lynch, 276-277; Rob MacDougall, 254, 256-257; Scott MacNeill, 250-251; Vickie Maloney, 124-125; Barbara Maslen, 328-329; John Mattos, 132-135; Julia McLain, 244-245; Dave Miller, 326-327; Kristen Miller, 170-171; Jonathan Milne, 178-179; J.T. Morrow, 62-63, 260-265; Christy Mull, 8-9; Alan J. Nahigian, 6-7, 38-39, 238-239; Susan Nees, 128-131; Tom Nikosey, 232-235; Stephen Osborn, 18-19; Julie Pace, 286; Nan Parsons, 60-61; Rodica Prato, 324-325; Mike Radenich, 292-293; Melaine Reim, 30-31; Anna Rich, 0-1; Ronald Ridgeway, 258-259; Ray Roberts, 46-47; Christian Rodin, 16-17, 196-197; Barbara Roman, 52-53; Marlene Ruthen, 313, 315, 316, 317, 318, 319; Lissi Sigillo, 68-69; Peter Spacek, 118-119, Richard Sparks, 154-155; Sandra Speidel, 72-73; Victor Stabin, 208-209; Tom Starace, 112-113; Jim Starr, 322-323, 410-411; Gary Symington, 40-41; David Taylor, 144-145; Joseph Taylor, 184-187, 306-307; Juan Tenorio, 2-5; Blake Thornton, 246-247; Leyla Torres, 174-175; Jenny Vainisi, 56-57; Mei Wang, 20-21; Elsa Warnick, 64-65; Vicki Wehrman, 58-59, 70-71; Peter Wells, 22-23; Dean Williams, 236-237; David Wisniewski, 218-219; Ted Wright, 192-194; Deborah Yellen, 74-75; Jeff York, 194-195.

Tech Art by TCA Graphics, Inc.

PHOTOGRAPHY

All photographs are by the Macmillan/McGraw-Hill School Division (MMSD) except as noted below.

i: instruments, Jim Powell Studio for MMSD. iv-v: instruments, Jim Powell Studio for MMSD. vi: t.l. instruments, Jim Powell Studio for MMSD. **Unit 1** 2: t. Bill Waltzer for MMSD. 4-5: Institute of Jazz Studies/Rutgers University. 8: Tony Stone Images. 10: Luis Villota/Stock Market. 13: Doug Bryant. 16-17: Morton Tadder/Archive Photos. 28-29: William Waterfall/Stock Market. 32-33: Dave Bartruff. 37: Edie Baskin/Onyx. 42: British Library, ADD Ms 18851. folio 184V. 43: The Bettmann Archive. **Unit 2** 50-51: Edie Baskin/Onyx. 51: b.r. Chuck Jackson Photo; t.r. Nick Elgar/London Features International. 54: t.r. Chris Michaels/FPG; t.l. Superstock. 56: Philadelphia Museum of Art: The Henry P. McIlhenny Collection in memory of Frances P. McIlhenny. 60: Scala/Art Resource. 76-77: t. Richard Kelly for MMSD. 77: b. © 1993 Craig Molenhouse. 80-81: b. Karen Meyers for MMSD; t. Jim Powell Studio for MMSD. 87, 88: Bill Waltzer for MMSD. 89: Glenn Velez. **Unit 3** 90-91: Scala/Art Resource. 92-93: Karen Meyers for MMSD. 95: Church Organ: Metropolitan Museum of Art, Purchase, Margaret M. Wess Gift, in memory of her father, John B. McCarty, 1982 (1982.54). 96: Metropolitan Museum of Art, The Crosby Brown Collection of Musical Instruments 1884 (1982.54). 96-97: l. Steinway & Sons. 97: r. Courtesy Yamaha International, Keyboards Division. 99: Giraudon/Art Resource. 102-103: Bridgeman/Art Resource; b. FPG. 104: t. Yamaha Corporation of America. 104-105: b. The Bettmann Archive. 107: Sydney Byrd. 109: Scala/Art Resource. 110-111: QRS Music Rolls Inc., Buffalo, NY. 112: Art Resource. 113: Metropolitan Museum of Art, Gift of Geraldine C. Herzfeld, in memory of her late husband, Monroe Eliot Hemerdinger, 1984. 114: Steve Pumphrey/Onyx. 116: Lisa Seifert. 120: Gerald Bourin/Explorer. 120-121: British Museum. 122, 123: John Cage/Artservices/Lovely Music. 125: M. Rosenstiehl/Sygma. 128: b. Ken Karp for MMSD. t. QRS Music Rolls Inc., Buffalo, NY. 129: b. Karen Meyers for MMSD; t. Giraudon/Art Resource. 130: l. Tony Freeman/PhotoEdit; r. Steinway & Sons. 132: Hooks Bros. © Michael Ochs Archives/Memphis Music & Blues Museum. 133: t. Michael Ochs Archives; b. American Stock/Archive Photos. 134, 135: Gene Martin. **Unit 4** 143: Tom & Michele Grimm/International Stock. 144: The Granger Collection. 162-163: Jim Powell Studio for MMSD. 165: Ken Karp for MMSD. 167: Mark A. Philbrick for MMSD. 168-169: Mark Lagerstrom. 170-171: Kevin King. 172, 173: Karen Meyers for MMSD. 175: David Muench. 177: Karen Meyers for MMSD. 181: r. Tom Owen Edmunds/The Image Bank; m. Jack Vartoogian; l. Bob Daemmrich/Stock Boston. 182: Phyllis Picardi/International Stock Photography, Ltd. 184: Musée National des Arts et Traditions Populaire © R.M.N. 185: Carol Simowitz. 186: M.L./Retna Ltd. 187: t. Blair Seitz/Photo Researchers, Inc.; b. Douglas Mason/Woodfin Camp & Associates, Inc. **Unit 5** 190-191: The Kobal Collection/Superstock. 196-197: Springer/The Bettmann Archive. 199: The Kobal Collection/Superstock. 203: Ron Scherl © 1982. 204-205, 207, 210-211: Martha Swope. 212: The Granger Collection. 213: The Bettmann Archive. 214, 215: Ron Scherl. 216-217: Ian Berry/Magnum. 217: inset Art Resource. 220: Jack Vartoogian. 221: t.l. Jack Vartoogian; t.r. Ron Scherl/The Bettmann Archive; m.r. Wu Gang/Gamma Liaison; b.l. Lee Snider/Photo Images. 228: l. E.J. Camp/Outline; r. Steve Granitz/Retna Ltd. 229: Obremski/The Image Bank. 230-231: Karen Meyers for MMSD. 232: Culver Pictures. 233, 234-235: The Bettmann Archive. **Unit 6** 238: The Granger Collection. 241: Bill Waltzer for MMSD. 243: Michael Ochs Archives. 246: t.l. Woody Guthrie Publications; b.r. Michael Ochs Archives. 247: Frank Driggs Collection. 252: Bill Waltzer for MMSD. 254: Culver Pictures. 255: Michael Ochs Archives. 258: t.l., b.l. Photofest; m.l. Brown Brothers; b.l. inset, m.r. NASA; t.r. Star File Photos; b.r. Photoworld/FPG International. 259: t.l., m.l., b.l., b.r., b.m. Photofest; t.r. The King Collection/Retna Ltd.; m.b. Star File Photos; t.m. James Pickerell/Black Star. 262: Zimmerman/FPG. 266: Bill Waltzer for MMSD. 270: Deborah Feingold/Outline Press. 271: F. Reglain/Gamma Liaison. 272-273: Jim Powell Studio for MMSD. 278: Bill Bernstein/Outline. 279: Kriss Kross/Outline. 280-281: Michael Putland/Retna Ltd.; t. DOD Electronics. 282-283: Stills/Retna Ltd.; t. DOD Electronics. **Celebrations** 286: Bill Hickey/The Image Bank. 288: l. A. Perez Bourse; r. Walter H. Hodge/Peter Arnold. 300-301, 304, 305: Nancy Palubniak for MMSD. 308: Chester Higgins, Jr./New York Times. 308-309 bkgnd., 310-311 bkgnd.: David Young-Wolff/PhotoEdit. 311: r. *Family* by Charles Alston, Collection of Whitney Museum of American Art, New York/Photography by Bill Jacobson, N.Y. 313: By permission of the Chinese Music Society of North America, Chicago, U.S.A. 314: l. Air India Library; r. Ken Karp for MMSD. 316: Bob Krist for MMSD. 318: Richard T. Nowitz. 320: The Bettmann Archive. 321: Flip Schulke/Black Star. 324: t. Tate Gallery/Art Resource; b. Ben Simmons/Paul Winter Consort/Living Music. 326: Black Star. 328: Bob Daemmrich Photos. 330: The Image Bank. 331: Tony Freeman/PhotoEdit. **Music Library** 410: Britain Hill Photography. 411: Christian Steiner. 412: r. Art Resource. 412-413: t. Courtesy The Selmer Company; b. Hutschenreuther U.S.A. 413: l. © 1946 by Hawkes & Son (London) Ltd. Copyright renewed. Reprinted by permission of Peter Bartok and Bela Bartok, Jr. and Boosey & Hawkes, Inc.; r. MMSD. 424: t. The Bettmann Archive; m. Herb Snitzer Photography; b.l. Ken Karp for MMSD.

Macmillan/McGraw-Hill School Division thanks The Selmer Company, Inc., and its Ludwig/Musser Industries and Glaesel String Instrument Company subsidiaries for providing all instruments used in MMSD photographs in this music textbook series, with exceptions as follows. MMSD thanks Yamaha Corporation of America for French horn, euphonium, acoustic and electric guitars, soprano, alto, and bass recorders, piano, and vibraphone; MMB Music Inc., St. Louis, MO, for Studio 49 instruments; Rhythm Band Instruments, Fort Worth, TX, for resonator bells; Courtly Instruments, NY, for soprano and tenor recorder; Elderly Instruments, Lansing, MI, for autoharp, dulcimer, hammered dulcimer, mandolin, Celtic harp, whistles, and Andean flute.

PRONUNCIATION KEY
Simplified International Phonetic Alphabet

VOWELS

ɑ	f<u>a</u>ther	æ	c<u>a</u>t
e	<u>a</u>pe	ɛ	p<u>e</u>t
i	b<u>ee</u>	ɪ	<u>i</u>t
o	<u>o</u>bey	ɔ	p<u>aw</u>
u	m<u>oo</u>n	ʊ	p<u>u</u>t
ʌ	<u>u</u>p	ə	<u>a</u>go

SPECIAL SOUNDS

β	say *b* without touching lips together; *Spanish* nue<u>v</u>e, ha<u>b</u>a
ç	<u>h</u>ue; *German* i<u>ch</u>
ð	<u>th</u>e, *Spanish* to<u>d</u>o
ṇ	sound <u>n</u> as individual syllable
ö	form [o] with lips and say [e]; *French* ad<u>ieu</u>, *German* sch<u>ö</u>n
œ	form [ɔ] with lips and say [ɛ]; *French* c<u>oeu</u>r, *German* pl<u>ö</u>tzlich
ɾ	flipped r; bu<u>tt</u>er
r̄	rolled r; *Spanish* pe<u>rr</u>o
ɬ	click tongue on the ridge behind teeth; *Zulu* ng<u>c</u>wele
ü	form [u] with lips and say [i]; *French* t<u>u</u>, *German* gr<u>ü</u>n
ü̆	form [ʊ] with lips and say [ɪ]
x	blow strong current of air with back of tongue up; *German* Ba<u>ch</u>, *Hebrew* <u>H</u>anukkah, *Spanish* ba<u>j</u>o
ʒ	plea<u>s</u>ure
'	glottal stop, as in the exclamation "uh oh!" [ˈʌ ˈo]
~	nasalized vowel, such as French b<u>on</u> [bõ]
˺	end consonants *k*, *p*, and *t* without puff of air, such as s<u>k</u>y (no puff of air after *k*), as opposed to *kite* (puff of air after *k*)

OTHER CONSONANTS PRONOUNCED SIMILAR TO ENGLISH

ch	<u>ch</u>eese	ny	o<u>n</u>ion, *Spanish* ni<u>ñ</u>o
g	<u>g</u>o	sh	<u>sh</u>ine
ng	si<u>ng</u>	ts	boa<u>ts</u>

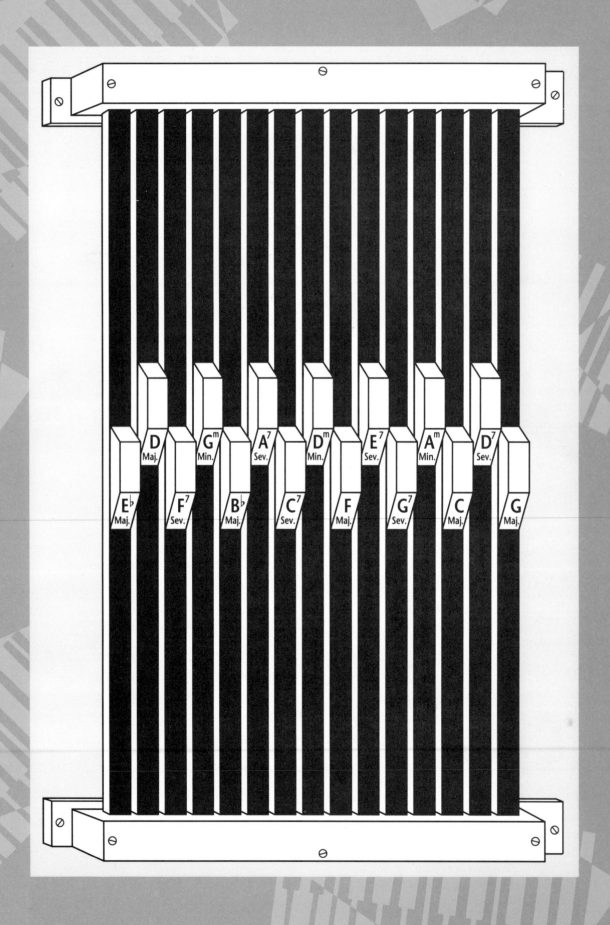